Fake PRESIDENT

Decoding Trump's Gaslighting, Corruption, and General Bullsh*t

MARK GREEN and RALPH NADER

Skyhorse Publishing

Skyhorse Publishing books may be purchased in bulk at special discounts for sales promotion, corporate gifts, fund-raising, or educational purposes. Special editions can also be created to specifications. For details, contact the Special Sales Department, Skyhorse Publishing, 307 West 36th Street, 11th Floor, New York, NY 10018 or info@skyhorsepublishing.com.

Skyhorse® and Skyhorse Publishing® are registered trademarks of Skyhorse Publishing, Inc.®, a Delaware corporation.

Visit our website at www.skyhorsepublishing.com.

10 9 8 7 6 5 4 3 2 1

Library of Congress Cataloging-in-Publication Data is available on file.

Cover design by 5mediadesign
Cover photo credit: Getty Images

ISBN: 978-1-5107-5112-5
Ebook ISBN 978-1-5107-5113-2

Printed in the United States of America

This book is dedicated to **Moses Gery Green**—born February 7, 2019—
and to all children who deserve lives of decency and justice.

It's also dedicated to Trump-leaning voters who should do some political homework to discover
how he's harming American families hoping for a better future.

CONTENTS

Photo by Chris McGrath/Getty Images

AUTHORS' NOTE & ACKNOWLEDGMENTS

W

e two have worked together for nearly 50 years on some 10 books and scores of causes.

Disgusted by Donald Trump's open war on truth and law in late 2018, we decided to collaborate on a Trump Bullshit Detector for the coming 2020 election. Our core premises: he is completely unfit to be President of the United States, and the 2020 election, as Jefferson said of the 1800 election, "would fix our national character and determine whether Republicanism or aristocracy would prevail."

Now, a year later, *Fake President* goes to production the month when House Democrats have announced a formal Inquiry into possible Articles of Impeachment, triggered by his admitted effort—can't say "no collusion!" this time—to pressure Ukraine to find dirt on a possible 2020 rival. That Inquiry appears likely to include other alleged crimes and abuses of power such as those detailed throughout this book.

While we each worked on all sections, Ralph's focus was on the introductory Essay and Epilogue and Mark's on the "Bullshit Detector" and chapters 1 to 17. We worked with a small team of excellent researchers/writers —Douglas Grant and Chris Gelardi primarily, with supplemental research and editing from Harut Manasian and Deni Frand (who moonlights as Mark's wife).

Fake President would not exist without the talent and devotion of publisher/agent Esther Margolis, whom we met at Bantam Books in 1972 while publishing our No. 1 bestselling *Who Runs Congress?*, and the very dynamic team at Skyhorse Publishing—especially publisher Tony Lyons and editors Michael Campbell and Julie Ganz—from acceptance through publication. All were patient and encouraging. We're grateful.

Unless otherwise noted, quotes are straight from the mouth (or tweet) of Donald Trump.

This small volume is illustrative but not exhaustive given the previously unfathomable number of lies and scandals that have pockmarked his presidency. For more encyclopedic compilations, please see Glenn Kessler's "Fact-Checker" collection in the *Washington Post*; Amy Siskind's *The List*; and Daniel Dale's continuing chronology in the *Toronto Star*.

If you'd like to add to your library of knowledge about this "unpresidented" man, we suggest that you look at two early, probing books: David Cay Johnston's *The Making of Donald Trump* and Tim O'Brien's *TrumpNation*.

More recently, there's Bob Woodward's *Fear: Trump in the White House*; David Corn & Michael Isikoff's *Russian Roulette;* Michael Wolff's *Fire and Fury*; David Cay Johnston's *It's Even Worse than You Think*; David Frum's *Trumpocracy*; Rick Wilson's *Everything Trump Touches Dies*; Vicky Ward's *Kushner, Inc*; Cliff Sims's *A Team of Vipers*; Joy-Ann Reid's *The Man Who Sold America*; Tim Alberta's *American Carnage*; Steve Kornacki's *The Red and the Blue*; Greg Sargent's *An Uncivil War: Taking Back our Democracy*; Laurence Tribe and Joshua Matz's *To End a Presidency*; Max Boot's *The Corrosion of Conservatism;* Stanley Greenberg's *RIP GOP*; Peter Wehner's *The Death of Politics*; Brian Klaas's *The Despot's Apprentice: Donald Trump's Attack on Democracy;* James Stewart's *Deep State;* Rick Stengel's *Information Wars*; and Susan Ohanian's *Trump, Trump, Trump: The March of Folly*.

And at the risk of being understood, Mark Green read biographies of Lenin, Hitler, and Mussolini during this book's gestation to learn from the worst authoritarians of the past century.

Mark Green
Ralph Nader
October 1, 2019

PROLOGUE: FAKING IT

Having won over 270 electoral college votes in 2016 (despite losing the popular vote by nearly three million), Donald J. Trump is of course the lawfully selected president of the United States...yet still a fake president. He's a PINO—a president-in-name-only.

Exactly a century ago, Woodrow Wilson was also a president in form but not function because a disabling stroke led his wife Edith to run the government behind the scenes during his final 18 months in office.

Trump similarly has the trappings of office. But due to a disabling "messianic narcissism" that allows his ego to warp his brain—as well as an unusual lack of knowledge, integrity, empathy, and stability—he can't perform many of the duties of office that the Constitution anticipated.

Staff sometimes remove papers from his desk or refuse orders they consider untenable or unconstitutional in the hope that he might neglect to follow up. Indifferent to the separation of powers, he repeatedly obstructs justice and intervenes in judicial proceedings based on partisan whim. He makes rash decisions that may cause irreparable damage to Americans for decades in order to please Fox's prime-time lineup. He feeds on and fuels hatred. He erupts with a daily lava of lies that aim to bury truth and progress.

Were a CEO, lawyer, or retail clerk to utter an average of 13 false statements a day at work, as Trump does, they wouldn't have shareholders, clients, or customers—they wouldn't have a *job*.

To amend the famous axiom, there are lies, damned lies... and frauds, the latter being an entirely different category. Not merely misstatements, mistakes, falsehoods, or white lies—Mark Twain generously called them "stretchers"— but a space where con artists keep playing catch-me-if-you-can to escape accountability. Nor can anyone act surprised that we've reached this low point with the 45th president. When a leader relies on repeated falsehoods without a capacity to learn or apologize—always doubling and quadrupling down to keep his credulous base satisfied—we almost inevitably end up with a president who keeps digging himself into ever-deeper holes.

Or, as the head of the Society of American Magicians once remarked, his members were popular because "people wanted a fraud they could believe in." In movies, Trump's the antihero.

Yet a Fringe Fourth of Americans according to all surveys have for now gone all in for his pretend presidency.

Based on his oath of office "to preserve, protect and defend the Constitution...against all enemies, foreign and domestic," Trump is having a hard time even getting by as a PINO. While prior presidents usually processed problems through such enlightenment values of fact, reason, and law, he instead sees everything through the filters of vanity, money, and revenge. These self-centered concerns inevitably generate disinformation—let's call them "fake news"—as Trump lies about his Inaugural crowd size, an official weather map about a monster hurricane, MBS's role in Khashoggi's murder, millions of immigrants who supposedly voted illegally for Hillary, pressuring other countries to interfere on his behalf in the presidential election, and so much more noted throughout this book.

How then can any rational actor now believe a word Trump says about Iran, the Taliban, his taxes, political rivals, trade wars, manufacturing, DACA recipients—anything?

He simply lacks the skill and focus to do the job, much as we don't expect a heart surgeon to be an opera singer. When someone spends so much time golfing, tweeting, and seething—he

Mark Taylor from Rockville, USA [CC BY 2.0 (https://creativecommons.org/licenses/by/2.0)]

once rage-tweeted Fox's Ed Henry 23 times in 23 minutes—it's not surprising that an incompetent poseur as president allows one-third of all Inspector General posts go unfulfilled and infuriates the Congress and allies by unending decades of Middle East policy after one call to Turkey's Recep Erdogan. Can anyone seriously imagine Trump as JFK, successfully working through a future version of the Cuban missile crisis?

For the first time in our history, the greatest danger *to* the United States is now the president *of* the United States. At issue is not just his voluminous lies, but the lives endangered at his intersection of mendacity, pathology, and ideology. Here's a partial scorecard:

- spurring white nationalist violence;
- pretending there's no climate crisis as fires, floods, and hurricanes intensify;
- withdrawing from a functioning Iran nuclear deal and increasing the risk of an eventual military conflict;
- transferring trillions in more wealth from 90 percent to the top 1 percent as real wages continue to stagnate;
- traumatizing millions of Latinx families with the threat of deportation because of manipulated crime statistics;
- undermining the Western military alliance that's held together for 70 years due to his bromance with a communist leader;
- endangering members of Congress and civilians by dehumanizing and ugly name-calling;
- and appointing revolving-door (de)regulators who allow powerful corporations to further jeopardize the

health, safety, and budgets of millions of defenseless families.

When called out for all the repeated lies and malign policies, he has so far evaded serious political and legal penalties by alternately bragging, bullying, blaming, and bullshitting (see his 21 favorite tricks in "Bullshit Detector" on page xxvi). Indeed, his disinformation is likely to get worse in a competitive 2020 presidential campaign. Based on his track record of cheating to win and penchant for drama to stay on offense, we can expect not just *an* "October" surprise, but periodic ones as he tries to muscle the mainstream media into being a conveyor belt of his fearmongering.

It's worked before. Remember Trump's assertions about Obama's birthplace, Hillary's emails, the Warren family ancestry? Trump's formula in 2020 should be no mystery: attack the Democratic nominee for some unproven and/or trivial offense, exaggerate whatever it is into a "potential Watergate," get his triumvirate of Giuliani, Hannity, Limbaugh, et. al.—and cabinet members acting as consiglieres to The Don—to demand an investigation "to get to the bottom of this," make sure Trump raises it in hyperbolic language at his WWF-like rallies so voters can't think of the opponent without first thinking of the charge ("but her emails!")—and if attacked first, demand that his Department of "Justice" investigate the investigators. Once he's established this "scandal," Trumpians then will wield it to counter his 12,000+ lies and other corruptions in a massive attempt at false equivalency.

So here we are: due to a once-in-forever fluke involving the confluence of Putin, Wikileaks, James Comey, the electoral college, and racially targeted voter suppression, the United States is for now stuck with the worst president in its history (according to a survey by the American Political Science Association). Former President Jimmy Carter, who's monitored elections around the world, believes that the combined impact of the above events damaged Hillary Clinton's candidacy in incalculable yet undeniable ways—and that Trump was, therefore, an "illegitimate" president who won by improper means.

Because he is uninformed, inexperienced, untruthful, and way over his head, it was predictable that a fluke candidacy would grow into a fake presidency.

Last, if using the adjective "fake" offends his acolytes, they need to explain his own prolific use of the word to undermine any media that dare criticize him. Here he operates in the tradition of two Russian leaders—Stalin in the 20th century, who also called them "the enemy of the people," and an 18th-century local Russian ruler who created facades now commonly called Potemkin Villages—huge murals of happy people put up in the distance—to hide bad conditions from travelers.

By gathering, explaining, and categorizing his "twistifications" (a Jefferson coinage) into one accessible volume, it is our hope that *Fake President* can help voters become their own Bullsh*t Detectors. Then they can better understand both impeachment proceedings and the Fall 2020 election, perhaps even winning over a Trumpian uncle or coworker along the way.

Like it or not, we're all in the absurd situation of dealing seriously—if not occasionally humorously—with a nasty miscreant who wouldn't be worth our time except for today's "tyranny of the minority" that gives him control of nuclear codes, the military, and law enforcement.

We nonetheless approach this stress test of democracy in the optimistic spirit of Benjamin Franklin, who concluded in 1732 that "when Truth and Error have fair play, the former is always an over-match for the latter." For in this culminating tug-of-war between Trumpism and Democracy—between a contempt for both truth and law and a belief in self-governance—only one can survive.

Mark Green and Ralph Nader

ESSAY:
DONALD TRUMP VS. OUR DEMOCRACY
BY RALPH NADER

We've had great presidents and awful ones. All had flaws. But never before has there been one so provably corrupt, impulsive, ignorant, incompetent, untruthful, work lazy, lacking empathy, antidemocratic, racist, sexist, ruthless, bullying, petty, arrogant, and endlessly self-centered and self-enriching. It's not easy to meld all these different handicaps into one sentient human form. Yet in a feat worthy of a mass illusionist, the current Oval Office occupant has nonetheless convinced millions—though still a minority of Americans—to support him to spite themselves.

Donald Trump is the David Blaine of politics...a master of misdirection and fakery.

Masterly is usually good...but not when it applies a batch of awful traits that we wouldn't accept in a friend, family member, coworker, or neighbor. And certainly shouldn't in a person chosen to govern nearly 330 million people in the world's oldest democracy. "Where other people have a soul," said the wise Bill Moyers, "Trump has a black hole."

Moyers observes what is perhaps Trump's core weakness *and* political strength—the near complete shamelessness of a comic book villain who doesn't morally flinch at mass lying or mass harm...while he invariably "doubles down" waiting for others to blink. And since a lifetime of cheating workers, consumers, bankers, and wives did not stop his ascension,

> "Facts don't cease to exist because they are ignored."
>
> Aldous Huxley

is anyone surprised that he thinks he can get away with just about anything?

There's a level of irony in all this that only a great novelist could portray. Trump embraces corporate capitalism and the American flag yet imitates the dictator's style of propaganda and unilateralism. He is a Niagara of fake information yet attacks "fake news" for accurately reporting on him. Those comforted by the cliché that "it can't happen here"—"it" being a blend of Monarchy, Authoritarianism, and Kakistocracy, i.e., "government by the worst"—it *is* happening here. Right now.

To better understand how this saga ends, let's look at the beginning—How did we get here? How does he, so far, overcome our constitutional system of checks and balances? Will a relentlessly dishonest president create a credibility gap so wide that nothing he says will be—or should be—believed? What can stop his intense drive to sabotage our democracy and steal our future?

I. LESSONS FROM 2016

Based on 44 prior presidents—few people would have anticipated that an Orange Unicorn would join an exclusive club including Washington, Lincoln, and the Roosevelts.

After the initial shock wore off, there was an early consensus about what actually occurred:

- following a two-term Democratic president, the public was ripe for a change rather than a "third" term;
- after decades of identifying with Wall Street plutocrats and war hawks, Hillary Clinton lost touch with working families. Bolstered by favorable polls, she ran a complacent big-money campaign without much get-out-the-vote energy;

- "trust in government" (and therefore in the "party of government") plunged from 70 to 17 percent from the 1960s to 2016 due to such shocks as Vietnam, Stagflation/Oil Embargo, the Nixon Watergate resignation, and the Iraq War criminalities;
- the lack of authentic language and the absence of long-overdue progressive proposals by the Democratic Party rendered it frozen in the headlights;
- GOP-sponsored voter suppression laws in key swing states had their intended effect of obstructing voting by large numbers of people of color;
- without James Comey's October 28th letter to Congress (released only ten days before the general election), which was interpreted as "reopening" the FBI probe of Clinton, Trump would have lost, according to polling specialist Nate Silver;
- just barely enough crossing over white working-class voters in a handful of crucial states—many economically aggrieved; many racially resentful; many both—combined to devastating effect;
- and an Electoral College, weighted to help slave states in 1789, for the second time in the past five national elections converted the loser into the winner.

That is, a "perfect storm" of implausible events elevated a figurative lounge club act and right-wing reality show host to become the 45th president. Lawful, yet—as noted—also "fake."

II. HOW HAS HE (SO FAR) SURVIVED?
"I could shoot someone on Fifth Avenue..."
Almost as confounding is how he has survived—albeit unusually unpopular in polls and at least until the House finally

began its Impeachment Inquiry—all the chaos, scandals, violations, and dissembling of his term in Office.

Donald Trump is, unarguably, a skilled "con artist"—the car salesman obsessed with getting you behind the wheel, whether the car is safe and affordable or not. Starting out as a local, grasping celebrity in earlier decades, he'd rely on such squalid artifices as pretending to be his own press agent whispering to columnists in a disguised voice how great he was in bed (really)—or enhancing the value of a Trump building by simply skipping floors 49 to 59 on the elevator's button panel...small potatoes stuff compared to today. For now as president, he enjoys exponentially greater power to dupe (which he relishes) yet is subject to far greater scrutiny (which he doesn't).

As when people ask magicians, "How do you *do* that?", we studied how Donald Trump games the system to get away with things considered unimaginable a few years or even months ago.

First, his power is amplified and protected by a billion-dollar media megaphone that all presidents enjoy, especially one so trained in the art of news manipulation—expanded by a huge Twitter-verse at his daily disposal.

Second, a couple of centuries of goodwill for the Office of President now allow this one to ignore many norms and laws. Like generations of heirheads, he has drawn down a family inheritance to maintain his extravagant habits.

Third, while all presidents can count on some political "base" of support—defined as people who stick with you no matter how often you screw up—Trump has a core of Republican voters who, due to economic grievances, religion, region, or race, comprise an unbreakable steady 25 percent of aggrieved Americans. That's the same percentage that supported Nixon as he waived good-bye from his helicopter in 1974. "I can't really say

White House photographer, via Wikimedia Commons

anything he says is true," said one admiring but representative Wisconsin woman in year two of his term, "but I trust him."

Such people comprise what journalist Peter Baker helpfully calls Trump's "United Base of America." They want to believe— and so *do* believe—that reverse racism is worse than racism, that white America is losing its Judeo-Christian culture, that gays shouldn't marry, that the federal debt only matters under Democratic presidents, that regulation kills jobs, and that an alien socialism is at the doorstep. Indeed, fully two-thirds of Republicans recently believed that Barack Obama was not an American while they now agree by 2-1 that Trump should be given an added two years at the end of his term in office, just because.[1]

At the same time, Trump has oddly immunized himself from standard criticism because of the very volume of his lies and scandals. "One death is a tragedy, one million a statistic" is an observation attributed to Stalin. Today, too many people come to expect—and therefore minimize—the huge cloud of sleaze enveloping Trump and his family.

Beyond such normal if tawdry political factors letting Trump get away with so many outrages, there are three other institutional ones that, of all modern presidents, together create a real and presidential danger to the American people. Consider briefly the Congress, the Supreme Court, and the Department of Justice.

---

1 Where does such irrationality come from? As behavioral historians Jonathan Haidt and William Davies discuss in their groundbreaking books—*The Righteous Mind and Dangerous States*, respectively—centuries of wars, religion, ethnic and racial hatreds, worsening economic inequality, extreme nationalism, and more recently terrorism have coalesced into a growing disdain for elites in our national psyche. If the "experts" who run government were so smart, thought millions of average families, why is mine barely getting by? For "five-minute voters," this intuition and anger were all that mattered.

- *Congressional Republicans* since January 20, 2017, have decided to ignore their oaths of office in order to protect their President's every outrageous word and deed, other than an occasional lamentation from the likes of Senator Susan Collins that some aberrant conduct "was unfortunate...regrettable...concerning." Led by Majority Leader Mitch McConnell cutting corners and changing rules, his Senate Republican Caucus has approved almost without dissent some of the least qualified and most corporate-conflicted executive and judicial nominees in recent memory.

  As for the constitutional obligation to perform Executive Branch oversight, committees chaired by Republicans didn't issue *a single investigative subpoena* in 2017–2018. But as soon as Democrats became the House majority in January 2019, the White House practiced constant stonewalling and disparagement of this coequal branch of government in the hope of slowing down or wearing down oversight committees. Trump's constant goading pushed the House to launch impeachment proceedings in the Fall of 2019.

  His party repeatedly shielded him from traditional accountability. Senator Lindsay Graham fulminated in 1999 about Bill Clinton's lie over a private affair yet now ignores Donald Trump's thousands of falsehoods about public affairs, giving hypocrisy an even worse name.

- *The Supreme Court,* after a two-century-plus run haltingly expanding democratic rights, can no longer even pretend to be an "umpire calling balls and strikes," to use John Roberts's disingenuous metaphor. To be sure, the five Republican justices—together comprising the most reactionary court since the 1890s, perhaps the 1850s—seem to be on a political mission to find any pretext in Common Law, 19th-century footnotes, dicta, new originalist theories, or "broad presidential discretion" to arrive at their verdict-first rulings against voting rights, consumer rights, environmental safety, campaign spending, unions, and poor people.

Masquerading ideology as law, their decisions reflect J. P. Morgan's insight about the value of false but plausible public rationales: "a man always has two reasons for something—a good reason and the real reason." Five to four decisions in favor of Trump's "Muslim Ban" and on racial gerrymandering, for example, are creating a Court acting more like the Republican National Committee than the heirs of John Marshall and Earl Warren.[2]

And while Justice Gorsuch in 2017 wondered why an exceptional American "would look to the experience of other countries rather than to our own in deciding cases," in 2019 that same jurist argued that "virtually every English-speaking country and a great many others besides ask this [citizenship] question in their censuses." Presto, they nearly brush off three lower federal court decisions and Commerce Secretary Wilbur Ross's documented falsehoods under oath (a.k.a., perjury).

Is President Trump right to believe that his

---

2 It was painful to watch self-proclaimed institutionalist Roberts twist himself into a jurisprudential pretzel to get to desired results. He ignored the president's openly flouted religious bigotry to justify a "Muslim ban" and gutted the Voting Rights Act (VRA) in *Shelby County* only to turn around and initially consider using the remains of the VRA to justify the "Citizenship" question. Heads I win, tails you lose.

Court—like "his" generals—will bail him out of other unprecedented misconduct? But a Supreme Court that becomes in effect Kavanaugh's Kangaroo Court—run by "unelected Republican politicians in fancy robes," in the words of writer Sean McElwee—will not long deserve or keep the trust of the American people.

- *The Department of Justice.* Attorney General William Barr's initially successful cover-up of the devastating Mueller Report made him look more like a presidential butler than an independent law enforcement officer.

  Barr maneuvered every which way—especially by adopting Trump's language that the FBI "spied" on Trump and twice mischaracterizing the Report to mislead public opinion and the Senate Judiciary Committee—to spare the President any legal or political fallout. Then when called out for being Trump's mini-me, he tried to explain himself on two media platforms, Fox and the *Wall Street Journal*, coincidentally both owned by Rupert Murdoch.

  After that, Barr got Trump to give him the authority to cherry-pick all confidential intelligence government-wide to support Trump's evidence-free assertion that the Mueller probe was illegitimate from the start. That is, having announced to Barr his desired conclusion, Trump launched an actual "witch hunt" of a Special Counsel investigation that wasn't a witch hunt.

  Barr's open cover-up—extending to his efforts to stonewall the whistleblower's complaint about Trump-Ukraine—is transforming the Justice Department from a presumed independent entity to what one Brazilian governor reported was his approach to

Photo by Chip Somodevilla/Getty Images

justice: "to my enemies, the law; to my friends, facilities." Trump has found someone who miraculously combines "his" Roy Cohn and *Showtime*'s Ray Donovan.

Conclusion: Trump is now looking to his Praetorian Guard of McConnell + Kavanaugh + Barr to do two things: first, recast the entire Executive Branch into his own Trump Organization, surrounded nepotistically by his children, consiglieres, and courtiers. Second, trash the Rule of Law to hold onto power in

2020 and thereafter...even as he still shouts that the system is rigged *against* him.

III. REELECTION OR REALIGNMENT?

When Trump lauded the Mueller Report's "conclusion on collusion" in April–May 2019 while simultaneously attacking it as "full of bullshit," it seemed fair to use his own framework in this book's subtitle. Face it, the man knows bullshit.

And most people know it. But there's nowhere a book that catalogues the worst ones and how they harm Americans and the world. Like truth, lies have consequences. At the same time, a kind of "BS fatigue" may exhaust normal citizens and create a more-is-less phenomenon that leads them to tune out so many outrages.

Because we concur with author Norman Cousins that "no one is smart enough to be a pessimist," we cannot ironically allow frequency to normalize corruption. Given the governmental disaster of Trumpism and the narrow margins that pick presidents—see George W. Bush and Trump—we are skeptical about cynicism.

First, everyone does *not* know—or knows it only hazily. So *Fake President* chooses a thousand examples, aggregates them by category, and explains each one and each category. In combination, it's clear that the whole of Trump's dishonesty is greater than the sum of its parts. Supporters may indignantly pluck out this one or that one on Twitter or radio as "locker room talk...a slip of the tongue...a joke," but fair-minded observers understand the irrefutable power of accumulated evidence. One brick is not a wall; 12,000 bricks are.

Second, since everything cannot be mandated by law and contract, our governing model needs the glue of trust so we all comply with mutual understandings...whether we win or

AlexanderGouletas, courtesy of Getty Images

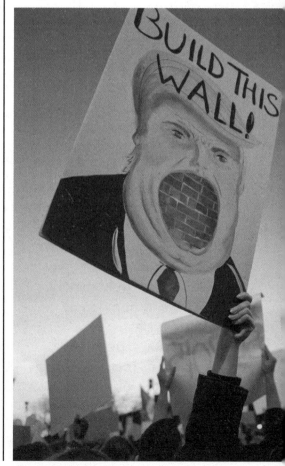

A ONE-MAN POLITICAL CHERNOBYL

Bok is right. Applying her fears to today, Trump has the potential to be a One-Man Political Chernobyl.

In the HBO series *Chernobyl,* German-made robots purchased to remove radioactive graphite near where the reactor exploded failed because the Kremlin gave the Germans a low but false propaganda level of radiation involved rather than the real higher amounts.

Should Trump's lying become "normalized," a tipping-point reached where officials routinely lie to themselves, the public, their staffs, their colleagues, the White House—then a spreading civic cancer could make a functioning democracy nearly impossible.

We don't expect leaders to be as reliable as the periodic tables. But we do not expect more falsehoods than facts coming from the

(continued next page)

lose any particular election, legislative vote, or court ruling. Democracy also needs to have confidence in reason and evidence, two of our original enlightenment values, in order to make the best policy. "Imagine a society where word and gesture could never be counted upon," wrote Sissela Bok in her worthy book *Lying: Moral Choice in Public and Private Life.* "Questions asked, answers given, information exchanged—all would be worthless."

Third, the same is true of diplomacy. If our allies know they cannot trust a president who may say or do one thing one day, and the opposite the next, the Western alliance that's held since World War II is in jeopardy. When Dean Acheson offered to show French President Charles de Gaulle the photographic evidence of Soviet missiles in Cuba in 1962, de Gaulle waved him off. "No, the word of the American president is enough."

Does anyone believe that exchange would happen today? Already the percentages of people who trust the United States in Western European nations have plunged by more than half since 2016—Germany going from 78 percent to only 30 percent; the UK from 70 percent to 32 percent. And as diplomacy falters, the possibility of war rises.

Trump's core betrayal is how he weaves together rhetorical populism for workers with policies for the corporate superrich. So far, he's gotten largely away with this continuing conflict with himself. In response, all of us need to pitch in to sway "public sentiment" in Lincoln's meaning as best we can. Politically, in 2020 that means aware Americans encouraging word-of-mouth neighbor-to-neighbor, as well as writing, advocating, litigating, investigating, marching, running for office, registering...and of course voting.

Success does not require convincing half his supporters that they've been duped, which is psychologically and politically impossible. Rather, what matters is small shifts at the margins, since, for example, water is liquid at 33 degrees but freezes at 32 degrees. So if a tough, talented Democratic nominee can get voters to ask themselves, "Whom do you trust?" and "Had enough?"—in conjunction with the likely higher turnout of new ascendant voters in 2020, as happened in 2018—there will be a reckoning, if not, conceivably, a realignment that not even the Electoral College can overrule.

While there's no guarantee, of course, that result is far more likely than the odds facing Susan B. Anthony or Martin Luther King, Jr. in their heroic efforts to change the way America treated women and people of color. In order to overcome, they regarded their causes in the last century as responses to big national emergencies. So must we in our own national emergency.

"History is like waves lapping at a cliff," French historian Henri See observed in the late 1890s. "For centuries nothing happens—then the cliff collapses."

White House, such as when Trumpers highlight (nonexistent) voter impersonation while ignoring climate violence.

Such intellectual corruption can provide a kind of permission slip to other policymakers state and local—and to children who are watching—that "dishonesty is the best policy" because we're in a "posttruth" world.

Will his poison spread or be contained?

YOUR OWN BULLSHIT DETECTOR:
21 FAVORITE TRUMP TRICKS TO DISTRACT, DEFLECT, DECEIVE

If Trump's institutional advantages described in the essay above don't completely insulate him, he is then forced to rely on his considerable guile and swagger to talk his way off of any cliff. For he is a world-class practitioner of George Bernard Shaw's timeless observation that "Political language is designed to make lies sound truthful and murder respectable and to give an appearance of solidity to pure wind."

It's not breaking news that Trump lies—his own lawyer, John Dowd, reportedly considered him "a fucking liar" and warned that he'd end up in "an orange jumpsuit" if he ever testified under oath to Mueller. But also his pace is both stunning and growing: from an average of eight lies or falsehoods a day in 2017 to some 22 a day by mid-to-late 2018. This strategic disinformation leads to gaslighting—when he pretends that the Mueller Report completely exonerated him, which it explicitly does not; or when he pretends that a White House transcript of that Trump-Zelensky June 25th phone call didn't prove that he was seeking the "favor" of getting political dirt on a potential rival in exchange for Ukraine obtaining its $400 million in essential military aid.

But his proven BS is not intended for everyone, only the 40 percent of Americans who are card-carrying members of Cult45 and are like worshippers everywhere who say, "Don't confuse me with the facts!" Their "motivated reasoning" means that getting Trump to stop dissembling will be harder than capping that pipe of gushing oil after the BP rig explosion in the Gulf.

But until then, imagine for a moment that you're Kellyanne Conway on your way to work on any morning wondering what idiotic thing your boss has tweeted or said that she'll have to figure out how to indignantly deny, sanitize, explain away, or counterattack. ("What's your ethnicity?" she asked a Jewish reporter who queried her about Trump's "go back to [your native country]" tweet.)

We don't feel badly for her since she long ago embraced the Faustian Bargain of trading reputation for prominence. Rather, we are concerned about millions of average citizens subjected to the rhetorical maneuvers that TeamTrump has road-tested over four years of campaigning and his presidency...and that he rotates daily or hourly to deflect questions on Twitter, on Fox, at rallies, or on the White House lawn en route to the helicopter, with rebuttals basically not permitted.

These enable Trump, in the still-relevant words of Jonathan Swift, "to argue that black is white or white is black, according to how they are paid." The first defense to such rhetorical magic is to expose beforehand what a trained magician will be doing—hence, here's a handy Bullshit Detector based on all the examples throughout *Fake President* so that starting now *you* can spot his tricks and provide real-time rebuttals.

1. **Cherry-Picking—The Black Swan Fallacy:** This is the phenomenon of spotting a black swan and then implying that all are black. The purpose is to replace analysis with anecdotage.

    For example, should Trump or a prominent Republican get in trouble because of some bigoted words or conduct, Fox's Sean Hannity will ride to the rescue to pugnaciously announce—*Hey, Democrat Robert Byrd was once a Klansman!* Which was true *100 years ago.* Yet it ignores the larger reality that Byrd often apologized for that lapse while serving 50 years as the highly regarded senator and majority leader from West Virginia.

And notice how Trump disparages reports of all bad polls as "fake," even if from Fox News. Yet whenever a Rasmussen Poll—understood to be a GOP outlier weighted some eight points in his favor—says that he's broken 50 percent, he tweets "THANK YOU RASMUSSEN"—as if that black sheep of polling reflected all pollsters.

2. **Assertions & Adjectives:** It takes enormous effort to enact a major law. That can be especially daunting to a president who gets to his office around 11 a.m. most days and also loses thousands of hours a year to golfing, tweeting, and Fox-watching. No surprise then that he has figured out that it's nearly as effective—and a whole lot easier—just to assert that he's done something really, really great.

E.g.: "we're going to have so much beautiful clean coal," "we're already building a big, beautiful wall," "we will always protect patients with preexisting conditions," "no president has been tougher on the Russians," his conversation shaking down the Ukranian president on the Bidens was "beautiful, perfect," "no president has suffered more than I have" (four were assassinated).

Two beauts tested our resolve not to fall to the floor laughing and gasping for air: *"To be frank, I'm a very honest person."* And after attacking four minority congresswomen with a famous racist trope, he defended himself with one of his routine self-acquittals: *"I don't have a racist bone in my body."*

The assertion trick goes into high gear whenever he discusses family members: "I thought Ivanka was amazing at the G20, and, I'll tell you, the foreign leaders loved her." "Jared will secure an Israeli deal which no one has managed to get." Here, Ivanka gets grandfathered in as the equivalent of a foreign leader, and Jared becomes Henry Kissinger. It's only a matter of time before he suggests that Nike reword its slogan to "Just *say* it."[3]

His overreliance on self-serving assertions to counter reality is getting close to the pathetic "Baghdad Bob" assuring his country in a TV interview that everything was fine at the Baghdad Airport as American troops were overrunning it in the background.

3. **Performance Artist:** *"There's no business like show business..."* "If you can fake sincerity," Ronald Reagan would half-joke, "you've got it made."

   Like Dutch Reagan, Trump too excels at talking like he means what he's saying, leading many people—unaccustomed in life to deal with a Ponzi-level fraudster—to marvel, "He tells it like it is!" But to be fair, it's an act that he's been doing his entire adult life to the point that it has become second nature.

   Like that other performer-president, 45 understands how to communicate messages by his use of voice,

---

3 This is a near-perfect trick when talking about the future, since people will associate the speaker with the superlatives without risk of contradiction. Then, when the braggadocio doesn't pan out, there's usually some other ploy to avoid accountability: Candidate Trump boasted that "all the jobs are coming back," yet three years later, GM shuttered its iconic Lordstown, Ohio, plant. *No problemo*—he quickly blamed the UAW local and took credit for a smaller, long-planned investment by Ford.

gesticulations, body language, smirks, and struts. At rallies he essentially does stand-up, as he'll invariably extend his arms palms up and lift his shoulders up in a "Come on, am I right?" plea, then shift to his "accordion" two-hand motion to coax approval. In interviews, he frequently barks, "Excuse me, excuse me!" if any journalist gets halfway through a sentence that Trump doesn't like in order to drown him/her out...all while making his points in a bellicose shout.

The poet Juvenal understood how easy it was to superficially appease everyday Romans with "bread and circuses." Trump apparently got the Juvenal memo because, on his first day in office, he told his staff that they should treat every day as another episode of a TV show. Which makes perfect sense since, in his mind, he's still primarily involved in entertainment, except now it's a *real* reality show.

Mark Burnett, producer of *The Apprentice*, told the *New Yorker* that Trump would never have become president without that show introducing him to millions of supporters who cared not at all about policy but dug his tough-guy "You're fired!" persona—a John Wayne for our digital age. It is odd, however, that so many believed in his fake persona as a scripted TV Boss even as he now calls nearly all journalists "fake." Supporters think what's fake is real and real is fake.[4]

An early Cassandra warning about the emergence

---

4 Here's Billy Bush, after his famous "Access Hollywood" tape scandal, explaining Trump's approach to TV and life: "He'd been saying it's No. 1 forever and finally, I'd had enough...I told him, 'Wait a minute, you haven't been No. 1 for like five years—not in any category, not in any demo.' He goes, 'Did you see last Thursday? Last Thursday, 18-49, the last five minutes?' 'Later, when the cameras were off, he said, 'Billy, look, you just tell them and they believe it. That's it. They just do.'"

of politics as entertainment came from Neil Postman's seminal 1985 book, *Amusing Ourselves to Death.* Now in 2019, James Poniewozik, the *New York Times* chief television critic, succinctly explained how Donald Trump had become the nightmare that Postman had anticipated: "The key is to remember that Donald Trump is not a person. He is a TV character." He cares about story arcs and performance—white hats and black hats—but policy not so much.

4. **The Insult Machine:** Think of Trump as a human monkey wrench waking up every day deciding who to throw himself at.

   Politico reported that fully a third of his first 2000 presidential tweets disparaged people—from the powerful to the little-known. (See Chapter 12, "Bully's Pulpit.") By the end of 2018, the list totaled a hard-to-believe 598 people and things. (When future dictionaries define "nasty," they may understandably add, "See Trump, Donald"; who else comes close?)

   Trump has learned from two mentors. First, he's channeling Roy Cohn, Senator Joe McCarthy's chief counsel who was later disbarred, when he often says, "If someone hits me, I hit them back 10 times harder." Second, he's updating the core observation of an Italian philosopher and politician five centuries ago, who wrote, "It's better to be feared than loved." Like Machiavelli, Trump loves being feared. And since a president's throw-weight can do real reputational damage, this thuggish tactic—giving extra meaning to the nickname *The Don*—can produce the desired effect of anticipatory genuflection by those fearing massive retaliation.

This applies especially to journalists or politicians who understandably don't want to be slandered in front of millions of voters, readers, friends, and family as well as receive death threats from unhinged Base voters. For example, the percentage of the 282 congressional Republicans in his first two years who said or wrote a critical word about him is near zero. Critics know that if "they go low," he will always enthusiastically "go lower." The adage about wrestling with a pig in the mud comes to mind.

In the modern era, Newt Gingrich unveiled this strategy, best described in Steve Kornacki's *The Red and the Blue,* brutally telling Republicans they should always refer to their rivals as "weak. pathetic, treasonous, unpatriotic, un-American, stupid. What Newt started, Donald is perfecting."

5. **The Unscientific Method—Figures Don't Lie, but Liars Figure:** In Trumpland, instead of facts leading to conclusions, conclusions lead to "facts." Among the worst examples in modern history was Lysenkoism, when the Soviet Union in the 1920s and 1930s insisted that learned habits could be genetically inherited because of the regime's ideological need to establish "the perfect Soviet Man."

Cut to the American version a century later. Due to a parallel political need to keep fossil fuel donors happy, the scientific near-unanimity about climate violence in 2019 is simply ignored as EPA and Agriculture Department climate studies are simply thrown out and deleted from government websites.

Other than Trump's inane comment that cold days

disprove global warming, the president simply cred-
its "my intelligence" for disagreeing with the White
House's own interagency report about increasing
weather-related calamities. (See #2 above, *Assertions.)*
"Don't take it personally," he'll be able to explain to his
grandchildren for putting Mara-a-Lago under water
and the planet at risk. "My base insisted that I own the
libs by denying climate change."

6. **Upside-Downism:** *"No, YOU'RE the puppet!"* In
an extremely deft maneuver, Trump will accuse
others of doing precisely what he does to preempt
expected attacks. See all those tweets announcing
that, if anything: "Black House Gov Ops chairman
Elijah Cummings is a "racist [and] brutal bully"...
Hillary colluded with the Russians...*Democrats* are
"obstructionists" and the actual "liars" who practice
"McCarthyism" (which is especially rich given Cohn's
tutelage)—and the *Mueller Report* was "treason" and
an "attempted coup." When *Speaker Pelosi* explained
her House Resolution to condemn a notorious Trump
tweet because it sounded like "he wanted to Make
America White Again," Trump attacked *that* comment
as racist because, in his world, even discussing racism
is construed as racist.

   See how often he'll just blame Obama for what he's
doing, as when he told NBC's Chuck Todd during
news reports of inhumane conditions for children at
Detention Centers, "You know, under Obama there
was a separation policy. I was the one who ended it. I
inherited separation from President Obama." To which
Obama's head of ICE responded, "That's categorically

Photo by Chip Somodevilla/Getty Images

false. Our policy was just the opposite, to do everything possible to keep families together."

There's also the probability that many busy people will throw up their hands when everyone's attacking everyone, and a tie usually goes to our one president. "I am completely confused as to who is lying and who is telling the truth," remarked Mary Linda Vetter from Woodhull, New York. "I just feel helpless."

7. **Rooster-Taking-Credit-for-the-Dawn:** With scant positive accomplishments (though many negative ones such as reversing health/safety rules and regulations), this president simultaneously takes credit for anything good in America "on my watch" while shunning responsibility for anything bad.

Although Trump weekly claims this is "about the best economy ever" and once said, "I'm the greatest jobs president God ever created," in fact the average number of jobs created, wage growth, and rate of GDP in the last two years of Obama were slightly better than Trump's first two years (an average of 220,000 a jobs a month for the 30 months of Obama vs. 191,000 jobs a month for the first 30 months of Trump). In fact, ever since Bush's recession of 2007–08 hit, it was Obama's stimulus and bailout policies that helped stave off a collapsed economy, with a largely steady, consistent growth from 2010 to 2019. *Post hoc, ergo propter hoc,* Trump seeks acclaim for staying on this upward trend while conveniently ignoring the huge spike in the federal debt as a result of his tax and spending policies.

One glaring examples is when in 2018 he bragged that there were no airline fatalities in his first year in office, as there hadn't been in any of the prior seven years. That boast, however, stopped after two crashes of Boeing 737 Max planes because of failures at the firm and FAA.

8. **Fear Itself:** Humorist Larry Wilmore joked that Trump indeed *was* our Roosevelt because "the only thing Trump has is fear itself." Indeed, 45 himself told author Bob Woodward, "Real power is—I don't even want to use the word—fear."

    Politicians appealing more to our amygdalas than our cerebellums is as old as...politics. There were patriotic newsreels during World War I against evil Huns; Gov. George Wallace said that "no one is going to out-n****r me" in case anyone was unsure; and LBJ's Daisy Ad in 1964, actually airing just once, helped turn GOP presidential nominee Barry Goldwater into a nuclear menace. But again, Trump has set the record for a modern version of "the Russians are coming"— only with hordes of brown people as, ironically, the Russians (since that country *did* invade the US digitally in 2016).

    In the weeks before the 2018 midterm elections, he mimicked Orson Welles in his famous 1938 radio broadcast "War of the Worlds" by daily, hourly shouting about a "caravan" of asylum-seeking families a thousand miles away "invading" our southern border. His fearmongering boomeranged, however, when it stampeded even more panicked families to flee Central American gangs before it was too late. He went on to declare that he might unilaterally end constitutionally protected "birthright citizenship," and he did spend tens of millions of dollars in a show of farce by sending 5,500 American troops to the border to do...nothing really, since by law they could not engage in domestic policing actions.

He huffed and puffed only to blow the (*Republican)* House down.

9. **Both-Sides-ism (a.k.a., What-About-ism):** A rhetorical sleight-of-hand related to "Black Sheep" is to ignore proportionality and imply that a flea is like an elephant, since both are in the animal kingdom. Lawyers call this the "slippery slope" where, because hard-and-fast distinctions are difficult to make, they are often not made.

The most famous example occurred after the clash at a protest rally in Charlottesville, Virginia, between Neo-Nazis chanting, "Jews will not replace us," and an antifascist group protesting *them*. It shouldn't be difficult to know the difference between a group carrying swastika signs and loaded guns and their targeted victims—indeed, one young protestor was murdered by a white supremacist when his car plowed into a group of them. Yet Trump belligerently insisted to reporters that there were "fine people on both sides."

Or when someone questions the intelligence of Trump or an ally, Sean Hannity usually hits back with the what-about-ism of that time when brainiac Barack Obama did mispronounce the word "corpsmen" as "cor*p*smen" (it's "coresmen").

That's supposed to equal the thousands of examples of dissembling, according to the *Washington Post*'s highly regarded "Fact Checker"?

Also, both-sides-ism can cut both ways: when the

Trump White House kept pushing the line that it was unethical or corrupt that the son of VP Biden during the Obama administration was doing business in Ukraine, it led CNN's Jake Tapper to ask a gulping Secretary Mnuchin, well, what about the president's two international business sons traveling around the world on the taxpayer's dime making deals that profit their father? Mnuchin replied that "I don't want to get into those details."

10. **Repetition:** When Trump decides on the story line of the day, he is a walking echo because a) as a student of advertising and rhetoric, he knows the goal is not originality but stickiness and b) he appears to lack the bandwidth to carry around too much information at any one time. Asked on C-SPAN about his goals for a second term, Trump replied, *"I think we're going to be very, very strong on health care. Very very strong because it is very important to me."* Here's a partial transcript of his first White House press conference on February 16, 2017, when he was struggling to explain why he issued an Executive Order ending the DACA program, since he really liked it:

> *We're doing to show great heart. DACA is a very, very difficult subject for me. I will tell you. It's one of the most difficult subjects I have...[it's] a very very difficult thing for me. Because, you know, I love these kids. I love kids. I have kids and grandkids. And I find it very, very hard doing what the law says exactly to do. And you know the law is rough. I'm not talking about new laws. I'm talking the existing law*

is very tough. It's very very rough.

For obvious example, there were also the thousands of times he said of the Mueller Report, "It's a witch hunt... it's a hoax...13 [or 18] angry Democrats...no collusion, no obstruction." While such repetition does induce millions to reflexively think of the phrase "witch hunt" whenever the word "Mueller" is uttered, it cannot erase Trump's 10 documented examples of obstruction, 77 instances of a Trump associate lying, 140 contacts with Russians during the 2016 campaign, and 34 indict-ments plus 7 convictions, all carefully documented in that report. As FDR observed about Joseph Goebbels, "Repetition does not transform a lie into the truth."

11. **Nicknames:** Trump has developed his own personal media—the nickname channel. He gives dozens of people unflattering monikers that the mass media happily recycle over and over—Crooked Hillary, Pocahontas, Crazy Bernie, Sleepy Joe, Low-Energy Jeb, Liddle Marco.
    Bush 43 did this as well, but usually from a jokey and not slanderous premise—Turd Blossom for Karl Rove, to take one oblique example. Despite many possibilities to respond in kind, targeted Democrats today rarely return the compliment so as not to remind everyone of their nicknames or compete in an arena where Trump is unarguably more skilled. This book, however, is under no such political constraint or modesty; hence, here are some whimsical entries: The Don, Corrupt Don, Cheatin' Don, Dangerous Don, Dictator Donald, Donald the Menace, Agent

Orange, Benedict Donald, Big Fat Liar (oh, sorry, Al Franken already used that one in a book about Rush Limbaugh).

12. **The Hyperbolic & Apocalyptic:** The man exaggerates exaggerations. "When Trump hears a number," says MSNBC's Chris Hayes, "he has to make it bigger"— one absurd example being that when he asked Putin how many Russians died in WWII and Putin, who should know, said "25 million," Trump responded, "I heard it was 50 million."[5]

   For those who think he's simply an ignorant egotist, please appreciate that there's also a method to his badness. The key to his style, he admits, "is bravado. I play to people's fantasies. People may not always think big themselves, but they can still get very excited by those who do. I call it truthful hyperbole. It's an innocent form of exaggeration—and a very effective form of promotion."

   We call it untruthful hyperbole: he claimed that Democrats engage in infanticide, that "almost everyone agrees that my Administration has done more in less than two years than in any other Administration in the history of our country," and that he has the world's "greatest memory" (except those 30 times he couldn't recall something in response to written questions from the Special Counsel). "He was the King of hyperbole,"

5 For another numerical grandiosity, here are his estimates of American jobs generated by pending arms deals with the Saudis:
March 20, 2018: "over 40,000"
October 17, 2018: "500,000"
October 19, 2018: "600,000"
June 23, 2019: "probably over 1 million"

columnist Liz Smith wrote, "and he had just the touch of Elvis vulgarity to endear him to the common man."

Then there are scores of examples (see Chapter 8, "Dumb & Dumber") where he says that nobody knows more about "drones, nuclear war, technology, banks..." than he does. Listen carefully, and you'll hear an Americanized version of Kim Jong-Un claiming he had five holes-in-one playing his first round of golf.

On the subject of Chairman Kim, Trump bragged that when he became president, "America was on the brink of nuclear war with North Korea," but, fortunately, he saved the day. Also, once he leaves office, the economy may "go to hell," which, if proven true, is the only argument so far for an Ivanka/Donald Junior dynasty. *Après moi, le deluge.*

13. **Rhetorical Questions:** Few politicians can resist this age-old device of planting a disputed premise in the form of a question in order to mislead listeners to an inevitable—if untrue—conclusion. With audiences trying to catch up to every sentence, it's very easy to go with the flow of falsehoods.

"What do you have to lose?" he asked a black audience in Detroit during a campaign stop (the answer turned out to be "plenty"). "*Why should I not like Kim?*" (perhaps because he's a murderous dictator?). "*Why would*" Putin try to interfere with the 2016 American presidential election? (Duh.) And most recently, when it appeared that he had indeed said something unlawful, foolish, or even impeachable in his now-famous July 25 phone call with the new Ukranian president, his best defense was "Is anybody dumb enough to believe that I

would say something inappropriate with a foreign leader while on such a potentially 'heavily populated' call?" (A majority of Americans would say, "YES!")

14. **Political Correctness:** Either party can overreact to "microaggressions" in order to ignore the content of a policy by sneering about its phrasing or source. If a reporter gets close enough to ask Trump about, say, "the impact of coal on the environment" or "voter suppression due to the ID laws," he can skate away by mocking such questions as merely "politically correct." Is that another way of saying—they're based on something that's true, popular, and unanswerable?

    This technique works especially well with rally audiences who supposedly resent condescending elites, calling out their racism or xenophobia. Consequently, Trump considers it a lay-up to invoke "PC" if something is uttered by Democrats, Hollywood, or liberals, or the trifecta of all three. Imagine a journalist asking, "Why did you give a speech on gun violence but not mention guns?" Answer: "That's sooo PC."

    Conveniently, it's easier to dismiss criticism than debate it...which can lead to obviously selective judgments. To Trumpers, every joke at his expense on *SNL* is ridiculed as "PC," but nothing said on Laura Ingraham's show is; anything said by Muslim Rep. Ilhan Omar about Israel or the Middle East is regarded as awful racism, but nothing white Christian Rep. Steven King says about Muslims is. When a cartoonist who drew an obviously anti-Semitic cartoon was disinvited to a social media gathering at Trump's White House, was that ok because anti-Semitism is

bad or PC because Trump surrendered to the Jews?
According to a venerable legal axiom, "To the jaun-
diced eye, all looks yellow."

15. **Conspiracy Theories:** Richard Hofstadter's 1964
essay and book *The Paranoid Style in American Politics*
famously explained that those who traffic in conspiracy theories display three habits: "heated exaggeration,
suspiciousness and conspiratorial fantasy." A half century later, they are flourishing in the soil of extreme
partisanship, with the Web and Trump as accelerants.

Conspiracy theories can justify the world to racists
who lack the mental acuity to connect cause and effect
and yearn for some unified field theory to explain their
fears. When Bill Clinton aide Vince Foster committed
suicide, several official inquires all dismissed theories of murder, yet Trump at that time provocatively
said, "There's something fishy here." He engaged in
the same fact-free innuendo about the 2018 caravans
("I wouldn't be surprised if Soros was paying for the
caravans. A lot of people say yes") and his retweets of
people speculating that the Clintons were involved in
the suicide of Jeffrey Epstein. "Murder," he wrote?

These grotesque comments would be startling
coming from a normal president if it weren't for his
years of birtherism that helped assure a high percentage of supporters that their anxieties were not base-
less. "The Deep State" has a ring of "Fifth Column"
mystery that similarly works without explanation.
He deploys two conspiracy theories in particular to
parry all bad news stories and bad investigations: viz.,
Trump-haters a) in the Mainstream Media generate

"fake news" (see below) and b) in the Mueller "cabal" make false accusations...never mind that nearly all decision makers in the Special Counsel's line of legal authority were lifelong Republicans.

Most prominently, according to his former Homeland Security advisor Tom Bossert, Trump keeps repeating the "completely debunked" conspiracy theory that it was Ukraine, not Russia, that hacked the DNC and then framed Russia.

This view is rejected by all American intelligence agencies and the entire Senate Intelligence Committee yet is the basis on which AG Barr traveled around the world in October, 2019, looking to find any evidence to support it. Nothing yet.

16. **Deny/Deny/Deny:** Recall that scene in *Chicago* when a wife walks in on her husband having sex with two women? She is outraged, shouting, "how could you do this!" While dressing, he says calmly and confidently, "Do what?" After he gaslights for several minutes, the wife calms down and begins to doubt if her dramatic encounter actually happened.

Cut to Trump being directly asked if he knew about hush money payments to his mistresses or the Trump Organization's financial involvement with Russian interests. He coolly denied both, even though he had personally signed at least six checks *while in the Oval Office* totaling $270,000 to Michael Cohen to pay off Stormy Daniels and others...and even though for the year before his election he had been negotiating with Putin-connected oligarchs to build a Trump Tower Moscow, signing a letter of intent. (All of which adds up to "Implausible Deniability," a coinage of Jelani Cobb of *The New Yorker*.)[6]

"Kiss-and-tell" author Cliff Sims, in *A Team of Vipers*, expressed his amazement watching firsthand in the White House at how Trump "would deny everything at first and revise as needed—[he] did this regularly."

17. **Block that Metaphor:** Metaphors aren't reasons but enable people to visualize and, therefore, better understand a problem. Lincoln's log cabin, Hoover's "a chicken in every pot," Churchill's description of the Soviet "iron curtain," JFK's "throwing our hat over the wall of space," Eisenhower's "domino theory" in Southeast Asia, and Reagan's composite "welfare queen"—they can substitute for, if not overpower, reason. And since evidence-based policy is not exactly Trump's forte, he often relies on metaphors to make his case.

The feral responses of his crowds to his incessant overuse of "We're gonna build the Wall...we're gonna drain the swamp" misled him to confuse good metaphors with good policies. But they do their job for Trump, which is to excite rather than to explain.

18. **The 180°:** Trump obviously enjoys hanging with

---

6 One variant, which *Washington Post* reporter Josh Dawsey named "selective amnesia," involves him separating himself from radioactive people by again and again shrugging and saying, "I hardly know the guy." He applied this trick to, among others, his interim AG Matthew Whitaker, Ann Coulter, Michael Cohen, Paul Manafort, Roger Stone, Cliff Sims, George Papadopoulos, George Conway, and even tried to get amnesia about Jeff Epstein: during his very bad week in mid-July when he was arrested on federal charges of running an underage sex ring, Trump remarked that "I was never a fan of his"; yet 15 years before, Trump said of Epstein, "He's a terrific guy [and] a lot of fun."

dictators, police, and soldiers as well as conveying toughness in his appearance and photographs. He scowls way more than he smiles because his brand is all about projecting strength. He's not Mr. Rogers.

Yet while conveying stubbornness in his base-pleasing views about immigrants and taxes, he will reverse himself on a dime when being chased by scandal and say anything necessary to survive to another day. He asserted in his campaign that he'd "absolutely" release his tax filings only to later retract; he said in 2017 that he'd "absolutely" submit to an in-person deposition with Special Counsel Mueller because, well, he doesn't cower; he repeatedly said in 2018 that he'd meet with Iran to discuss sanctions and nukes "without preconditions," which his Secretary of State and National Security Adviser repeated in September 2019...until Trump tweeted a few days later that he'd never held this view that was being reported by the "fake media"; twice after mass killings, the president said (following the El Paso massacre) that he liked the idea of universal background checks. "I'm looking to do background checks...like we've never done before. Congress is getting close to a bill." Within a day of each statement and after talking to the NRA, he dropped the idea.

There's a political expression in Japan: "After six months, no one remembers." That seems to reflect Trump's thinking, except it's not "after six months," but more like after six days or six hours.

19. **The Fake Media:** There indeed is such a thing as "real" fake media, which used to apply to Russian troll

farms pushing out obvious lies on social media, such as "Pope Francis Endorses Trump!" (No, he didn't.)

Trump's appropriation of this term is the trick that keeps on giving. He privately admitted to Leslie Stahl of *Sixty Minutes* that he relentlessly pounds away at all journalists as "fake media" to "discredit" them so readers don't believe their criticisms of him. (See "Media," Chapter 10.) So whenever there's a serious accusation against him, Trump—sparing himself any need to explain or document something—simply sneers, "That's fake media," as he glides away.

While of course journalists on deadlines make mistakes, the *New York Times,* to take one prominent example, will acknowledge them in a "Corrections Box" within a few days. There is no equivalent mechanism in the Trump White House, if for no other reason than he openly says he never apologizes for anything. Like yelling *leper* on the streets of London five centuries ago, the mere invocation of "FAKE MEDIA" provokes a predictable Pavlovian reaction among his true believers without having to even bother with a factual reply.

Of course, this whole idea is ridiculous. The term "fake news," wrote Never-Trumper David Frum, author of *Trumpocracy*, basically translates to "true though embarrassing." The chance that numerous journalists and platforms would somehow conspire among themselves to take a similar tack is nonexistent, yet Trump's gullible base swallows this contrivance whole.

20. **The Lyin' King:** This is Trumpers' go-to escape from most unanswerable questions, especially if the lie is

the first (mis)characterization of something, e.g., AG Bill Barr twice spinning the Mueller Report in his own words before it was released. His strategy was straight from Mark Twain: "A lie gets halfway around the world before truth puts on her boots."

When one of the authors asked a prominent conservative magazine editor during the 2016 election, "Do you really think that Hillary Clinton lies more than Donald Trump?" he laughed. "No one lies more than Donald Trump."

Why? Because it works. There's a "liar's dividend" that rewards untrue, unrebutted statements made to people unaccustomed to dealing with pathological liars—think those "Swiftboat Veterans" who smeared John Kerry for two weeks without challenge because the Kerry camp couldn't believe anyone would take them seriously—which smears are then perversely further spread by people earnestly trying to debunk them. Those who simply believe that Trump is an "idiot" do not fully appreciate that his falsehoods are willful, strategic, incessant, made not to win a particular argument, but to create an entirely false reality.

On two rare occasions, however, Team Trump finally admitted the obvious—whenever possible, they prefer lying to a base that's unusually gullible, uninformed, and enthralled. "I love the poorly educated," he exulted in his February 24, 2016, victory speech after winning the Nevada caucuses. And son-in-law Jared Kushner admitted to Elizabeth Spiers, the editor of the local newspaper he owned, the *New York Observer*, that his father-in-law of course didn't believe in birtherism but

Brit Hume of Fox: "Trump's claims about the *NY Times* losing $$ are so easily checked that one wonders why he keeps repeating them."

Preet Bharara, former US Attorney: "Because he's a liar."

"he just knows that Republicans are stupid and they'll buy it."

Some previous presidents took a very different approach. According to FDR speechwriter Robert Sherwood, in *Roosevelt and Hopkins:* "The *New York Times* can make mistakes—but the president of the United States must not make mistakes. This constant thought imposed a harrowing responsibility. After 1940, the White House had its resident statistician, Isador Lubkin, the Commissioner of Labor Statistics, who was constantly available and incalculably valuable to Roosevelt and to Hopkins in checking every decimal point."

Kellyanne Conway is no Isador Lubkin—and DJT no FDR.

21. Last, there is a final sleight-of-hand to help this Political Houdini slither away.

*Where there are no facts or words to explain some crazy comment—from buying Greenland to nuking a hurricane to going to war—Trump will invariably grab onto this life preserver: "Let's see what happens."

There's no way to rebut a person who hints either that he knows something's around the corner or *could* be around the corner to salvage any filthy lie. After all, the Giants did come from 13½ games back to beat the Dodgers in a three-game playoff in 1951 on Bobby Thomson's "shot heard 'round the world" in the rubber game, and Franco Harris made that "Immaculate Reception" in 1972 to beat the Oakland Raiders with five seconds remaining. There's a reason that the New York Lotto slogan is "Ya Never Know."

*He can also do a version of the old "Borscht Belt" favorite, "Do you love your wife?" "Compared to who?" Which translates to "If you think I'm bad, take a look at X." Then he will happily assert, evidence not required, that someone did something, maybe, similar or wrong. Most recently, Hunter Biden served his purpose after the whistleblower's credible complaint. Otherwise just saying words like "Obama," "Hillary," "AOC," or "socialists" is enough to adequately rile up his rallies so they forget what Trump was originally caught doing or saying.

*Finally, there's always the option of simply admitting the scandal—yeah it was that Russian thing, yeah I spoke to President Zelinsky about the Bidens—and then saying or implying, "So what?", as if admitting the crime excuses it. Don't try it under oath, but, in the world of political BS, this has a surprising success rate for people in MAGA hats eager to swallow his word salads.

Anderson Cooper, CNN: "If the president doesn't acknowledge his lies and his supporters don't care–then what?"
John Dean: "We're in trouble."

U.S. Air Force Tech. Sgt. Trevor Tiernan

1.
HEALTH INSURANCE
"OBAMACARE IS DEAD." (NO, IT'S NOT.)

The children of Donald Trump's late brother Freddy Jr. were mostly left out of Fred Trump's will. They sued, alleging that the reason they were excluded was that the will was "procured by fraud and undue influence" by Donald Trump and his siblings. Freddy's grandson, also excluded from the will, suffered from seizures and cerebral palsy. Donald Trump cut him off his health insurance and bragged about it to the papers: "Why should we give him medical coverage? They sued my father, essentially. I'm not thrilled when someone sues my father."

The suit was later settled and sealed. But it proved to be good practice for trying to deny health insurance to millions of Americans.

"If you can't take care of your sick in the country, forget it, it's all over. I mean, it's no good. So I'm very liberal when it comes to health care. I believe in universal health care. I believe in whatever it takes to make people well and better." —Donald Trump, Larry King Live, *1999*

"We're going to have insurance for everybody. There was a philosophy in some circles that if you can't pay for it, you don't get it. That's not going to happen with us." —Donald Trump, five days before taking office. (1/15/17)

Obamacare

"Obamacare covers very few people—and remember, deduct

"It's very easy to disguise a medical program as a humanitarian project. Most people are a little reluctant to oppose anything that suggests medical care for people who possibly can't afford it."

Ronald Reagan, 1961

from the number all of the people that had great health care that they loved that was taken away from them—it was taken away from them." (2/24/17)

Trump doing math is always a dangerous proposition. That "very few people" the Affordable Care Act covers? Obamacare has added about 20 million people to the insurance rolls— about the combined populations of Wisconsin, Michigan, and Kentucky, states that handed the presidency to Trump. The number of people who lost insurance from plans that were not ACA-compliant (about 2.6 million) is just a portion of that. And after the outrage over the plan cancellations, most were issued a waiver so that they could keep plans continuing until late 2017.

"It's an unbelievably complex subject. Nobody knew that health care could be so complicated." (2/28/17)

Tell that to Barack Obama. He had his integrity questioned during a joint session address by a House member yelling from the well ("You lie!") and still managed to pass the bill after a 14-month slog and no Republican votes. He could also ask Hillary Clinton, who tackled the country's most vexing public policy challenge with vastly different results from Obama and was pilloried and taunted by seething crowds for the crime of trying to expand health care access. Trump promised the moon and the stars, and "great health care" in the 2018 midterms, but could only deliver the House to the Democrats.

Actually, fellas, Obamacare is not a disaster. While there are negative anecdotes (Trump's wheelhouse), the Association of American Medical Colleges says there's "no significant number" leaving because of Obamacare. In fact, the number of physicians has actually increased 8 percent under the Affordable Care Act, and medical school applications are at an *all-time high*, up 25 percent since 2009.

#20. The Lyin' King: *"Together we're going to deliver real change that once again puts Americans first. That begins with immediately repealing and replacing the disaster known as Obamacare...You're going to have such great health care, at a tiny fraction of the cost—and it's going to be so easy." (10/25/16)*

"I never said I was going to repeal and replace in the first 61 days." (3/24/17)

Sure he did. He famously and repeatedly promised his crowds that the Affordable Care Act would be "immediately" repealed and replaced, with something "terrific" in its place. In the run-up to his swearing-in, President-Elect Trump and his team prepared the country for a whirlwind of activity that would make FDR's first hundred days look like a weekend at Mar-a-Lago: he supposedly considered calling Congress into a special session to repeal Obamacare on Inauguration Day, perhaps allocating money for the Great Wall in tuxes and gowns at the evening's inaugural balls. Instead, he stewed over inauguration crowd sizes and forced his press secretary to begin his relationship with the press on the wrong foot by falsely insisting that more watched the president's inauguration than any before in history:

"And they just fell a little bit short, and it's very hard when you need almost 100 percent of the votes and we have no votes, zero, from the Democrats. It's unheard of." (3/24/17)

"The longer I'm behind this desk and you have Obamacare, the more I would own it." (4/12/17)

"I couldn't afford to have regular mammograms. In 2014 I signed up for Obamacare. I was diagnosed with breast cancer in September of last year. The lumpectomy alone was billed at $40,000. I have four more chemo sessions to go, and after that, I have to do radiation. Luckily my cancer is only a stage one, so my prognosis is pretty good. But it is really scary thinking about my insurance being taken away. This is a fight for my life."

Claudette Williams, 58,
Orlando, FL, 2017

It's unheard of—if only you redact the prior eight years of American history before Trump took office, which saw an obstinate opposition party opposed to matters of routine (that ensure the full faith and credit of the US, like a vote to raise the debt ceiling) or on action that would help the country avert a great depression (like the stimulus) or, for the constitutional purists that Republicans purport to be, allow a president to fill a Supreme Court vacancy on his watch and with his entire presidency being defined by trivialization of the Senate's filibuster. Other than *that*, it's unheard of.

"Obamacare will explode and we will all get together and piece together a great healthcare plan for THE PEOPLE. Do not worry!" (3/25/17)

"Obamacare is dead. Some of you folks have yourself—you have family members that have suffered greatly under Obamacare. It's dying. It's just about on its last legs. If we did nothing, if we did absolutely nothing, Obamacare is dead." (3/17/17)

Reports of the Affordable Care Act's demise have been greatly exaggerated—especially by Donald Trump. The Congressional Budget Office's numbers indicate it's not imploding and is sustainable for the foreseeable future. It's not even down for the count, and it's definitely not out, despite the Trump White House's best efforts, such as slashing enrollment advertising by 90 percent. And slashing by 70 percent the "navigators" who help individuals sign up for health insurance.

"I think we're probably in that position where we'll let Obamacare fail. We're not going to own it. I'm not going to

own it. I can tell you, the Republicans are not going to own it." *(7/18/17)*

Forget Trump's flip-flops. Trump owned Obamacare at noon on January 20, 2017, regardless of whatever damage he could inflict on it, or how many times he could separate people from their healthcare, a dry run perhaps for wresting parents from their children at the border. No matter how many times he's tried to deny it, it's now his.

The Senate bill "will provide emergency relief for [Obamacare's] victims." *(7/24/17)*

The summer 2017 Senate GOP's "skinny repeal" bill contained $158 billion in funding that states could use for a variety of purposes, like lowering premiums, according to the Congressional Budget Office.

However, the money is temporary and more than offset by reductions in spending elsewhere: the measure would reduce spending on subsidies to purchase private insurance and lower deductibles by $396 billion over a decade and reduce spending on Medicaid by $756 billion over a decade in comparison to Obamacare.

Seventy-eight percent of Americans want Trump to make the health care law work while a nihilist few say that Trump should sabotage the law so that it fails and can be replaced later.

#12. The Hyperbolic: *"So pre-existing conditions are a tough deal. Because you are basically saying from the moment the insurance, you're 21 years old, you start working and you're paying $12 a year for insurance, and by the time you're 70,* *you get a nice plan. Here's something where you walk up and say, 'I want my insurance.'" (7/19/17)*

Somehow, somewhere, Donald Trump won a reputation for "telling it like it is." Sure, he would exaggerate, according to his famous "truthful hyperbole," but at least he was *authentic.* Here, he's authentically out to lunch. Almost as if he lived most of his adult life in a gilded, tacky tower. It's the same world where you need ID to buy groceries, and at that same supermarket, they let you add to the tab when you're strapped for cash. It's a nice world, but it's not the real world. Suffice to say, most 21-year-olds don't spend $12 a year on health insurance. For a 21-year-old earning $25,000, it's more like an average of $282 monthly, which is a mere 300x higher.

Trump's health care promises made it seem like he was doing his best impression of a snake oil salesman:

"[C]ross state lines, where you have—where it's almost impossible for insurance companies to compete in different states....We're putting it in a popular bill, and that will come. And that will come, and your premiums will be down 60 and 70 percent. People don't know that. Nobody hears it. Nobody talks about it." (7/19/17)

A couple of things here: the bill's not popular (the Republican bill had about a 20-point lower approval rating than Obamacare), and no study has remotely supported his claim that premiums would see such a drastic drop under the Republican bill. Purchasing insurance across state lines has been just about the only Republican idea on health care over the past three decades, beyond just repealing Obamacare, and there is no proof that it would cause premiums to plummet. The author of a study supporting buying insurance across state lines and who believes it would decrease premiums says a drop would likely depend on age and that such a steep fall seems "a little unreasonable."

"Health care didn't go down. We have the votes." (9/28/17)

There is a crazed bullishness to his boasts on a subject for which he had no experience until January 20, 2017. This "we have the votes" bravado came more than two months after his Senate repeal of the Affordable Care Act was torpedoed by John McCain's thumbs down. It famously didn't work... because they *didn't* have the votes. This was despite Trump's claims, among them that the repeal attempt that fall would have passed if Thad Cochran (R-MS) wasn't in the hospital (he wasn't). This new bill actually lost three Republican votes, when the party had only 52 senators, leaving them clocked in at 49 votes, where Mike Pence couldn't help.

"It is time to liberate our communities from this scourge of drug addiction." (10/16/17)

As a candidate, Trump said he "will give people struggling with addiction access to the help they need." He hasn't—and he's gone to great lengths to do the opposite. Trump enlisted his counselor and ex-pollster Kellyanne Conway—not Kellyanne Conway, MD—as the White House Opioids Policy Coordinator, showing that he sees it simply as a publicity issue, not a medical crisis on the level of the AIDS epidemic. Trump has not taken the issue seriously, appointing a 24-year-old former Trump campaign staffer whose main qualifications for a public health emergency was coordinating a golf tournament

In her *New York Times* column, Maureen Dowd discussed a *Washington Post* article headlined "Risk of Premature Birth Increased for Latinas After Trump's Election."

The story explained that "Researchers have begun to identify correlations between Trump's election and worsening cardiovascular health, sleep problems, anxiety and stress, especially among Latinos in the United States."

and a veterans charity, to help troubleshoot the crisis. Conway herself has been accused of freezing out experts, excluding the Office of National Drug Control Policy, from key decisions and strategy plans.

Nevertheless, the number of opioid overdoses total all US Vietnam War deaths each year, and in spite of Trump declaring a public health emergency, Trump proposed a 95 percent cut to the Office of National Drug Control Policy after his plan to strip 24 million of their health insurance failed. This was after firing the Obama-appointed Surgeon General after the publication of his own in-depth report on the opioid epidemic. That proposed 95 percent cut would reduce the Office of National Drug Policy staff by half and also close its drug-free communities initiative and anti-drug trafficking programs.

Preexisting Lies

"But when I watch some of the news reports, which are so unfair, and they say we don't cover pre-existing conditions, we cover it beautifully." (4/28/17)

"All Republicans support people with pre-existing conditions, and if they don't, they will after I speak to them. I am in total support." (10/18/18)

#10. Repetition: *"Republicans will totally protect people with Pre-Existing Conditions, Democrats will not! Vote Republican." (10/24/18)*

Republicans will not!

The midterms were a busy time for Trump's mendacity: the "caravan" of migrants coming for America might have grabbed the most attention—and activated the white supremacists' fevered imaginations of a browner America—but the brazenness of his health care lies were among the most galling. Republicans made a few facetious gestures toward protecting people with preexisting conditions, throwing in $8 billion to cover the care, but that fell far short of what was necessary. Their focus wasn't on protecting care, but repealing Obama's crown jewel.

Trump knew that health care was voters' most important issue and that 14 percent of Americans called it the "single most important" issue, which is why he and the Republicans sextupled down on the lie in the campaign's final weeks. They do not—and will not—protect people with preexisting conditions, which is estimated at anywhere from 50 to 129 million Americans (53 percent of US households report a preexisting condition). Indeed, the Trump administration is supporting a lawsuit—led by Republican AGs—that claims that the ACA's protections for people with preexisting conditions are *illegal*. If they win, those protections are gone—and insurance companies will again be allowed to deny people coverage. As of this writing, Trump's White House has made no alternative plan to keep those protections in place.

Single-Payer

#2. Adjectives & Assertions: *"You go and you look at countries where they have single-payer tax care, single-payer health care. If you look at it, they're a disaster." (10/11/18)*

Here's the lie Republicans have told themselves for generations: that countries from France to Sweden have largely government-provided universal health care and that they hate it,

Approximately 15,600 people died between 2014 and 2017 as a result of their states refusing to expand Medicaid coverage under the Affordable Care Act, according to a new working paper by the National Bureau of Economic Research… Today, 14 states have not adopted Medicaid expansion."
–*Mother Jones*

instead craving America's byzantine healthcare bureaucracy that costs far more than that of other advanced countries, covers fewer people, and provides worse outcomes. Donald Trump continued this Grand Old Party tradition.

As doctors Adam Gaffney, Steffie Woolhandler, and David Himmelstein explain, single-payer shifts how we pay for health care without actually increasing costs, far from a "disaster," and actually saves Americans more than $2 trillion over a decade. But don't just take their word for it. Take the word of people who actually live with single-payer care: one poll shows that 86.2 percent of Canadians want to strengthen their public health care rather than try out for-profit American health care. For some perspective, 86.2 percent of Americans probably don't agree that there are 50 stars on the flag.

> *"In recent years we have made remarkable progress in the fight against HIV and AIDS. Scientific breakthroughs have brought a once-distant dream within reach. My budget will ask Democrats and Republicans to make the needed commitment to eliminate the HIV epidemic in the United States within 10 years. Together, we will defeat AIDS in America." (2/5/19)*

The day after making this Kennedy-esque moonshot, Trump's own Department of Justice filed suit to stop a needle exchange program. Such efforts have made drastic strides in reducing HIV transmission. The DC needle exchange (once a congressional ban was lifted) produced a 70 percent decrease in HIV transmission over two years. Trump's budget request announced not long after that it would slash the National Institutes of Health by $5 billion. So how exactly will he stop HIV/AIDS? Let alone in the next decade?

"Federal health officials reported that, for the first time since enactment of Obamacare in 2011, the number of uninsured Americans grew—by 2 million to 27 million."
—*Politico* (9/10/19)

2.
CLIMATE VIOLENCE
WHAT, ME WORRY?

#15. Conspiracy Theory: *"The concept of global warming was created by and for the Chinese to make U.S. manufacturing non-competitive." (11/6/12)*

This comment in 2012 was not made by Alex Jones, but rather by a NYC real-estate developer who went on to be elected President of the United States.

"I was elected to represent the citizens of Pittsburgh, not Paris." (6/1/17)

This was Trump's alliterative attempt to justify withdrawing the United States from the historic Paris Climate Agreement. But since pollution, storms, and blistering heat don't stop at national borders, we can only hope that this won't be the sentence surviving historians use to illustrate the beginning of the end of civilization. But it could be if American energy policy continues to be effectively run by fossil fools.

"We don't want other leaders of other countries laughing at us anymore. And they won't be... I promised I would exit or renegotiate any deal [the Paris Agreement] which fails to serve America's interests." (6/1/17)

Unlike Trump, the 195 other world leaders who signed the Paris

Agreement realized that climate violence affects the entire globe. To these leaders—who, more or less, consider this issue to potentially be on the same level as a world war—Trump's chesty "America First" approach translates to "Screw You."

> *"[The Paris Agreement] includes yet another scheme to redistribute wealth out of the United States through the so-called Green Climate Fund—nice name—which calls for developed countries to send $100 billion to developing countries all on top of America's existing and massive foreign-aid payments."* (6/1/17)

Not only did Trump trivialize a global existential threat during his Paris Agreement withdrawal speech, he also flat out lied about international efforts to mitigate it. The Green Climate Fund, formed in 2010 by the United Nations Framework Convention on Climate Change, contains around $10 billion (not $100 billion) in funds from 43 countries, and the United States has only pledged $3 billion.

> #5. Unscientific Method: *"It's really cold outside, they are calling it a major freeze, weeks ahead of normal. Man, we could use a big fat dose of global warming!"* (10/19/15)

> *"Large parts of the Country are suffering from tremendous amounts of snow and near record setting cold. Amazing how big this system is. Wouldn't be bad to have a little of that good old-fashioned Global Warming right now!"* (1/20/19)

That Trump is a climate-change denier is terrifying enough. But the way he goes about his denial is grossly stupid and trivializing. He thinks he's being clever when he employs sarcasm to mock those who believe in climate disruption. But the joke's on him, since, as seemingly every serious news outlet has pointed out, the president routinely repeats global-warming skeptics' cardinal fallacy: confusing climate with weather.

The country laughed when, in February 2015, Senator Jim Inhofe (R-Florida) brought a snowball onto the Senate floor and used it to disprove the "eggheads" at "science laboratories" who were peddling global warming during a bout of "very unseasonable" cold in DC. Rational people pointed out that wide variations in weather are completely compatible with a warming climate; that, despite a temporary cold streak, 2014 was the warmest year on record at the time; and that "temperatures in February are supposed to be cold in the Northern Hemisphere, since it is a season called 'winter.'" Inhofe was properly shamed, but two years later the country inaugurated a Republican president who makes Inhofe-esque gaffs on a regular basis.

The administration's denial isn't just rhetorical, either. In 2019, the Agricultural Department began to refuse to "publicize dozens of government-funded studies that carry warnings about the effects of climate change, defying a long-standing practice of touting such findings by the Agriculture Department's acclaimed in-house scientists," according to *Politico*.

"You know, the windmills, boom, boom, boom [mimicking windmill sounds], bing [mimes shooting a gun], that's the end of that one. If the birds don't kill it first. The birds could kill it first. They kill so many birds. You look underneath some of those windmills, it's like a killing field of birds." (8/20/18)

"They want to have windmills all over the place, right? When the wind doesn't blow, what do we do? Uh, we got problems.

According to an analysis by *Vox*, between 2011 and 2015, Trump tweeted climate skepticism 115 times.

"Man, this guy hates windmills worse than Don Quixote. Did a windmill kill his dad or something?"

John Leguizamo (4/9/19)

When there's thousands of birds laying at the base of the windmill, what do we do? Isn't that amazing? The environmentalists, 'We like windmills.' Oh, really? Try going to the bottom of a windmill someday. It's not a pretty picture." (8/30/18)

Forget the millions of people living on coasts who are set to lose their homes to ocean rise, or the air and water being polluted by fossil-fuel extraction and burning, or the dying ecosystems—what about the birds? (FYI, several times more birds are killed by flying into tall buildings—like Trump's towers—than are killed by windmills.)

"If you have a windmill anywhere near your house, congratulations, your house just went down 75 percent in value. And they say the noise causes cancer. You tell me that one, okay— [imitates windmill sound with looping hand gesture]. You know, the thing makes so much noise and of course it's like a graveyard for birds." (4/2/19)

What is up with Trump's war on windmills? In 2006, he had a tiff with a company that wanted to build an offshore wind farm in Scotland that, Trump claims, would have spoiled the views at a luxury golf course he was building in the area—perhaps he's never gotten over that.

Whatever the case, his claims about windmills are demonstrably false. We've already addressed the bird issue, but the noise-cancer issue is tin-hat crazy—one often peddled by anti-wind power groups.

As *New York Magazine*'s Jonathan Chait wrote, "Wind turbines do not cause cancer...A power source that does cause many health problems, including cancer, is coal, an extremely dirty fuel Trump loves and has attempted to bolster."

One time, apparently, someone explained to Trump the actual concept of "clean coal"—the still very small-scale and experimental process of taking the carbon emissions from coal plants and storing them deep underground. But instead of nodding his head and politely saying, "interesting," like any rational human, Trump took the idea and ran with it, akin to giving birth in one month, not nine. Now, according to his rhetoric, all coal—literally the world's dirtiest mass-energy source—is "clean."

#16. Deny/Deny/Deny: *"After I left, [the death toll in Puerto Rico from Hurricane Maria] was 16 people that died. The 16 people was then lifted a couple of months after to 64 and that was the official number. And then all of a sudden, I read a report, many, many months later—a long time later—that they did a report that 3,000 people died. And I was like, 'Wait a minute, you went from 16 people to 64. We did a great job, and then you went from 64 to 3,000. How did that happen?' And they couldn't explain it. If you read that report, it's not explainable." (9/24/18)*

Puerto Rico was just a taste of the climate violence yet to come as the Earth continues to warm. The US response was wholly inadequate, so, in his typical fashion, Trump simply asserted conspiracy theories to smear his enemies and the victims of his failures:

"I think something's happening. Something's changing and it'll change back again. I don't think [climate change is] a hoax, I think there's probably a difference. But I don't know that it's man-made." (10/14/18)

Ocean acidification, glacier melting, sea-level rise, increased precipitation, increasingly violent weather, coral-reef death, droughts, wildfires, habitat destruction, rising temperatures, irregular animal migration—yeah, something's happening. And it's not going to "change back again."

"Nobody's seen anything like it." Increasingly extreme weather events—it's almost like the climate is... changing. Also, note how Trump "loves" people in Florida's Panhandle. This sudden ersatz compassion, so out of character for a man without apparent empathy, seems always reserved for people suffering in states that Trump carried in 2016. Any examples of him loving people in, say, California or Washington, DC?

More and more US homes—particularly those near coasts—are going to be subject to climate violence as the planet's average annual temperature continues to rise. According to a report from Climate Central:

> *"You'd have to show me the scientists [who say climate change is man-made] because they have a very big political agenda." (10/14/18)*

Well, for a start, there are the government's own NASA and National Oceanic and Atmospheric Administration scientists the interviewer—Lesley Stahl of *60 Minutes*—mentioned in the question Trump is answering here. There are also the scientists who conducted 97 percent of climate studies that took a position on climate change. And there's the Intergovernmental Panel on Climate Change—a United Nations body—that says we have less than 12 years to meaningfully address the matter before it becomes largely—if slowly—irreversible.

> *"One of the problems that a lot of people like myself—we have very high levels of intelligence, but we're not necessarily such*

"If an asteroid were spotted hurtling toward Earth, we wouldn't argue over whether asteroids exist. But that's basically what the politicization of science has done to the public discussion about climate change."

Susan Hockfield, former MIT president

believers. You look at our air and our water, and it's right now at a record clean. But when you look at China and you look at parts of Asia and you look at South America, and when you look at many other places in this world, including Russia, including—just many other places—the air is incredibly dirty."

"And when you're talking about an atmosphere, oceans are very small. And it blows over and it sails over. I mean, we take thousands of tons of garbage off our beaches all the time that comes over from Asia. It just floats right down the Pacific, it flows, and we say, 'Where does this come from?' And it takes many people to start off with." (11/27/18)

Climate disruption real? Oceans small? None of those science bloviations are as impressive as Trump's near-superhuman ability to name countries and continents.

"The Paris Agreement isn't working out so well for Paris. Protests and riots all over France. People do not want to pay large sums of money, much to third world countries (that are questionably run), in order to maybe protect the environment. Chanting 'We Want Trump!' Love France." (12/8/18)

Climate policy is hard. There will be kickback if you place a disproportionate amount of the burden on working-class people. That's what happened with the yellow-vest protests in France: President Emmanuel Macron enacted a gas tax that took a heavy toll on everyday car drivers in the country. Saving the planet will require smart decisions, bold policy, and political nuance.

Trump is neither smart, bold, nor nuanced. His response

THE TRUMP ADMINISTRATION IS MORE ANTIREGULATION THAN AUTOMAKERS.

After years of fighting fuel economy standards, four major automakers in 2019—Ford, Honda, Volkswagen, BMW of North America—cut a side deal with the California Air Resource Board to produce more fuel-efficient cars for their US fleets than required by federal agencies. An angry White House got the DoJ to investigate whether the agreement to reduce auto pollution was a possible antitrust violation even though the obvious purpose was not to boost prices.

to the yellow-vest protests was to mock the idea of any climate-change policy at all—to resign himself to watching the world burn and to make up stories about protesters chanting his name.

> *"The fire in California, where I was, if you looked at the floor, the floor of the fire, they have trees that were fallen, they did no forest management, no forest maintenance, and you can light—you can take a match like this and light a tree trunk when that thing is laying there for more than 14 or 15 months. And it's a massive problem in California... And it was very interesting, I was watching the firemen, and they're raking brush—you know the tumbleweed and brush, and all this stuff that's growing underneath. If that was raked in the beginning, there'd be nothing to catch on fire. It's very interesting to see." (11/27/18)*

The Green New Deal has nothing on Trump's plan to mitigate environmental disasters: massive government investment in... rakes.

> *"And [the Green New Deal] would force the destruction or renovation of virtually every existing structure in the United States. New York City would have to rip down buildings and rebuild them again. I don't think so." (3/2/19)*

> *"I think it is very important for the Democrats to press forward with their Green New Deal. It would be great for the so-called 'Carbon Footprint' to permanently eliminate all Planes, Cars, Cows, Oil, Gas & the Military—even if no other country would do the same. Brilliant!" (2/9/19)*

Though Republicans would never admit it, Donald Trump is taking their party to its logical conclusion—what historian Greg Grandin has described as a nihilistic "death cult."

In making progressive Democrats' plan for a "Green New Deal" seem nonsensical by deliberately misrepresenting its proposals, Trump, like most of the conservatives in power in Washington, is saying that the United States is incapable of mobilizing like it did during World War I, or World War II, or the original New Deal. He's saying that the plutocratic status quo is a greater priority than ecological disaster. He's saying that the world isn't worth saving.

What the Experts Think

"At about two degrees Celsius of warming, just one degree north of where we are today, some of the planet's ice sheets are expected to begin their collapse, eventually bringing, over centuries, perhaps as much as 50 feet of sea-level rise. In the meantime, major cities in the equatorial band of the planet will become unlivable... in India, and even in the northern latitudes, heat waves will kill thousands each summer. This is probably our best-case scenario." David Wallace-Wells, The Uninhabitable Earth

"We live in a world where we are acidifying the oceans, where there will be few places cold enough to support year-round ice, where all the current coastlines will be underwater, and where droughts, wildfires, floods, storms, and extreme weather are already becoming the new normal." Dahr Jamail, The End of Ice

"It is estimated that one-third of all reef-building corals, a third of all fresh-water mollusks, a third of sharks and rays, a quarter of all mammals, a fifth of all reptiles, and a sixth of all birds are headed toward oblivion." Elizabeth Kolbert, The Sixth Extinction

"Rapid, far-reaching and unprecedented changes in all aspects of society" are needed to avoid the worst consequences of climate change. *The United Nations Intergovernmental Panel on Climate Change, "Global Warming of 1.5"*

The July 2019, UN Report concluded that the current rate of global warming would push 120 million into poverty by 2030 alone and create a "climate apartheid" where the wealthy pay to escape overheating, hunger and conflict while rest of world suffers.

#8. Dumb & Dumber: Trump isn't the only one in the White House making ludicrous statements about climate violence. In February 2019, the *Washington Post* revealed that Trump was preparing to form a Presidential Committee on Climate Security, apparently in an effort to discredit intelligence agencies' assertion that climate change is a threat to national security. To head that committee, the president was set to appoint Dr. William Happer, a National Security Council senior director and emeritus professor of physics at Princeton University. Though Happer's credentials sound impressive, his past statements on climate are not. Here are two:

#12. The Hyperbolic and Apocalyptic: "The demonization of CO2 and people like me who come to its defense... differs little from the Nazi persecution of the Jews, the

Soviet extermination of class enemies, or ISIL slaughter of infidels." (1/20/17)

"From the point of view of geological history, we are in a CO_2 famine... There is no problem from CO_2... The world has lots and lots of problems, but increasing CO_2 is not one of the problems." (1/25/18)

"We've ended the war on beautiful, clean coal, and in just the last year, our coal exports have skyrocketed." (9/29/18)

"Clean coal. I say beautiful, clean coal. And we have more of it than anybody." (10/18/18)

So wind power isn't clean, but coal is?

Large environmental-protection rollbacks proposed or implemented by the Trump administration:

- Freezing Obama-era greenhouse-gas emissions standards for automobiles
- Relaxing requirements for energy companies to monitor and repair methane leaks
- Rolling back the Obama administration's Clean Power Plan
- Boosting the coal industry by deregulating coal-fired power plants
- Lifting a moratorium on new coal leasing on federal lands
- Rescinding the 2013 Climate Action Plan, thus curbing climate regulations on private business
- Disbanding the Council on Climate Preparedness and Resilience

"I know more about renewables than any human being on earth." (4/13/16)

"You know what fires cost CA last year? $400 billion. So when Republicans talk about a switch over to renewables [or a Green New Deal] and ask, 'Well, how are you going to pay for it?' we should say, 'Well, how are you going to pay this?'"

Bill Maher (2/22/19)

"It's not that global warming is like a world war. It is a world war. And we are losing."

Bill McKibben

- Opening up Alaska's Arctic National Wildlife Refuge to oil and gas drilling
- Opening up nearly all US waters to oil and gas drilling

According to a *New York Times* analysis, as of December 2018, the Trump administration had rolled back 47 environmental rules and was in the process of rolling back 31 others.

The week of Labor Day, 2019—as the Amazon was burning, Greenland's glaciers were melting, and a Category 5 Hurricane bore down possibly on Florida, its winds accelerated by ocean warming—this is when the Trump Administration announced its reversal of Obama's Methane Rule designed to reduce global warming.

3.
WOMEN

WHEN NOT "GRABBING THEM BY THE PUSSY," TRUMP MAINTAINS THAT "NOBODY HAS MORE RESPECT FOR WOMEN THAN ME. NOBODY."

This would be news to *most* American women who, for the eighteen months prior, watched candidate Trump suggest that a woman asking him pointed questions must have been menstruating, called a female rival unattractive, suggested that he couldn't have sexually assaulted a woman because she was bad-looking, alluded to Hillary Clinton using the restroom as "disgusting," later said that she didn't look "presidential," referred to her as a "nasty woman" in a presidential debate, and then insisted that no one *respects or "cherishes" women more than he does.*

Oh, and a woman credibly accused him of a rape that she said took place in 1996—and told two prominent women in media at the time what Trump had done. Trump denied ever meeting her; photos show Trump and his accuser together in 1987.

Wonder what he'd be saying if he didn't respect them the mostest.

#4. Insult Machine: *"I heard poorly rated @MorningJoe speaks badly of me (don't watch anymore). Then how come low I.Q. Crazy Mika, along with Psycho Joe, came to Mar-a-Lago 3 nights in a row around New Year's Eve, and insisted on joining me. She was bleeding badly from a face-lift. I said no!" (6/29/17)*

George Washington warned of entangling alliances, Abraham Lincoln began his second term extending an olive branch to the

A man who allegedly groped a woman during a flight told authorities after he was arrested that "the president of the United States says it's OK to grab women by their private parts," according to a complaint by the FBI.

—The *Huffington Post*

"I hate the concept of abortion. I hate it. I hate everything it stands for, I cringe when I listen to people debating the subject, but you still—I just believe in choice."

Donald Trump, interview with Tim Russert, 1999

Writer: "O.K., I guess I'm asking, do you consider yourself ideal company?" Trump: *"You really want to know what I consider ideal company? A total piece of ass."* (1997)

South—"with malice toward none, with charity for all"—and the person in that same office in 2017 began his first Fourth of July holiday weekend as president by attacking a cable news anchor for her alleged face-lift.

> *"Women are very special. I think it's a very special time, a lot of things are coming out, and I think that's good for our society and I think it's very, very good for women, and I'm very happy a lot of these things are coming out. I'm very happy it's being exposed." (11/21/17)*

Trump's unusual syntax aside—who else would whimsically refer to the revelations of the #MeToo movement as a "very special time"—he said this in the aftermath of Democratic politicians facing allegations of sexual misconduct, evidently reveling in attention shifting away from the many women who had accused him.

> *"[S]omeone who would come to my office 'begging' for campaign contributions not so long ago and would do anything for them." (12/12/17)*

This was a presidential statement about a sitting United States Senator, Kirsten Gillibrand. Try to imagine Richard Nixon, for all his myriad faults, making a public statement about Margaret Chase Smith and throwing a clear illusion to a sexual favor into the public record. But for Donald Trump, that was called a Tuesday.

THE WOMEN WHO HAVE PUBLICLY ACCUSED TRUMP OF SEXUAL MISCONDUCT:

Jessica Leeds	Natasha Stony
Kristin Anderson	Jennifer Murphy
Jill Tarth	Juliet Huddy
Lisa Boyne	Rachel Crooks
Mariah Billado	Samantha Holvey
Victoria Hughes	Ninni Laaksonen
Temple Taggart	Jessica Drake
Cathy Heller	Summer Zervos
Karena Virginia	Cassandra Searles
Tasha Dixon	Alva Johnson
Bridget Sullivan	Ivana Trump
Melinda McGillivray	E. Jean Carroll

"Federal Judge throws out Stormy Daniels lawsuit versus Trump. Trump is entitled to full legal fees." @FoxNews "Great, now I can go after Horseface and her 3rd rate lawyer in the Great State of Texas. She will confirm the letter she signed! She knows nothing about me, a total con!"

Donald Trump, 10/16/18

Go ahead and ask any Trump supporter reading this—what's the chance that at least one accuser is telling the truth? Infinitely likely. Or the odds that most or nearly all are? Extremely likely, right?

"As we mark International Women's Day, we remain committed to the worthwhile mission of enhancing women's leadership in the world and building a stronger America for all." (3/8/18)

His annual platitudinous statements every March 8 about cherishing women's leadership and expanding opportunity always have the unfortunate effect of brushing up against what he's actually *doing* on a daily basis as president: appointing two Supreme Court justices (one credibly accused of sexual assault, for good measure) who lick their lips at the prospect of overturning *Roe*, stacking the Department of Health and

Human Services with antichoice advocates, cutting off birth control access based on the objections of women's employers, universities, or insurers and blocking a refugee from obtaining an abortion.

> #18. The 180°: *In 2002, Donald Trump heaped praise on his old friend Jeffrey Epstein, who later pleaded guilty to charges of solicitation of prostitution and procurement of minors for prostitution and committed suicide in a federal jail in the summer of 2019: "I've known Jeff for fifteen years. Terrific guy. He's a lot of fun to be with. It is even said that he likes beautiful women as much as I do, and many of them are on the younger side."*

Epstein, faced with a life sentence for sexual abuse of minors and a 53-page sex crimes indictment in 2007, instead received a stunningly light sentence: 13 months in a private wing of the Palm Beach county jail, complete with work release for 12 hours a day, six days a week in a "comfortable office." The US attorney arranged for a nonprosecution agreement, shielded from view of the victims, which would keep them from challenging it. (A judge would later rule that in keeping this from Epstein's 30 victims, the US attorney had broken the law.) That US attorney, Alexander Acosta, would later be appointed by Donald Trump as his secretary of labor, after his first choice's alleged spousal abuse was revealed.

> *"When I ran for office, I pledged to stand for life, and as president, that's exactly what I have done. Today, we have kept another promise. My administration has proposed a new rule to prohibit Title X funding from going to any clinic that performs abortions." (5/22/18)*

"Earlier in the [1990s], Trump had been in such bad shape I felt compelled to refer to him as a 'financially embattled thousandaire.' Trump sent me a copy of that column with an arrow pointing to my face, on which he had written 'the face of a pig.'"

Gail Collins, *New York Times*

The prolife crowd cheers this as a de facto defunding of Planned Parenthood because the organization already gets $50 to $60 million a year through the Title X program. Guess who isn't cheering this decision. The millions of low-income young, mostly people of color who rely on Title X for their reproductive health care needs and services like providing access to birth control, mammograms, and other cancer screenings. "The most prolife president?" Depends on how you define prolife.

> *"Every life is sacred, and ... every child is a precious gift from God. We know that every life has meaning and that every life is totally worth protecting." (5/22/18)*

This is a welcoming statement that, when uttered by Donald Trump, begs for fact-checking and stretches any rational idea of credulity. It's a beautiful sentiment, but one that lives on teleprompters but not in Trump's mind.

That "every life" standard comes with a big asterisk reserved for, but not limited to: black lives (police brutality never condemned by Trump), migrant children (families broken apart, including six children who have died in detention), Muslims, American school children traumatized by school shootings (2018 marking the worst year for US school shootings), American women (he once insisted that there "has" to be some punishment for women for having an abortion), women globally (exemplified by the Mexico City policy that bans any funding that may go to abortion services worldwide), the families of terrorists ("you have to take out their families"), American consumers, and servicemen's widows (ask Myeshia Johnson).

For Donald Trump, life that has value has a distinct look and a lighter hue.

"Look at that face! Would anyone vote for that? Can you imagine that, the face of our next president?!"

Donald Trump, on Carly Fiorina, 2015

"Of all the ugliness in politics, the utter disrespect George Conway shows toward his wife, her career, place of work and everything she has fought SO hard to achieve, might top them all."

Eric Trump

"If he thinks that's horrible, wait until [Eric] hears what Daddy and Auntie Stormy did to his step-mommy Melania. Talk about disrespectful."

Jimmy Fallon

"It is a very scary time for young men in America, where you can be guilty of something you may not be guilty of. This is a very, very—this is a very difficult time. What's happening here has much more to do than even the appointment of a Supreme Court justice." (10/2/18)

You call tell a lot about a person by where his sympathies lie (see "very fine people" in Charlottesville). Note where his sympathies didn't lie, even after they had been exonerated by DNA—viz. the Central Park Five.

#4. The Insult Machine: *"Thirty-six years ago this happened. I had one beer, right? I had one beer. How did you get home? 'I don't remember.' How'd you get there? 'I don't remember.' Where is the place? 'I don't remember.' How many years ago was it? 'I don't know. I don't know. I don't know. I don't know.' What neighborhood was it in?' I don't know.' Where's the house? 'I don't know.' Upstairs, downstairs, where was it? 'I don't know. But I had one beer. That's the only thing I remember.'" (10/2/18)*

The *New York Times* headline after Trump's routine read, "Trump Taunts Christine Blasey Ford at Rally." If you're bad with names, the headline should more accurately read, "Trump Taunts Victim of Alleged Sexual Assault at Rally." Mr. Sensitive here chose a rally of thousands of people in Mississippi as the right time to debut his new material mocking Brett Kavanaugh's accuser, the very one he earlier had called "believable."

Trump rarely speaks without verbal crutches, a limited vernacular, or mindless repetition, but never more lucidly than when mocking another person. Among those rare people who don't laugh, he can successfully get other people in stitches when he's mocking a disabled man or a woman accusing a Supreme Court nominee of a sexual assault in high school. Maybe Trump saw in Brett Kavanaugh a kindred spirit: a man educated at the "best schools," deep in debt, and accused by multiple women of sexual impropriety.

> *"It's a tough thing going on. You can be an exemplary person for 35 years, and then somebody comes and they say you did this or that, and they give three witnesses, and the three witnesses at this point do not corroborate what you were saying, that's a very scary situation where you're guilty until proven innocent." (10/2/18)*

Trump deserves credit for discovering the presumption of innocence, though a generation too late (again, see his public taunts of the falsely accused and exonerated Central Park Five). He's applied this standard to anyone who may resemble a supporter or an employee of his: Bill O'Reilly, Roy Moore, Rob Porter (accused of abuse by not one, but two wives), Steve Bannon (charged with domestic violence and battery), Andrew Puzder, who was the initial nominee for Labor Secretary (accused of domestic abuse by his ex-wife), and Corey Lewandowski, who was charged with battery against a Breitbart reporter.

> #7. Rooster Dawn: *"No one has benefited more from our thriving economy than women, who have filled 58 percent of the new jobs created in the last year. All Americans can be proud that we have more women in the workforce than ever before." (2/5/19)*

It should have been an easy applause break, but it was wrong: 76.8 million are employed, and that is more women than ever

> *"I honestly think this president loves his family, and I think it has as much to do with trying not to have public discussions about something that is, for him, a private matter that he didn't want to have discussed with his family."*

Senator Mike Rounds, Republican of South Dakota, on why Trump sent payments to Stormy Daniels following their affair

> *"I'm telling you that we want the votes in the Senate to get this tax bill through."*

Kellyanne Conway, on why the White House held firm in its support of Roy Moore for Senate in Alabama despite allegations of sexual misconduct with underage girls—that is, pedophilia.

"Well, I'll tell you the funniest is that I'll go backstage before a show, and everyone's getting dressed and ready and everything else, and you know, no men are anywhere. And I'm allowed to go in because I'm the owner of the [Miss Universe] pageant and therefore I'm inspecting it. You know, I'm inspecting, I want to make sure that everything is good. You know, the dresses. 'Is everyone okay?' You know, they're standing there with no clothes. 'Is everybody okay?' And you see these incredible looking women." (2005)

"...Ivanka does have a very nice figure. I've said if Ivanka weren't my daughter, perhaps I'd be dating her. Isn't that terrible? How terrible? Is that terrible?"

before, but that comes to 57.5 percent of American women participating in the labor force (below the male rate of 68.3 percent), below the peak of 60.3 percent in 2000, putting the United States in ninth place, behind Germany, Canada, and Australia—and to the point where Japan has mocked America's track record in female labor participation. Japanese Prime Minister Shinzo Abe boasted that Japan's female labor participation rate, at 67 percent, is significantly higher than the United States.

> *"Women have one of the great acts of all time. The smart ones act very feminine and needy, but inside they are real killers. The person who came up with the expression 'the weaker sex' was either very naive or had to be kidding. I have seen women manipulate men with just a twitch of their eye—or perhaps another body part."*—Donald Trump, *The Art of the Comeback,* 1997

As articulated in a William Saletan *Slate* piece, "People may disagree on when life begins, but everyone agrees, at least in principle, on the sanctity of human life.

"Everyone, that is, except Trump. He treats human life as expendable, not just in the womb or in infancy, but in childhood and adulthood. He condones killing people in ..." several contexts: capital punishment and the families of terrorists—and is an apologist for people he likes (Prince Mohammed bin Salman and Vladimir Putin) who are known to have murdered political opponents.

> #12. The Hyperbolic: *"The baby is born. The mother meets with the doctor. They take care of the baby. They wrap the baby beautifully. And then the doctor and the mother determine whether or not they will execute the baby."* (4/28/19)

Photo by Chip Somodevilla/
Getty Images

Maybe with Bill O'Reilly forced off the airwaves, someone
needs to fill the void to defame abortion providers and cook
up paranoid fan-fiction about reproductive health practices in
America.

Through the mid-2000s until April 2009, O'Reilly assailed
George Tiller—Kansas physician and medical director of
Women's Health Care Services—fully 29 times on the most

popular cable news show in the country, claiming he was "operating a death mill," "executing babies about to be born," and compared him to Hitler, even using syntax almost indecipherable from how Trump speaks: "And if I could get my hands on Tiller—well, you know. Can't be vigilantes. Can't do that. It's just a figure of speech. But despicable? Oh, my God. Oh, it doesn't get worse. Does it get worse? No."

In May 2009, a rabid antichoice extremist shot Tiller to death while he was at church.

Now Trump is trying his hand at it, assailing the Wisconsin governor for vetoing a bill that would imprison doctors for life for not providing medical care to infants born alive after a botched abortion attempt. In Wisconsin, where Trump was making the claims, only about 1 percent of abortions happen after 20 weeks of pregnancy and it's exceedingly rare for this to happen, and doctors do not "execute" the infant. Some conditions can kill mother and fetus, and the only treatment is delivering the child.

The *New York Times* elaborated, "If it seems unlikely that the baby will survive, the family may choose to provide just comfort care—wrapping and cuddling the baby—and allow the child to die naturally without extreme attempts at resuscitation. The bill that the governor vetoed would force the baby to be resuscitated—even against the wishes of the family or the mother. Trump doesn't explain this distinction and rolls the dice with people's lives."

4.
RACE

"I AM THE LEAST RACIST PERSON IN THE WORLD."

While many supporters make a show of anger if anyone says that Donald Trump is a racist, let's be adults in this chapter, given three extremely well-known facts: he milked the fantastic lie for years that an American president—who happened to be the first black president—was not an American; at his 2015 presidential announcement, he essentially said that Mexicans were "rapists"; and in mid-2019, he previewed his 2020 core strategy by relentlessly and brutally attacking minority members of the House as radical, stupid, corrupt people who should "go back" to their original countries.

He knew his audience, knew what he was saying, and knew what he was doing.

What he was doing is what he's always done—dig his finger in the wound of race to advance his political interest at the expense of a *united* states.

THE NEW YORK YEARS

"My legacy has its roots in my father's legacy" (8/10/15)

From the *New York Times*, June 1, 1927: "Fred Trump, of 175-24 Devonshire Road, Jamaica, was dismissed on charge of refusing to disperse [from a KKK] parade when ordered to do so."

The family name first appears in the *New York Times* that June day in 1927 in an article about Fred's arrest at a Klan rally that spawned brawls over Memorial Day weekend. The family has insisted he had nothing to do with the rally, and there's no one around to say whether that's true or not. It's conceivable he was just curious about the commotion and was an innocent bystander...or that this is yet another dog-ate-my-homework explainer, since, at the least, he *was* "arrested at a Klan rally," later excluded people of color from his apartment buildings, and his son couldn't take sides when neo-Nazis marched in Charlottesville.

For a lot of people, seeing your name in the *New York Times* is a pinch-me moment, a measure of how far you've made it. Donald Trump's story was a little different. Fred's son Donald's own maiden mention in the Paper of Record—on the front page, no less—also concerned race and racism. How coincidental. It occurred when the Nixon administration twice sued him (in 1973 and 1978)—and his father, Fred—for housing discrimination against black tenant applicants at their dozens of apartment buildings across New York City.

Trump employees were instructed to mark applications with a "No. 9" or "C" for colored (subtlety has never been a Trump trait). Black applicants were told available apartments had already been rented. One young black nurse filled out what the rental agent called a "beautiful application" in Queens in the hope of landing a one-bedroom in Trump Management's Wilshire Apartments. The agent asked Fred Trump what to do and got his answer: "Take the application and put it in a drawer and leave it there."

After the Justice Department sued, a public battle ensued and a consent degree was later signed, without an admission of guilt, which was and still is a common practice in such filings. But old habits die hard—the DoJ found new discrimination against potential black tenants and therefore brought a second suit in 1978. This time, although their applications were approved, African American tenants were confined to a few complexes in poor conditions, with falling plaster and bloodstained floors. The case was finally settled by another consent decree in 1982, not long before Trump Tower opened.

"Bring Back The Death Penalty!" (5/1/89)

In April 1989, a white woman was raped and nearly beaten to death in New York's Central Park. Five black teenagers were arrested and charged. Their coerced confessions, brought after long hours away from lawyers, were soon followed by their convictions. Donald Trump, a famous real estate developer just months from his first bankruptcy, seized the public spotlight and spent $85,000 on full-page ads at four New York-area newspapers (see headline above) calling for the death penalty for the teenagers. After the Central Park Five spent a decade in jail, the confession of the real attacker as well as DNA evidence exonerated them in 2002. Instead of admitting he got caught up in the uproar against a brutal crime, Trump called their exoneration "the heist of the century."

If he had his way, today they would be ashes mixed with dirt.

"I've got black accountants at Trump Castle and at Trump Plaza. Black guys counting my money! I hate it. The only kind of people I want counting my money are short guys wearing yarmulkes.... Those are the only kind of people I want counting my money. Nobody else... Besides that, I tell you something else. I think that guy's lazy. And it's probably not his fault because laziness is a trait in blacks." (1990s)
"What Donald Trump has said about Jews." *The Week.* April 18, 2019.

You have to give him credit. To combine two insidious stereotypes into just a few sentences about disparate groups is not

"[Trump] would say racially insensitive things that made me uncomfortable. I don't think he ever said anything in that room like 'African-Americans are inferior' or anything about rape or grabbing women, but of those two hours every other day in a room with him, every 10 ten minutes was fingernails on a chalkboard."

Penn Jillette, comedian who was regularly on *The Apprentice*

that easy. But Donald Trump has a self-acknowledged "very big brain," at least when it comes to bias.

"I heard he was a terrible student. Terrible. How does a bad student go to Columbia and then to Harvard?" (4/26/11)

This is an early appearance of documentation based on "I heard…," which is pretty difficult to peer-review. Barack Obama, constitutional law professor and perhaps the best writer in the presidency since Abraham Lincoln, didn't pass the intellectual smell test for one Donald Trump, who gets bored by dialogue in Jean-Claude Van Damme movies and has to fast-forward to action scenes.

#6. Upside-Downism: Another key to Trump's vault of lies is that he accuses others of what he himself has done. Within days of Trump attacking Obama for not releasing his academic records, he sent the later-infamous Michael Cohen to his former schools—the New York Military Academy and Fordham University—to threaten lawsuits if his records were ever released. To date, they haven't been. Why this concern for privacy? Either it's based on a principled view that such matters are no one else's business...or they're so awful that they disprove his repeated claims of brilliance—"I'm very smart."

Campaign 2016

2000: "The Reform Party now includes a Klansman, Mr. Duke, a neo-Nazi, Mr. [Patrick] Buchanan, and a communist, Ms. [Lenora] Fulani. This is not company I wish to keep." (2/13/00)

2016: "Well, just so you understand, I don't know anything about David Duke. Okay? I don't know anything about what you're even talking about with white supremacy or white supremacists. So, I don't know. I don't know, did he endorse me or what's going on, because, you know, I know nothing about David Duke. I know nothing about white supremacists. (2/28/16)

Trump blamed a faulty earpiece for his confusion. But the declarative sentence *"I know nothing about David Duke"* came not out of an earpiece, but out of his mouth. Two years later, the day after his comments about *"very fine people...both sides"* of the neo-Nazi march in Charlottesville, Duke took to Twitter to thank Trump, "for your honesty and courage." Message received.

#1. Cherry-picking: *Pointing to a black person at a Trump rally: "Look at my African-American over here." (6/5/16)*

Even beyond the plantation locution, the aforementioned African American was never "his," as Gregory Cheadle was a black Republican candidate for Congress who opposed Trump in the campaign and was at his rally passing out pamphlets for his own campaign.

"Dwayne [sic] Wade's cousin was just shot and killed walking her baby in Chicago. Just what I have been saying. African-Americans will VOTE TRUMP!" (8/27/16)

Trump took days to disavow David Duke and the tiki-torch-bearing neo-Nazis in Charlottesville before equivocating but wasted no time (misspelling Wade's name) to exploit an NBA star's family tragedy. In the new racial landscape of

"Donald Trump said recently he has a great relationship with the blacks, but unless the Blacks are a family of white people, I bet he is mistaken."

Seth Meyers

After a CNN interview with Pat Buchanan in 1999, Trump commented: *"He's a Hitler lover. I guess he's an anti-Semite. He doesn't like the blacks. He doesn't like the gays. It's just incredible that anybody could embrace this guy."*

Trump on Pat Buchanan in 2016: "Way to go Pat, way ahead of your time!"

the right wing, "Chicago" is a foghorn in the way Ronald Reagan's "welfare queen" was a dog whistle.

#13. Rhetorical Question: *"You're living in poverty, your schools are no good, you have no jobs, 58 percent of your youth is unemployed. What the hell do you have to lose?" (8/19/16)*

As a piece of propaganda, his use of the rhetorical question brilliantly allowed any credulous African Americans in his audiences to instinctively think that they could get out of the hellscape he described. But other than claiming credit for the historically low level of black unemployment that occurred under Obama, it's hard to see any uptick in their quality of life since his election. It's even harder to spot the presence of black people in his administration (no black senior White House staff), and just 8 percent of people of color have been appointed judges.

#2., #4., #12., #15. Assertion, Insult Machine, Hyperbolic, Conspiracy Theory: *"Hillary Clinton meets in secret with international banks to plot the destruction of U.S. sovereignty." (10/13/16)*

With language seemingly lifted from the *Protocols of the Elders of Zion*, Trump galvanized the alt-right in the closing weeks of the 2016 campaign. Also wink-winking Jewish memes was a tweet with a photo of Hillary Clinton surrounded by a Star of David with a pile of cash nearby.

RACIST PRESIDENT—2017

"Racism is evil. And those who cause violence in its name are

criminals and thugs, including the KKK, neo-Nazis, white supremacists, and other hate groups that are repugnant to everything we hold dear as Americans." (8/14/17)

Let's take what Trump himself said about his own statement forthrightly, if belatedly and almost through clenched teeth, condemning white supremacist terrorism: "I don't know about this....This doesn't feel right to me." That's how he felt before finally, after much staff pressure according to author Michael Wolff, delivering a rare condemnation of racism. It might not feel right for someone who opened his candidacy by calling Mexican immigrants rapists and whose campaign inspired such

"Claiming a person can't do their job because of their race is sort of like the textbook definition of a racist comment."

Paul Ryan, on Trump's comments about Judge Gonzalo Curiel

Photo by Chip Somodevilla/Getty Images

"Mr. Trump is a racist. The country has seen Mr. Trump court white supremacists and bigots. You have heard him call poorer countries 'shitholes.' He once asked me if I could name a country run by a black person that wasn't a 'shithole.' This was when Barack Obama was President of the United States. While we were once driving through a struggling neighborhood in Chicago, he commented that only black people could live that way and, he told me that black people would never vote for him because they were too stupid."

Michael Cohen, 2019

a surge in attendance at white supremacist think tanks (National Policy Institute's attendance jumped 75 percent in 2016) and in traffic at neo-Nazi websites like Stormfront, which required the purchase of new servers and is linked to nearly 100 murders.

"Why do we need Haitians? Take them out....Why are we having all these people from shithole countries come here? We should have more people from places like Norway." (1/11/18)

Trump's particular antipathy toward Haitians, famously observing the eighth anniversary of the 2010 earthquake, is inexplicable...except that, unlike those from Scandinavian countries, they are People of Color. He's done more than just fulminate, however, terminating Temporary Protected Status for about 300,000 immigrants from countries like El Salvador, Haiti, Honduras—thereby blighting America's reputation as a refuge from oppression, per Emma Lazarus's immortal words on the base of the Statue of Liberty.

"Wouldn't you love to see one of these NFL owners, when somebody disrespects our flag, to say, 'Get that son-of-a-bitch off the field right now. Out! He's fired. He's fired!'" (9/23/17)

"The NFL players are at it again—taking a knee when they should be standing proudly for the National Anthem. Numerous players, from different teams, wanted to show their 'outrage' at something that most of them are unable to define." (8/10/18)

Trump willfully misconstrued the meaning of Colin Kaepernick's protest—against police brutality, not against the stars and stripes. (Kaepernick began the protest sitting on the sidelines before he consulted with veterans and started to kneel during the national anthem, to show respect.) Trump's remark is peak Trump-era Republican, made to an Alabama crowd in support of a senator who would get defeated by an alleged child molester. He tellingly challenged black Americans' intelligence—inexplicably claiming that black athletes are unable even to define police brutality. Could *Trump* define it?

#4. Insult Machine: *"LeBron James was just interviewed by the dumbest man on television, Don Lemon. He made LeBron look smart, which isn't easy to do. I like Mike!" (8/14/18)*

"Congresswoman Maxine Waters, an extraordinarily low IQ person, has become, together with Nancy Pelosi, the Face of the Democrat Party." (6/25/18)

Trump has repeatedly played into an age-old trope that black people are of inferior intelligence. Perhaps he was lashing out after his porcelain ego was bruised by his staff's own estimation of his intelligence: "idiot," "moron," "dope," "dumb as shit." That was before scholars rated him last in presidential intellect in a list that includes Andrew Johnson. That must hurt.

"I have asked Secretary of State @SecPompeo to closely study the South Africa land and farm seizures and expropriations and the large scale killing of farmers. South African Government is now seizing land from white farmers." @TuckerCarlson @FoxNews (8/22/18)

By 51 percent to 45 percent in an August, 2019 Quinnipiac poll, a majority of Americans believed that Donald Trump was a

"How many black people were in Abraham Lincoln's West Wing?... Is Abraham Lincoln a racist because he didn't have a black person in the White House?"

Katrina Pierson in 2019, national spokesman for Donald Trump's 2016 presidential campaign

"When such violent demeaning words come from the President of the United States, they are a clarion call, and give cover, to white supremacists who consider people of color a sub-human 'infestation' in America....The question is less about the president's sense of decency but of our own."

Statement of the Washington National Cathedral, 2019

#17 Block that Metaphor: "Mr. Trump was reportedly energized by his Tuesday performance, which he saw as a rebuke to politically correct forces that he thinks are determined to topple him. He crashed ahead, attacking critics on all sides and delivering Twitter bursts of anti-historical nonsense. Not the least of these was his repetition, shortly after the terrorist attack in Barcelona on Thursday, of the canard that Gen. John Pershing, known as 'Black Jack,' had stopped Islamic terrorists in the Philippines by killing dozens of them with bullets dipped in pigs' blood, a strategy Mr. Trump thinks worthy of emulation."

The *New York Times,* editorial

racist; 41 percent of Americans in 1968 thought that Alabama's segregationist governor George Wallace was a racist.

Two big differences: First, Wallace would mock groups generically but never name individuals who were the subject to his scorn. Trump, however, usually names names of black people he mocks for their intelligence: Don Lemon, LeBron James, Maxine Waters, black journalists…

Second, Wallace lost. Trump became president, despite or because of his racial hostility.

The 2020 election may answer which it was.

Trump managed to unearth a racist conspiracy theory from the swamps of the Internet and bring Stormfront-user jargon to the broader public, swayed, as is standard, by the Fox News primetime lineup. He mainstreamed a cause célèbre of the alt-right and assorted Neanderthals, namely, that minorities will "replace" whites in various societies. If this racism-without-hoods works to boost Tucker Carlson's ratings, it appears that Trump hopes it can do the same to his polls.

#1. Cherry-picking: *"Democrats let him into our country. Democrats let him stay." – GOP campaign ad featuring undocumented immigrant convicted of killing a police officer (10/31/18)*

#12. The Hyperbolic: *Just days before the 2018 midterms, Trump doubled down on fear-mongering about the Central American caravan that was still hundreds of miles from the US border, with a stunningly racist ad featuring an unrepentant cop killer in the country illegally celebrating his murders. In the ad, the killer says he'll break out of prison and kill more. It then charged Democrats for letting him kill and stay in the country, though the link is tenuous —the killer was in the US illegally during the Clinton and Bush presidencies and was picked up by Maricopa County police, home of Trump booster (and pardon recipient) Joe Arpaio.*

The ad tied one killer's horrible actions with the thousands of poor desperate immigrants fleeing violence-racked Central America. The ad was rejected by networks for its "insensitive nature" (they mean racist), and in doing so, Trump set a new record: being too racist for Facebook or Fox News.

According to multiple reports, Trump's father repeatedly sought to conceal the fact that he was the son of German immigrants. Fred Trump sought to pass himself off as Swedish amid anti-German sentiment sparked by World War II. According to [Trump biographer] Gwenda Blair, Fred Trump denied knowing German and did not teach it to his children. John Walter, a Trump family historian and one of Donald Trump's cousins, said this was an effort to not offend his Jewish customers. "He said, 'You don't sell apartments after the war if you're German,'" Walter said in the *Boston Globe* article. "So he's Swedish, no problem."

#6. Upside-Downism: *"I don't know why you say that, that is such a racist question." Trump to Yamiche Alcindor (11/9/18)*

#4. Insult Machine: *"What a stupid question that is. What a stupid question. But I watch you a lot, you ask a lot of stupid questions." Trump to Abby Phillip (11/11/18)*

"[April Ryan] doesn't know what the hell she's doing. She gets publicity and then she gets a pay raise, or she gets a contract with, I think, CNN. But she's very nasty and she shouldn't be.

"Donald Trump will not offer a full-throated condemnation of white supremacy for two reasons. 1. It will result in his political destruction. 2. At his core he is a white supremacist."

Rob Reiner

#20. The Lyin' King: *"An 'extremely credible source' has called my office and told me that @BarackObama's birth certificate is a fraud."*

Tweet by Donald Trump, 2012

"If you own a business that attempts to keep black people from renting from you and if you are reported to say that you don't want black people counting your money. If you just come out and say someone can't judge their case because they're Mexican. If your response to the first black president is that they weren't born in this country, despite all proof. If you say they weren't smart enough to go to Harvard Law School and demand to see their grades. If that's the essence of your entire political identity, you might be a white Supremacist."

Ta-Nehisi Coates

You've got to treat the White House and the office of the presidency with respect." –Trump on April Ryan (11/11/18)

Trump heaps scorn on almost anything that questions his awesomeness—the Oscars, Saturday Night Live's comedy chops, and nearly 600 people, places, and things as of late 2018. His backers argue that this mountainous volume shows he's an equal opportunity offender, that it is part of his authentic charm—except when it comes to women, people of color, and specifically black people. Especially black women and black journalists. His attacks on Yamiche Alcindor, Abby Phillip, and April Ryan followed his midterm wipeout. Using his common technique of accusing others of what you're doing, he called Alcindor racist after spending the better part of 2011 through 2015 asking for Barack Obama to show his papers.

"If you buy a box of cereal—you have a voter ID. They try to shame everybody by calling them racist, or calling them something, anything they can think of, when you say you want voter ID. But voter ID is a very important thing." (11/14/18)

Beyond the inanity of thinking you need an ID to buy cereal or any food—which Trump has repeated in his pained effort to support laws to stop eligible voters from voting—there's the obvious racial motive. Voter *suppression* might be the most "important thing" to Trump's Republican Party given their registration disadvantage and polls showing the popularity of progressive proposals on guns, environment, choice, immigration, taxes. Looks like they've decided to become the party of subtraction, not addition. This single-minded focus has helped turn losses into narrow wins in governors' races in Florida and Georgia in 2018.

Voter fraud in the form of requiring voter ID contributed to a sharp decline in presidential black voter turnout: Wisconsin, which Trump won by just 10,000 votes, saw a 27-point decrease; 2016 saw the first decrease in African American voter turnout since 1996 (when voter turnout overall was notoriously low, not even cracking 50 percent of voters). In Kansas, after enactment of its strict voter ID law, black turnout fell by 3.7 percentage points more than white voters'. So yes, this is "a very important thing."

We have people coming into the country, or trying to come in—and we're stopping a lot of them—but we're taking people out of the country. You wouldn't believe how bad these people are. These aren't people. These are animals. And we're taking them out of the country at a level and at a rate that's never happened before." (5/16/18)

Trump has a thing for dehumanizing language—but he doesn't only reserve it for black people. He says that members of MS-13 "aren't people." His apologists correctly point out that he's referring to a brutal street gang implicated in horrific crimes. But he said those words in an immigration roundtable about sanctuary cities, which don't protect undocumented immigrants who have committed 800 crimes, as MS-13 allegedly has, including domestic abuse, sex offenses, child abuse, torture, burglary, kidnapping, and murder.

"When you give a crazed, crying lowlife a break and give her a job at the White House [he said of Omarosa Manigault Newman after she wrote a tell-all book]...Good work by General Kelly for quickly firing that dog!" (8/14/18)

"He trusts his gut on issues surrounding race, because he's got a simplistic, deterministic, and racist perspective on who people are. I think at his core he has a genetic understanding of what makes people good and bad or successful. And you see it all the time—he talks about people having good genes. He looks at the world that way. He's got a very Aryan view of people and race."

Tim O'Brien, Trump biographer

"Really bad news! The Baltimore house of Elijah Cummings was robbed. Too bad!"

Donald Trump (8/2/19)

DONALD TRUMP AS TA-NEHISI COATES:

Speaking at a Black Leadership Summit in late 2019, Trump lauded how unheralded black Americans "helped build the White House" in 1799, starting off with No. 6 John Adams." No. 6?

In a poll of the Louisiana Senate race in 2016, supporters of white supremacist David Duke voted for Donald Trump over Hillary Clinton by a margin of 81 percent to 6 percent. In his campaign for Louisiana governor in 1991, Duke won 55 percent of the white vote.

Trump thinks he's delivered the most savage insult imaginable—comparing a black person to a dog, an animal to which he is famously averse. While he enjoys deploying dehumanizing language, it may be a tell. As a domestic animal researcher told *Vice*, "Recent studies have shown that affection for pets goes hand-in-hand with concern for the natural world."

"You're not gonna support me because I don't want your money. You want to control your politicians, that's fine...I'm a negotiator like you folks, we are negotiators. Is there anybody that doesn't renegotiate deals in this room? This room negotiates them—perhaps more than any other room I've ever spoken in." (12/3/15) Spoken with stereotypical candor to a room of only Jewish Republicans.

#20. The Lyin' King: *"The Democrats hate Jewish people."* (3/10/19)

"The 'Jexodus' movement encourages Jewish people to leave the Democrat Party. Total disrespect! Republicans are waiting with open arms. Remember Jerusalem (US Embassy) and the horrible Iran Nuclear Deal!" (3/15/19)

"I think any Jewish people that vote for a Democrat—I think it shows either a total lack of knowledge or great disloyalty." Disloyalty to whom, Trump was asked. "Yes Israel." Speaking of "lack of knowledge," was he even remotely aware that charging Jews with a dual loyalty to U. S. and Israel has been an anti-Semitic trope for decades?

In a 2019 poll, the group with the highest disapproval numbers for Trump—outside of African Americans—was Jewish

Americans with a 71 percent negative view. And he expects them to oppose Democrats to show their loyalty to *Israel?* Fugeddaboudit!

The 80 percent of American Jewish voters who regularly do vote blue presumably reject the assertion of Democratic anti-Semitism, especially when it comes from the Steve King-Steve Bannon-Donald Trump party that spent the six months prior using George Soros as a boogeyman and after a white nationalist lauding Trump killed 11 in a Pittsburgh synagogue.

Senate Minority Leader Chuck Schumer (NY) explained why Trump's comments on Democrats hating Jews was so wrong and hurtful: "Those who seek to use Israel as a means of scoring political points do a disservice to both Israel and the United States...we must pledge to one another that we will keep the polarization from Washington away from poisoning the bipartisan support that Israel has always enjoyed. It will always be wrong to use anti-Semitism as a political weapon. Always. And let me tell you: if you only care about anti-Semitism coming from your political opponents, then you are not fully committed to fighting anti-Semitism."

> *"Number one, you need [Citizenship census data] for Congress—you need it for Congress for districting. You need it for appropriations—where are the funds going? How many people are there? Are they citizens? Are they not citizens? You need it for many reasons." (7/5/19)*

Trump gave away the store, admitting how he was weaponizing the Census to give Republicans an advantage by disenfranchising and undercounting people of color when mapping congressional districts. Typical Republican stuff. Faced with a

STANDARD #6 UPSIDE-DOWNISM ON "WHO'S A RACIST?"

Given the evidence in this chapter plus his racist binge in mid-2019 on denouncing those four minority women members as "The Squad," Trump resorted to calling others what he is. Here are a few of the 22 people and things he considers "racist": Barack Obama, Spike Lee, Elijah Cummings, Jon Stewart, Elizabeth Warren, the TV show *Black-ish*, and Hollywood. Convinced?

"America's always trying to find this gotcha moment that shows Donald Trump is racist—you know, let's find this one big thing. Let's look for that one time when he burned a cross in someone's yard so we can now finally say it. People refuse to see the bread crumbs that are already in front of you, leading you to grandma's house."

Kwame Jackson, contestant on *The Apprentice*

"I imagine one of the reasons people cling to their hate so stubbornly is because they sense, once hate is gone, they will be forced to deal with pain."

James Baldwin

changing country, Trump and his party are pulling out all the stops to give themselves a cheating edge.

Nonetheless, the *Washington Post* reported in mid-August that Trump was "livid" that so many people were calling him a racist—indeed, half the Democratic presidential field agreed that he was a "white nationalist." He appeared to assume that only *he* was entitled to engage in political insults. In this case, his tactic of Upside-Downism—of calling numerous others racist to strip the word of any meaning—wasn't working. His own political staff was openly admitting, albeit anonymously, that they were aiming to turn out "Wallace-like voters" in key Midwestern states to replicate their 2016 electoral college win.

We consider that immoral...but was it politically irrational if you're a Republican running in 2020? With many of the core principles holding up the GOP for a half century gone—no Soviets as an "axis of evil," no pieties to balanced budgets, few seriously pretending that tax cuts for the rich paid for themselves, homophobia largely played out—the race card was among the few left in their deck.

The bottom line: Trump may not like the stink from segregationist Wallace to Nixon's Southern Strategy to his attacks on "The Squad" urging them to "go back to" their "shithole" countries. But "racist" is the phrase that fits and that will likely stick—the skunk smell on a suit that won't go away.

5.
CRIME & GUNS
LESS CRIME! MORE GUNS!

For Donald Trump, race, immigration, and crime are inextricably linked, since it's politically advantageous for him to blame the first two for the third as an easy pander to his white base. An early tell: he kicked off his discussion of crime in the presidential campaign with a retweet that wildly inflated crime statistics for African Americans, placing 97 percent of white murders at the hands of black Americans. In actuality, it's less than a half of one-third of that number. It's no surprise that he picked as his campaign manager Steve Bannon, whose Breitbart platform had a section subtlety devoted to "black crime." (See, also, chapters on Immigration & Race.)

On the Campaign Trail

"We've also seen increasing threats against our police and a substantial rise in the number of officers killed in the line of duty—a very big rise." (7/11/16)

"We must discuss, as well, the ongoing catastrophe of crime in our inner cities. Our inner cities are rife with crime. According to the Chicago Tribune, *there has already been more than 2,000, 2,000 shooting victims in Chicago alone this year. This epidemic of violence destroys lives, destroys communities, and destroys opportunity for young Americans. Violent crime has increased in cities across America. The New York Times described 'the startling rise in murders' in our major cities." (7/11/16)*

On the one hand, it's a relief that Trump is reading at all, let alone reading the *New York Times* (we thought he regarded it as both fake and failing). But on a bigger hand, the "startling" increase in murders he refers to are across a single-year period in several cities, not a broad, long-term trend and not sufficient to deduce troubling trends.

#5. The Unscientific Method: Beginning around 1991, the American crime rate peaked, with New York City alone seeing more than 2,200 murders as the crack cocaine epidemic sent violent crime soaring. But the next generation saw a dramatic plunge in crime, with a 42 percent drop by the close of the 1990s that kept going through the boom times of the 1990s and the Great Recession even as unemployment topped 10 percent nationally.

Criminologists have plumbed data for what caused the decline—income growth? less alcohol consumed in recent decades or is it the widespread use of CompStat, a police data tool? was it the *Roe v. Wade* ruling reducing the number of babies and, later, teenagers? might it have been the removal of lead in gasoline that one economist has attributed a 56 percent drop in violent crime? Needless to say, be assured that Donald Trump is not seriously analyzing causation and data before he becomes a human accelerant spreading the fires of racial fear and resentment. For Trump, this good news is politically unhelpful since it undermines his efforts to whip up fear, especially in cities (think Chicago) that his base considers synonymous with black people.

Conclusion: it's ok to accurately warn about rising crime but, since this is 2019 not 1909, not OK to spur racial antagonism in order to harvest white voters.

"Q: How do you heal the racial divide?
A: We need law and order. If we don't have it, we're not going to have a country. I just got today the endorsement of the Fraternal Order of Police. We have endorsements from

almost every police group, a large percentage of them in the US. We have a situation where we have our inner cities, African-Americans, Hispanics are living in hell because it's so dangerous. You walk down the street, you get shot." First presidential debate (9/26/16)

In that debate, Trump then pivoted from a discussion of race to crime, revealing the inherent link in his mind...which is odd if you contrast what became his ethics-busting presidency and his foundational views on "law and order." Painting a view of black and Hispanic life in America as a living hell might not be the best ploy for their votes, but they do excite the confirmation biases of some white Americans. No matter that it's not a reflection of reality: in America, while black Americans endured the highest murder rates, crime rates have plummeted across all races since the 1990s, as noted above.

"And the murder rate in the United States is the highest it's been in 45 years and the dishonest media, they never tell you that." (10/21/16)

#20. The Lyin' King: The murder rate for 2015, the last year available when he made these claims, was *lower* than at any time between 1965 and 2009. Even accounting for a nearly-65 percent increase in population from 1970 (203 million to 320 million), the United States had fewer raw numbers of murders in 2015 (15,696) than in 1970 (around 16,000). The grain of truth he was referring to was that the murder rate in 2015 was 10 percent higher than in 2014, the highest one-year increase in nearly 50 years. Since he uses this tactic frequently, it's a strong example of "Figures don't lie, but liars figure."

In the White House

"... for too many of our citizens, a different reality exists: Mothers and children trapped in poverty in our inner cities; rusted-out factories scattered like tombstones across the landscape of our nation; an education system, flush with cash, but which leaves our young and beautiful students deprived of knowledge; and the crime and gangs and drugs that have stolen too many lives and robbed our country of so much unrealized potential. This American carnage stops right here and stops right now." Inaugural Address (1/20/17)

Context counts. This *could* be read as an empathetic read on communities that are crime-ridden yet neglected—say a page from Ramsey Clark's 1970 *Crime in America*...until you consider who is saying it. "American carnage"—the banner headline of Trump's inaugural address as well as a likely epitaph for his presidency to come—focused on distorting crime statistics while ignoring the rise in mass murders. Indeed, 2017 would go on to be America's worst year for mass shootings, only to be followed by 2018, distinguished as the worst year for school shootings. Yet because of his own supine fear of the NRA, this wasn't the focus of his assertions.

"Right now, too many families don't feel secure. Just look at the 30 largest cities. In the last year alone, the murder rate has increased by an estimated 14 percent. Here in Philadelphia, the murder rate has been steady, I mean, just terribly increasing." (1/26/17)

Although January 2017 was an unusually violent month for Philadelphia, any statistician worth their salt knows not to follow short-term crime trends because they are often misleading and far too small of a sample size. (Worth noting: Trump is not a statistician and is not worth any salt.) In Philadelphia, for example, in September 2016 the murder tally was 9 percent higher than the year prior, and still the city ended 2016 with fewer murders overall than 2015.

"The murder rate in our country is the highest it's been in 47 years, right? Did you know that? Forty-seven years. I used to use that—I'd say that in a speech and everybody was surprised, because the press doesn't tell it like it is. It wasn't to their advantage to say that. But the murder rate is the highest it's been in, I guess, from 45 to 47 years." (2/7/17)

#5. Unscientific Method: We didn't know that because it's not true: even while population jumped 25 percent from 1993 to 2014, the number of murders has dropped by 42 percent. Yet he claimed the highest rate in 47 years, using an accurate dateline for the statistic he's warping, the biggest one-year increase in 45 years. But no matter. He's still wrong.

"The eight-year assault on your Second Amendment freedoms has come to a crashing end. You have a true friend and champion in the White House. No longer will federal agencies be coming after law-abiding gun owners. No longer will the government be trying to undermine your rights and your freedoms as Americans. Instead, we will work with you, by your side." (4/29/17)

For once, Trump wasn't lying. Not about that eight-year assault on gun rights (one of President Obama's earliest moves on guns was to expand gun rights, eliminating a ban on firearms

"The White House's response to the New Zealand attack more broadly fits into a by-now-expected pattern. When an apparent terrorist or hate attack has been committed by a Muslim, Trump is quick to draw attention to it. When it targets Muslims, however, Trump's responses are slower and totally different. That pattern itself helps bolster questions about Trump's willingness to condemn violence against Muslims."

Editorial in
the *Washington Post*

"Although assault weapons account for less than 1 percent of the guns in circulation, they account for nearly 10 percent of the guns traced to crime....While we recognize that assault weapon legislation will not stop all assault weapon crime, statistics prove that we can dry up the supply of these guns, making them less accessible to criminals. We urge you to listen to the American public and to the law enforcement community and support a ban on the further manufacture of these weapons."

Ronald Reagan, Gerald Ford, and Jimmy Carter in joint letter to Congress, 1994

in national parks), but about the alliance that exists between the Trump White House and the NRA. The NRA invested $30 million in Trump's campaign—three times what they spent on Mitt Romney's race—and for their money they've reaped two Supreme Court justices on the Court to uphold "gun rights." In the face of Parkland, Las Vegas, Sutherland Springs, and Pittsburgh, he's considering adding firearms training to teachers' already endless tasks.

For a candidate who won plaudits for claiming he'll "bomb the shit" out of ISIS, his fealty to the NRA leaves Americans as sitting ducks, as terrorists exploit our permissive gun laws. In 2011, one terrorist, Adam Gadahn, an American recruit by al Qaeda, on video explained it simply: "America is absolutely awash with easily obtainable firearms....So what are you waiting for?"

And when you see these towns and when you see these thugs being thrown into the back of a paddy wagon—you just see them thrown in, rough—I said, please don't be too nice. (Laughter.) Like when you guys put somebody in the car and you're protecting their head, you know, the way you put their hand over? Like, don't hit their head and they've just killed somebody—don't hit their head. I said, you can take the hand away, okay? (7/27/17)

Aside from lifting a famous Jerry Seinfeld routine during a speech in Suffolk County, Long Island, the comedy-allergic president (see his tweets fuming at an SNL rerun) might find it news to learn that suspects are not the same as criminals and are afforded innocence until they are proven guilty. Although Trump has made no effort to condemn police misconduct, even when captured on body cameras, here the local police department called him out, as police officials condemned this Trump misconduct: "The Suffolk County Police Department has strict rules and procedures relating to the handling of prisoners, and violations of those rules and procedures are treated extremely seriously. As a department, we do not and will not tolerate 'rough[ing]' up prisoners."

#9. Bothsides-ism: *"There were people in that rally—and I looked the night before—if you look, there were people protesting very quietly the taking down of the statue of Robert E. Lee. I'm sure in that group there were some bad ones. The following day it looked like they had some rough, bad people—neo-Nazis, white nationalists, whatever you want to call them. But you had a lot of people in that group that were there to innocently protest, and very legally protest—because I don't know if you know, they had a permit. The other group didn't have a permit." (8/15/17)*

After a domestic terrorist attack in Charlottesville, Virginia, killed a young woman, Heather Heyer, and crowds of neo-Nazis and assorted racists chanted, "Jews will not replace us!," the president seemed to care more about permits than deaths: he might be the living embodiment of white extinction anxiety as he searches for some good apples in a large rotten barrel of riotous racists. But even on this ancillary point, Trump's lying or at best wrong: they *did* have a permit.

"We'll be talking about gun laws as time goes by." (10/3/17)

He said this in the aftermath of America's worst-ever mass shooting, in Las Vegas, which took 58 lives in 2017. "Talking about" proved to be a stalling tactic—after 14 months of foot

"My daughter's right to life was God-given, however, because of a bastardized 2A interpretation pushed by gun sellers like this Congressman, she is dead."

Fred Guttenberg, father of Jamie Guttenberg, who was killed at Parkland

"We think it's reasonable to provide mandatory instant criminal background checks for every sale at every gun show. No loopholes anywhere for anyone..."

NRA executive vice president Wayne LaPierre, 1999. Those were the days.

"Mar-a-Lago, Trump's posh Florida club, doesn't allow guns, a hotel staff member told ABC News. Nor does Trump National Doral, in Miami, Florida. The resort would 'much rather not have guns on the property,' said a security official with the hotel, who noted that guns are 'not to be carried on our property.' A security worker at Trump National in Jupiter, Florida, said 'no' when asked if guns were allowed on premises by citizens who are licensed to carry them."

ABC News (5/20/16)

dragging, the bump stocks that enabled that attack were banned. He did briefly offer platitudes and condolences after the Las Vegas slaughter...but then spoke far more frequently and with more fervor when a jihadist's car attack in New York City a few weeks later tragically took eight lives.

#13. Rhetorical Questions: After making positive statements about President Obama's response to the Newtown tragedy, by 2015 Trump had adopted a nihilist attitude toward the national crisis of routine mass shootings: "It's the same old story. But what are you going to do? There are many people like that and what are you going to do? Institutionalize everybody? So you're going to have difficulties," he said. These "difficulties" include 345 mass shootings in 365 days in 2017. But on November 14, 2017, Trump tweeted his too-routine condolences for a school shooting in California. *Except* he copied and pasted the tweet from the wrong mass shooting in Texas, from nine days before. Maybe the monotony of mass shootings is the real national emergency.

"You know why [Senator Pat Toomey didn't address raising the age for purchasing rifles]? Because you're afraid of the NRA." (2/28/18)

Again, Trump has a gift for projecting onto others his own pathologies, e. g., accusing the philanthropic Clinton Foundation of being a "criminal enterprise" (while his own Trump Foundation folded following the exposure of a multitude of fraudulent activity) and accusing Democrats of being "treasonous" after the Mueller Report cleared him of conspiracy with Russia to hack the election.

Trump's finger-wagging comment to Toomey came at his White House meeting following the Parkland schools shooting.

He then turned the technique against his own party, telling them while the NRA has "great power over you people, they have less power over me." Then he went far out on a limb on age limits for firearms: "It should all be at 21," Trump said. "And the NRA will back it."

Not exactly, really not at all. Following Trump's televised bravado, the NRA provided its astute medical opinion on the issue: "Raising the age is not going to solve psychosis," according to its spokeswoman Dana Loesch. And that was that. After a White House lunch, an NRA chieftain tweeted that Trump and Mike Pence "don't want gun control," and Trump withdrew his limp support for raising the age of gun purchases. The ties that blind.

#20. The Lyin' King: *"My Administration is determined to do everything in our power to protect our students, secure our schools, and to keep weapons out of the hands of those who pose a threat to themselves and to others. Everyone must work together at every level of government to keep our children safe." (5/18/18)*

These are admirable goals—and the bare minimum—any civilized society's leaders should strive for. Yet Trump has not—indeed, he's actively worked against them by signing his first bill, with no fanfare, that reverses an Obama-era rule that keeps guns out of the hands of people with mental illnesses and instead toys with the idea of arming teachers. He's right, though: everyone must work together to keep children safe... since he hasn't.

"LONDON needs a new mayor ASAP. Khan is a disaster—will only get worse!" (6/15/19)

"The Republicans walk the NRA line and refuse even limited restrictions....I generally oppose gun control, but I support the ban on assault weapons and I support a slightly longer waiting period to purchase a gun. With today's Internet technology we should be able to tell within 72 hours if a potential gun owner has a record."

Donald Trump, 2000

"We don't plan to release the picture at this time."

Sarah Huckabee Sanders, commenting on a photo showing the signing ceremony of a law President Trump signed in February 2017 that makes it easier for mentally ill people to purchase guns. The law repealed an Obama administration regulation that put the names of some people with mental illnesses on criminal databases.

Trump tweeted about a story concerning knife killings in the UK posted by racist British Gen X Tomi Loren. London's knife murders are sort of conservatives' scaremongering about Chicago gone global. Here, it contains a trifecta of right-wing schizophrenia—one that blends Islamophobia (London's mayor, Sadiq Khan, is Muslim), mania about gun control ("see, even without guns, England is a war zone"), and immigration.

It's also a chance to draw attention away from America's shame of gun violence while also ignoring facts helpfully pointed out by a political scientist: the United States has five times the population of the UK but *469 times* the number of the UK's gun homicides.

It took one mass shooting—killing 50 people in a nation of under 5 million people, their 9/11—and just three weeks for New Zealand to act. By a vote of 119-1 Parliament passed a ban on most semiautomatic weapons and assault rifles. Since Sandy Hook, the United States of America has had at least 2,029 mass shootings.

6.
THE RULE OF LAW(LESSNESS)
"A SHOCKING PATTERN OF ILLEGALITY"

Donald Trump frequently referred to himself as the "law and order candidate." The part about "order" was accurate, but the "law" part, not so much. When it comes to respect for the Rule of Law, Richard Nixon is Justice Oliver Wendell Holmes, Jr. compared to Donald Trump.

The Rule of Law depends not only on police, prosecutors, and courts enforcing statutes but also on all of us voluntarily respecting rules and norms in our billions of interactions daily. Not Donald John Trump. Whether in his business career or presidency—especially his presidency—he often shuns the letter or spirit of the law. Yet he has largely escaped legal accountability because of a supine GOP Senate, an attorney general who performs as his butler, a base full of "grudge voters," and, ironically, scandal fatigue.

Again, more is less, since each new scandal crowds out scores of prior ones—or what Bill Kristol calls "the routinization of corruption." Consider how one Monica Lewinsky stands out more than 23 women accusing Trump of sexual assault.

Trump also evades many charges of corruption by rakishly admitting them "in plain sight." He acknowledges on national TV that he fired James Comey to derail the probe of Russia's role in the 2016 election and then acts indignant when people believe him. His AG says it's wrong to "politically weaponize" the Department of Justice as Trump then tries to politically weaponize the DoJ to investigate and jail political rivals. And he tells border agents they should just unlawfully turn away asylum seekers while hinting at pardons if necessary.

"Oh my god. My presidency is over. I'm fucked."

Donald Trump, on being told that Robert Mueller III had been named as Special Counsel

To Trump, "a lawyer is a person who helps you evade or violate the law and then helps you get away with it."

Richard Stengel,
former executive editor,
Time magazine

Allow this thought experiment. If President Obama told police officers in a city not to arrest black men buying drugs as an exercise in "legal reparations"—while winking at the cops that he'd have their backs—exactly what would Newt Gingrich have said?

Do we have a Rule of Law or a Law of Rule, in the Louis XIV sense of "L'Etat c'est moi"? Does Trump take the constitutional requirement that he faithfully "execute" the law only literally? What happens when perhaps the most corrupt person in America is also the only one who can't be (federally) indicted...and runs the "Justice" Department?

We report—you decide.

Business Career

"C" for colored. As also discussed in Chapter 5 on Race, he and his father were twice sued by President Nixon's Department of Justice in 1973 for willfully excluding African American applicants to their housing units, designating them with the code word "c" so even slow staff could get it—sort of a "racism for dummies" approach. The Trumps eventually agreed to two consent decrees where they promised not to do it again, (presumably) ending the practice.

Trump "University." For years Trump laughed off a lawsuit filed by the NY AG and two class actions against his Trump University for fraudulent misrepresentations. *"I could have settled this case many times but I don't want to when we are right,"* he told a crowd in May, 2016. *"And when you start settling cases, you know what happens? Everybody sues you because you get known as a settler. One thing about me—I am not known as a settler."*

But a raft of depositions revealed that some 7,000 victims paying up to $35,000 apiece were promised teachers and courses that didn't materialize. Never settling, it turns out, meant not until just *after* the 2016 presidential election and a week *before* a scheduled jury trial, when he personally agreed to pay $25 million to the State of New York and individual claimants in restitution.

Not a model agency. As part of his anti-immigrant campaign in 2017, Trump said that he would crack down on visitors who overstayed their US visas because when any citizen "loses their job to an illegal immigrant, the rights of that American Citizen have been violated."

Compare that declaration to the so-called Trump Model Management—started in 1987 and 85 percent owned by him. It turned out to be "like modern-day slavery," according to Rachael Blais, a former executive who worked there. In *a Mother Jones* exposé, she reported that very young girls, some as young as 14, lived in cramped quarters at high rents while being paid very low wages. They usually worked illegally since they needed work visas, which the agency never sought, and were instructed to lie on customs forms about where they intended to live. "Honestly, they are the most crooked agency I've ever worked for," added Blais, "and I've worked for quite a few."

Trump on Women. "They're all horrible, horrible liars," claimed the candidate about the now-23 different women publicly accusing him of sexual assault, adding with bravado that he'd be suing all of them when the campaign was over.

#20. The Lyin' King Really? All of them lying when they've publicly put themselves in the line of sight of not only one of most litigious bullies ever, but also millions of his online trolls? At the same time, he can't shed his boys-will-be-boys Howard Stern skin in the #MeToo era. Among men criticized for mistreatment of women or girls, Trump has come to the defense of Roy Moore, Brett Kavanaugh, Roger Ailes, Bob Kraft, and—a decade ago—Jeffrey Epstein. If the credo of the

#MeToo movement has been "believe the women," Trump's is "believe the men."

  * *"Illegals" bad, unless they're working for DJT.* When a contractor on his 58-story Trump Tower hired 200 unauthorized Polish workers in the mid-1980s for as little as $4 an hour to work 12 hours a day in often dangerous circumstances—and even then shortchanged those wages—many of them sued. Trump claimed no knowledge, but several plaintiffs reported that they saw him often visiting the site, and one foreman testified under oath that Trump told him, "Those Polish guys are good, hard workers." In 1991, Federal Judge Charles E. Stewart, Jr ruled that there was "strong evidence" he had conspired with the contractor to hire the workers and awarded them and a union pension fund $324,000 in damages—100 percent of what was claimed.

His public denunciations of undocumented workers *and* his private employment of them continued into his business presidency. Pulitzer Prize-winning investigative journalist David Fahrenthold and Univision did pieces in 2019 showing such workers without papers—and usually lacking benefits and health insurance—at six of his golf clubs and wineries, as well as at Mar-a-Lago. They were often told to work off the clock for little or no pay, classic "wage theft" in violation of state labor laws. In heartbreaking interviews on the record, they explained how their supervisors knew their status for years—one former manager said the attitude at his Trump club was "don't ask, don't tell"—firing them with no notice after *Washington Post* articles appeared about them.

In August, 2019, just days after the El Paso shooting, ICE's raid of a poultry processing plant in Mississippi picked up 680 undocumented workers. Trump defended the raid because it served as a "very good deterrent" and will somehow dissuade families fleeing violence in their home countries...as for traumatizing children for a lifetime, well, that's the price of progress. Left untouched: the processing plant's owners—and Trump properties' *own* management—who have obviously been unlawfully hiring such people for years.

#6. Upside-Downism: *Trump "Foundation."* Candidate Trump claimed that the Clinton Foundation was a crooked enterprise, despite its "A" rating from the American Institute of Philanthropy Charity Watch. Yet it was the Trump Foundation and its board of directors that were sued in 2016 by New York State Attorney General Barbara Underwood "for being little more than a checkbook to serve Mr. Trump's business and political interests [in a] shocking pattern of illegality."

His repeated self-dealing included the purchase of a $10,000 portrait of Trump displayed at one of his golf clubs and the expenditure of $100,000 to resolve a legal dispute between the Town of Palm Beach and his Mar-a-Lago resort; also, campaign manager Corey Lewandowski personally dictated the size and timing of $2.8 million in "philanthropic" grants in order to advance Trump's political prospects before particular primaries.

Although it would be hard to more blatantly violate the laws governing charities, Trump attacked "sleazy New York Democrats" for suing his, vowing, "I won't settle this case!" Six months later, he agreed to settle by dissolving the foundation entirely and allowing the AG office to oversee distribution of all remaining funds. One more thing: Underwood sued to prevent Trump and his family from serving on any foundation boards for 10 years. The upshot: while he was constitutionally empowered to run the federal government, he was found to lack the character to run a charitable organization in New York State. Sad.

"These super PACS are a disaster, very corrupt. There is total control of the candidates. I know it better than anybody that probably ever lived…[When] I was a businessman, I gave to everybody. When they call, I give. And you know what? When I need something from them, two years later, three years later, I call and they are there for me. And that's a broken system."

Donald Trump (3/15/97)

Tax Fraud. An extensive piece in the *New York Times* on April 10, 2019, reported that Trump family members created a shell company that enabled them to fake invoices in order to hide gifts and charge rents higher than allowed in their residential buildings. Coowners included Donald as well as his sister, 3d Circuit Court of Appeals judge Maryanne Trump Barry. Ten days after the article appeared, four different people filed charges against her in the Judicial Conduct Council. Ten days later, at age 82, she resigned, mooting the inquiry.

Presidency

As "the Child is father of the Man," wrote William Wordsworth, Trump's persistent contempt for law before 2017 proved to be only a start—if not a template—for how he would behave with the public powers of the presidency at his disposal. Imagine if Senator Joseph McCarthy got elected president and appointed Roy Cohn as his AG—both deploying their now-infamous array of innuendo and conspiracy theories. We are roughly in that situation now with Trump-Barr, or certainly would be if 45 wins reelection, though without any Republican Senators like Maine Republican Margret Chase Smith to call out the sleaze and self-dealing.

Analogies don't do Trump & Barr justice. So let's go to today's videotape. Even putting numerous ethical violations in a separate chapter, here is part of the rap sheet of a person whom both former FBI director James Comey and former CIA chief John Brennan compared to the head of an organized crime family:

1. *Alien Invasion.* The president clearly cares far more about appearing tough on undocumented immigrants—calling them "animals…murderers…invaders…

[from] shithole countries"—than being faithful to the letter and spirit of the law.

Trump's "Muslim" ban failed in several federal courts until it got to the Supreme Court—and then for a second time—when Justice Gorsuch-not-Garland made the difference in his 5–4 win. But his Executive Order denying lawful status to 800,000 DACA children has now been struck down four times by different courts. 45's attempt to turn away all asylum seekers, despite the obvious law to the contrary, was

stayed by a temporary injunction in late 2018, then upheld by the Supreme Court. Three months later, his effort to turn down hundreds of visa applications of children who had been abused, neglected, or abandoned under the US Citizenship & Immigration Services was rejected by a federal judge.

That March also saw US District Court Judge Dana Sabraw require his administration to reunite thousands of children, including toddlers, unlawfully separated from their parents at the southern border and put into cages at different locations throughout the United States. Sabraw, appointed by President George W. Bush, wrote:

> *The hallmark of a civilized society is measured by how it treats its people and those within its borders. That defendants [may have to undertake additional efforts] does not render modification of the class definition unfair; it only serves to underscore the unquestionable importance of the effort.*

In May, 2019, Trump visited the border and told a group of border guards, "Listen, just turn them [asylum seekers] away—tell them no room." After he left, border officials were put in the awkward position of telling the guards to ignore their commander in chief.

"If the president does it, that means that it is not illegal."

Former president Richard Nixon, The Nixon-Frost Interviews, 1977

Somewhere Emma Lazarus was weeping.

2. *Nepotism.* The reasons against it are self-evident. Even if the relative in a particular case—say, Hillary Clinton or Robert F. Kennedy—possesses presidential-level talents, when an officer holder appoints a family member to a taxpayer-funded position, the motive will certainly appear to be favoritism, not merit. Hence the 1967 Federal Anti-Nepotism law prohibiting it.

To Donald Trump, however, laws are not mandates, but inconveniences to circumvent. How was he able to appoint both his completely unqualified daughter (who made clothes) and his completely unqualified son-in-law (who made bad real estate deals) to senior White House positions? *No problemo.* The day after his inauguration, an official in the now-Trump Justice Department reversed a decades-long determination to conclude instead that the law barring relatives applied only to agencies *across* the government but not the office *in charge of* the government.

What happened next was a reminder why "nepotism" is such a pejorative. It took numerous do-overs for the couple to complete federal financial and ethics forms that

"I'd say, Mr. President, I understand what you want to do but you can't do it that way. It violates the law. It violates treaties."

Rex Tillerson, President Trump's first secretary of state, after leaving office.

Photo by Mark Wilson/Getty Images

Treasury Secretary Gerald Cohn was appalled, as reported in Vicky Ward's *Kushner, Inc,* "when he heard the two discussing who [between them] might run for president someday." Though less weird than Emperor Caligula famously appointing his beloved horse as First Counsul, Cohn hadn't previously appreciated the dynastic presumptions of this privileged couple.

carried criminal penalties for inaccuracies. Even then, many conflicts were reported by the media—such as China rewarding Ivanka valuable copyrights on the day the Chinese and American presidents met for dinner at Mar-a-Lago and Jared using Saudi financing to sell his troubled 666 Madison Ave. property while ostensibly negotiating a Middle East peace.

And then, like a Forrest Gump appearing here-there-everywhere, Ivanka showed up on her father's arm at the G-20 meeting in June 2019 looking like a head of state, which didn't much impress the actual heads of state. (Not to mention that she had trademarks in 18 of the 20 nations attending.)

But Daddy thinks that she's Wonder Woman. So he asked her, according to her, to lead the World Bank,

*COUNTRIES IVANKA TRUMP HAS VISITED AS A WHITE HOUSE OFFICIAL:	*COUNTRIES VISITED THAT RECOGNIZE A TRADEMARK FROM IVANKA'S BUSINESS:
Saudi Arabia	Saudi Arabia
Israel	Israel
Poland	Poland
India	India
Japan	Japan
South Korea	South Korea

Source: Citizens for Responsibility & Ethics

According to Noah Bookbinder, former federal corruption prosecutor and executive director of the Citizens for Responsibility and Ethics, Ivanka and Jared "show why nepotism laws exist. This is not only an ethics issue but a national security issue. They have received special treatment, including security clearance and apparently can't be fired." According to the files of ranking White House advisers John Kelley and Don McGahn, a White House adviser overruled the advice of the office determining security clearances to provide the couple desired credentials, at the president's specific insistence, although he publicly denied having done so.

Photo by Aaron P. Bernstein/Getty Images

explaining that "you're good with numbers." In a world of renowned economists and finance ministers, Donald Trump settled on fashion designer Ivanka Trump. She declined, indicating that she did have *some* public—though still not much financial—savvy. Yet when asked in a Fox interview her opinion of the jobs guarantee in the Green New Deal proposal, this lifetime heiress opposed it because "Americans like to work for what they have."

3. *President Buttinski.* American legal tradition and practice has historically shied away from chief executives interfering in law enforcement matters as an obvious violation of fair and impartial justice. When President (and lawyer) Richard Nixon blurted out at a press conference his opinion about the guilt of Lt. Calley in

his trial for the My Lai massacre, Nixon realized his mistake and the next day retracted his comment.

For a litigious Donald Trump, however, having his own Department of 9,000 lawyers was intoxicating, even for a teetotaler like him. He intuitively assumed that the Department was his, like everything was more or less "his" in his private business career.

#4. Insult Machine: He was infuriated when AG Jeff Sessions properly recused himself from the Mueller special counsel investigation, since he had been a top official person in the campaign under investigation. Said Trump, privately, publicly, repeatedly, "If I knew I'd never have appointed you"—the clear implication being that he wanted not neutral law enforcement, but rather an AG and probe that he could control. Of course, he fired FBI Director James Comey after the director couldn't promise fealty when it came to going easy on Michael Flynn and, as he told NBC's Lester Holt, because of "this Russia thing."

You don't have to be a barrister in England to know that, since Common Law, it has been accepted wisdom that "no man can be the judge of his own case." Trump, however, cared not about several hundred years of legal tradition, but his own hide and political needs. And he was guided by a different ethic entirely. As former Senator Warren Magnuson (D-WA) once put it, almost anticipating Trump, "all anybody wants in life is an unfair advantage.

He pressured Treasury Secretary Gary Cohn, then director of the National Economic Council, to tell the Justice Department to bring an antitrust case against the ATT-Time Warner merger, not because of the real problems of vertical integration of the combination, but due to his hatred of Jeff Bezos, the world's richest man and owner of the equally despised *Washington Post*. Giving away his motive, Trump also personally urged US Postmaster Megan Brennan to double the rate charged Amazon and other firms to ship packages, which would have cost these firms billions of dollars. Brennan refused.

#1. Cherry-picking: He intervened in major military cases, including the well-known trial of Sergeant Bowe Bergdahl, who walked off his post in 2015 in Afghanistan, was captured and held by the Taliban for five years, and then released. At his capture, Trump called him "a traitor, a no-good traitor, who should have been executed." When a military court fined him $10,000, downgraded him to private, and dishonorably discharged him, 45 was furious: "The decision on Sergeant Bergdahl is a complete and total disgrace to our Country and to our Military." Except the military, in the form of a Military Tribunal on this matter, disagreed.

Trump repeatedly attacked judicial rulings when they didn't go his way, as courts will occasionally do to any POTUS. He referred to Judge Gonzalo Curiel as a "Mexican judge" (he's a US citizen born here) in a border case that he lost; and he's constantly belittled the 9th Circuit Court of Appeals in California for overruling Administration actions.

Chief Justice John Roberts, a conservative Republican chosen by Bush 43, had had enough. "We do not have Obama judges or Trump judges, Bush judges or Clinton judges," he said in a rare, if not unprecedented, rebuke by the head of the Judiciary to the head of the Executive Branch. "What we have is an extraordinary group of dedicated judges doing their level best to do equal rights to those appearing before them. That independent judiciary is something we should all be thankful for."

Should a black person get entangled with the law—like actor Jussie Smolletts claiming that he was attacked by two homophobic assailants—Trump seems eager to jump right in such local law enforcement matters to urge prosecution; but when a white person is accused of some act of domestic terror, such as the Trump-quoting murderer of 11 at a Pittsburgh synagogue, there's largely silence.

"Thank you to all of America's brave police, deputies, sheriffs, and federal law enforcement on National Law Enforcement Appreciation Day! We love you and will always support you." Donald Trump (1/29/19).

Except the FBI, when the president to an unprecedented level reached down into its bureaucracy to railroad and cashier officials—and denounce them repeatedly to his Twitter army—who were part of the team investigating him.

Last, unrelenting attacks on his own Department of Justice, especially the FBI, shook morale in both places. "Disgusting, disgraceful" were among his go-to adjectives to disparage the Bureau for investigating him as part of a lawful law enforcement action. All of which was odd, since the FBI has a reputation as a nonpartisan law enforcement agency (at least since J. Edgar Hoover), staffed largely by white male Republicans and run by Republican directors (Robert Mueller, James Comey, Christopher Wray). If there were any tilt in 2016, it was when Comey twice felt it necessary to publicly discuss Clinton's email probe during the election but never the far more serious counterintelligence investigation of Trump.

#6. Upside-Downism: After forcing Jeff Sessions out, Trump found his man in Washington attorney and former AG Bill Barr, who time and again has proven to be a White House mouthpiece rather than an independent law enforcement official. Although Barr piously warned against "weaponizing and politicizing" the system of justice, he followed Trump's lead in pushing for probes into why the FBI investigated Trump in the first place—a move that will surely chill any future potentially career-ending effort to investigate an allegedly corrupt president. Trump and he agreed to what had been previously inconceivable, that the president could recommend prosecution of his political rivals, as Trump did when he urged Sessions to criminally charge Hillary Clinton for something-or-other and pushed Barr to look into the financial dealings of Joe Biden's son in Ukraine. Biden? Rings a bell.

4. *Mueller Report*. Donald Trump has so far politically survived this potentially catastrophic investigation due to a multipronged defense: a party-over-country

When Linda E. McMahon, a wealthy supporter of candidate Trump and one of only five female cabinet officers, retired in early 2019, the *New York Times* ran this headline: "Small Business Chief, Who Avoided Scandal, Resigns." Apparently, after messrs Manfort, Flynn, Gates. Porter, Pruitt, Price, Zinke, etc., it was considered newsworthy that a Trump appointee was *not* implicated in wrongdoing.

GOP Senate majority making conviction of any Article of Impeachment unlikely; Attorney General William Barr shilling for Trump like any $1,000-an-hour criminal defense lawyer *cum* publicist; and a Dudley-Do-Right special counsel who played by the rules—can't indict a sitting president, won't leak, won't subpoena the president—while Trump brought a chain saw to their knife fight.

#20. The Lyin' King: The result? An asymmetrical gaslighting allowed Trump-Barr to repeatedly shout "no collusion, no obstruction, total exoneration!" for weeks while they lied about the hidden report before anyone could even read it.

> "There is no statute against helping a foreign hostile power meddle in an American election. What Donald, Jr.—and Kushner and Manafort—did may not be criminal. But it is not merely stupid. It is also deeply wrong, a fundamental violation of any code of civic honor."
>
> Conservative columnist Charles Krauthammer

WHEREIN DONALD, JR. LAMENTS "LIE AFTER LIE" ABOUT HIM. NO, REALLY.

The *Washington Post* called this exchange "cringeworthy" when one reads it, aware of a) Junior's *prior* email eagerly anticipating receiving "dirt" on Hillary Clinton at the Trump Tower meeting and b) every US Intel agency agreeing that Russia intervened in 2016 to help Trump win:

CNN's Jake Tapper: [The Clinton campaign manager] seemed to be suggesting that this is part of a plot to help Donald Trump and hurt Hillary Clinton. Your response?"

Donald Junior: "Well, just goes to show you their exact moral compass. They'll say anything to be able to win this. This is time and time again, lie after lie....It's disgusting. It's so phony."

But, alas, accurate.

Remember Ben Franklin's axiom about "truth vs. error" from the preface? Here's the truth based on under-oath witnesses and documentary evidence:

- Team Trump claimed that they "rebuffed at every turn" all Russian overtures. #20. The Lyin' King: Actually, while Mueller concluded there was no provable criminal "conspiracy," there was plenty of cooperation between Russian interests and a welcoming Trump Campaign: who can forget the nominee saying on July 17, "Russia, if you're listening..." ...or Don Junior emailing "I love it" when offered what he thought would be dirt at his Trump Tower confab (see adjacent exchange between Jake Tapper and Junior)—and then lying that it was only about "adoptions."
- And what *was* campaign chair Paul Manafort doing traveling to a The Grand Havana Room, a cigar bar in Manhattan, to share polling data state-by-state with a Russian oligarch tied to Putin? In all, Mueller found 140 documented contacts with Russian nationals—or 140 more than Obama and Romney combined in 2016.
- Trump Team asserted that there can't be any Obstruction charges, since Mueller concluded that there was no underlying crime. Actually, even conveniently forgetting the crimes of Manafort, Cohen, Flynn, Papadopoulos, Gates, and Stone, that's wrong as a matter of black-letter law—did Barr not have access to any lawyers in his office *at the Department of Justice* to tell him about Martha Stewart?

Two months before Mueller was appointed, President Trump called Mike Rogers and Richard Legett, #1 and #2 at the National Security Agency, to ask them to publicly deny news stories that the Trump campaign had ties to Russia. Said Legett: It was "the most unusual request I had ever heard in my 40 years in intelligence."

@WalterDellinger, former U S Solicitor General under President Clinton, May 15, 2019: "The Mueller Investigation fully established not merely crimes, but the betrayal of the president's office: a failure to defend the country's electoral system from foreign attack and acts of interference with justice that shred the rule of law." Retired Judge Andrew Napolitano, the Fox News judicial analyst: "When the president asked Corey Lewandowski...to get Mueller fired, that's obstruction of justice. When the president asked his last White House Counsel to get Mueller fired and then lie about it, that's obstruction of justice..."

- #16. Deny/Deny/Deny: They also pretended that there was no evidence of Obstruction. Actually, Mueller provided 10 examples in detail and discussed several pieces of evidence in his famous testimony before the House Judiciary Committee on July 24, 2019. Or do Trump's lawyers think it kosher for him to ask Don McGahn to lie about his request to fire Mueller? Do they think it all right for Trump to order private citizen Corey Lewandowski to fire AG Sessions to help Trump purge the DoJ during Mueller's investigation?
- Team Trump claimed that they fully cooperated with Mueller's inquiry, so there should be no follow-up investigations or an impeachment process—i. e., no "do-overs." Actually, that was true...if you don't count Senior and Junior refusing requests to answer questions in person, dictating the false Trump Tower meeting cover-up story, lying to the public about the Trump Moscow project, and the 1,100 times over 22 months when they called the Special Counsel probe "18 angry Trump-hating Democrats...witch hunt, hoax, etc." Doesn't sound very cooperative.
- As for do-overs, Mueller was charged with looking into Russia's possible intervention into the American election, which they concluded had occurred, but nothing else about, say, Trump's taxes, finances, emoluments, pardons, etc.
- #6. Upside-Downism: Trump tweeted after release of the Report: "*Everyone is asking how the phony and fraudulent investigation of the No Collusion, No Obstruction Trump Campaign began. We need to*

know for future generations." Hence, Trump-Barr announced several investigations into the FBI investigators.

- How did it begin? Answered David Corn of *Mother Jones*, "It's pretty simple. You kept saying positive things about a foreign adversary attacking the United States. And then the FBI learned one of your foreign policy advisers was in touch with a Russian cut-out and discussing dirt on Hillary Clinton."
- The Trump administration, however, isn't really looking for the origins of a law enforcement proceeding when they announced their counterinvestigations. Rather, they're hoping and expecting to produce headlines for months—à la Benghazi—before issuing a Friday afternoon press release in 2020 that indeed FBI lovers Peter Strzok and Lisa Page didn't literally start the whole thing.
- And in a political version of *Catch-22,* Barr creatively argued that a) a president has the authority to end any investigation into him if HE thinks that he's falsely charged ("Mr. Madoff, you say that you're innocent of these charges and emotionally spent by them? Sounds good. You may go now."), b) he can claim exoneration, since Mueller didn't indict him because of a DoJ rule that Barr could change any morning, and c) Congress cannot investigate the president for corruption or other crimes, since those are exclusively law enforcement, not legislative, matters.
- Yet in the view of Chuck Rosenberg, an ex-FBI official who had worked with Mueller, "but for the

William Barr, in 1996, testified that "the greatest threat to free government, the Founders believed, was not tyranny but personal licentiousness." To which Bill Maher responded, "The Founders believed in this so strongly that they wrote it down...*nowhere!*"

"The United States suffered the worst, most effective, attacks on our democracy in our history. And the AG is very concerned that people may have investigated that." @LOLGOP

Campaign aide Sam Nunberg sat with nonlawyer Donald Trump in 2015 to get him to read and understand the Constitution better. "I got as far as the Fourth Amendment before his finger is pulling down on his lip and his eyes are rolling back in his head."

OLC regulation, a person doing that would be in handcuffs."

- "That's called a monarchy," explained author and commentator Joy-Ann Reid. Trump and Barr are relying on the profound "content bias" of Trumpers to swallow whole their excuses in order to draw attention away from what is the greatest exposé of presidential corruption in American history.

5. *Speech.* Trump appears to take a narrow reading of the First Amendment—viz., everyone's entitled to his opinion. His views on matters involving constitutionally protected speech are not criminal, of course, merely ridiculous and chilling:
   - Annoyed by an SNL satirical sketch about him, Trump tweeted that they had "no right" to do that and threatened to "open up" federal libel laws to make it easier to sue news outlets and "win lots of money." #6. Upside-Downism:
   - When the father of a slain Muslim American soldier criticized him from the podium at the Democratic National Convention, he complained that the father *"had no right to stand in front of millions of people and claim that I have never read the Constitution"* (thereby proving that...he had never read at least the First Amendment).
   - When a cast member of the Broadway musical *Hamilton* called out Vice President Pence during a curtain call for his indifference to fundamental civil rights, Trump tweeted that such confrontations "should not happen."

- He argued that "Nobody should be allowed to burn the American flag. If they do, there must be consequences—perhaps loss of citizenship or year in jail." (Attempted political assassinations do not even lead to loss of citizenship.) The Supreme Court, with Justice Scalia in the 5–4 majority, concluded that burning the American flag was a form of protected speech.

- He cannot stop attacking NFL quarterback Colin Kaepernick and others for silently kneeling during the playing of the national anthem in order to protest police violence, saying that he'd "like to fire the son-of-a-bitch."

- He has repeatedly called the media (using Stalin's abhorrent phrase) "the enemy of the people." Worse, here's how he explained away his continuing praise of Putin despite accusations that he ordered the murder of journalists: "What, you think we're so much better?" he told a clearly surprised Bill O'Reilly on Fox. At a political rally in December 2015, after denouncing journalists as "disgusting people," he showed his soft side by adding that as president he would "never kill" them. Then he paused, smirked, and appeared to jokingly reconsider. *"Uh, let's see...No, I would never do that."*

- Showing profound confusion and/or disregard for the First Amendment protection of individual speech, Trump used his office to promote Fox News 1,000 times and then announce in the summer of 2019 after Fox interviewed some Democrats and reported on bad poll numbers, "Fox isn't working for us anymore...we have to start looking for a new network."

- The White House withdrew the credentials of two reporters after they wrote articles that displeased Trump—most notably CNN's Jim Acosta—and twice courts reinstated them.
- When 100 heads of state, led by France's Emmanuel Macron and New Zealand's Jacinda Ardern, signed an agreement to try to encourage social media platforms to establish rules to keep hate speech, conspiracy theorists, and white supremacists off social media platforms, Trump's White House refused to join, citing its free speech concerns. Free speech for Alex Jones but not Alec Baldwin?

6. *Cases: A Judicial Batting Average of .060.*

No person or institution can win them all, but, in one study, the Trump administration had a six percent win rate in federal courts as compared to 70 percent for prior presidents. *To repeat: that's 6% vs. 70%!* As of May 2019, the Administration had lost 63 times in federal court, for an average of twice a month, a success rate well below the infamous '62 Mets, that being its expansion year.

But with a Supreme Court and federal judiciary both now stacked due to bad luck and malice (the butterfly ballot misdesign of 2000 and McConnell's stalling of 44's federal picks while rushing 45's through), Trump is openly panting to be rescued from his worst offenses by a 5–4 Republican Supreme Court (watch for *ACA, Roe*, and *Affirmative Action* decisions to come).

7. *Stormy Daniels.* The saga of their relationship and legal wrangling is well known and mentioned above in Chapter 3, "Women." But it bears repeating, as MSNBC's Lawrence O'Donnell stressed on *The Last Word:* for how often does a president lie about an affair AND then sign at least six hush money checks totaling $270,000 while in the Oval Office? Like, never?

> April 5, 2018, aboard Air Force One:
> #16. Deny/Deny/Deny: *Q: "Mr. President, did you know about the $130,000 payment to Stormy Daniels?*
> Trump: "No, no. What else?"*
> *Q: "Then why did Michael Cohen make those if there was no truth to her allegations?"*
> *Trump: "Well, you'll have to ask Michael Cohen. Michael is my lawyer. And you'll have to ask Michael Cohen."*
> *Q: "Do you know where he got the money to make that payment?"*
> *Trump: "No, I don't know. No."*

8. *Pardon Power.* Leave it to Donald Trump to figure out how to violate a constitutional power that is specifically unlimited.

   The pardon power originates from common law in England, where it was meted out to fix an injustice or extend mercy. Of course, any authority can be abused. Consider the example of former Illinois governor and *Celebrity Apprentice* contestant Rod Blagojevich. When his Senate appointment power was first explained to

"As has been stated by numerous legal scholars, I have the absolute right to PARDON myself, but why would I do that when I have done nothing wrong? In the meantime, the never-ending Witch Hunt, led by 13 very Angry and Conflicted Democrats (& others) continues into the mid-terms!"

Donald Trump (6/4/18)

the governor, he was pleasantly amazed. "Hey, this is golden..." So he apparently offered for sale the vacant Senate seat of Barack Obama and was consequently convicted for corruption.

This chapter and the previous one draw the portrait of a profit-maximizing cheat—as his lawyer of 10 years described him to a House heading—who at the least is smarter than saying out loud the monetary value of presidential pardons. While prior presidents almost always had a formal process for reviewing pardons to help assure that they weren't given out fecklessly or never, Trump, however, established no process other than his own whims and advice from friendly celebrities. Eight of his first big nine pardons went to criminals who were either prominent conservatives or major supporters of his.

- Joe Arpaio is an unrepentant racist convicted because he violated a court order intended to stop racial profiling. Can there be any other reason for this pardon than the fact that he had been a Trump loyalist for years?
- Right-wing author and filmmaker Dinesh D'Souza was found guilty of funneling thousands of dollars to a Senate candidate without disclosing that he was the actual donor and ripping through campaign finance limits for individual contributions. Although D'Souza never asked for one or offered a statement of contrition, Trump gave him a full pardon.
- Lewis "Scooter" Libby, a former aide to vice president Dick Cheney, was convicted of perjury and

obstruction of justice during the investigation of leaks of the identity of CIA agent Valerie Plame, the spouse of a prominent anti-Bush43 critic.

- Conrad Black was a 74-year-old business tycoon and media magnate convicted of fraud and obstruction of justice involving two business partners in a Chicago skyscraper deal.

- Trump "was a legal friend in my legal troubles," said Black, who wrote a hagiography of 45 with the title *Donald J. Trump, A President like No Other.* After he freed Black three years into his five-year term, Trump White House press secretary Sarah Sanders put on her game face, explaining that the felon was "an entrepreneur and a scholar who had made a tremendous contribution to business, as well as to political and historic thought."

- Reports out of the White House indicate how Trump lawyers would "dangle pardons" to targets of the Special Counsel probe in what appears to be witness tampering. For example, a cocounsel with Rudy Giuliani emailed Michael Cohen in the Spring of 2018, according to *CNN*, that he could "sleep well tonight" since he had "friends in high places." In the context of the list above, what could that mean?

- Finally, the *Washington Post, Axios,* and *CNN* all reported in late August 2019 that Trump had several times urged DHS officials to build at least some of his cherished wall by 2020, despite budget laws, and to "take" land illegally if necessary, and that he'd pardon them if later prosecuted. The White House admitted it, adding that *he was joking!* At

"I am not a crook."
　　　　　　–Richard Nixon, 1973

"Case closed. Case closed."
–Sen. Majority Leader Mitch
McConnell, after the publi-
cation of the *Mueller Report,*
May, 2019

"I don't do cover-ups."
　　　　–President Donald Trump

the risk of seeming tendentious, three questions: Did those at the meeting think it funny? Did they think that it might be an instruction? If Richard Nixon had laughed off his taped comment that paying hush money was obviously "a joke," would he have escaped the impeachment process?

- And a fourth question: Does the Trump White House think Americans are idiots?

9.　*Emolumental Greed.*

> *"It's very possible that I could be the first presidential candidate to run and make money on it." (4/3/00, in Fortune)*

> *"As the president, I could run the Trump Organization—great, great company—and I could run the country. I'd do a very good job. But I don't want to do that..." (1/11/17)*

Photo by Alex Wong/Getty Images

Yes, he did. Which is how we now have the first for-profit presidency.

Article I, Section 9, Clause 8: "[N]o Person holding any Office of Profit or Trust under them, shall, without the Consent of the Congress, accept of any present, Emolument, Office, or Title, of any kind whatever, from any King, Prince, or foreign State."

This foreign-emoluments clause (and a parallel domestic one) deals with a federal officeholder's legal obligation to separate him- or herself from any business dealings with foreign governments and state officials in order to avoid bribery or conflicts of interest. It basically prohibits the president and other officials from taking gifts—including, most Constitutional scholars agree, in the form of business transactions—from state actors who might want something in return. Given the Founders' deep concern about meddling by foreign entities, a 1994 Department of Justice opinion said, "the language of the Emoluments Clause is both sweeping and unqualified."

It appears that Trump likes DoJ opinions that won't let him be indicted, but not those that won't let him milk public office for private gain.

This has barely been an issue historically, since no federal officeholder has so blatantly tried, in his words, "to run a company and the country." Like Trump, Washington made his fortune in owning property (and marrying wealth); he wrestled with whether mixing business and his governmental connections—especially with British ministers who had authority in areas where Washington owned land—was improper. That decade also saw Benjamin Franklin, as ambassador to

France, ask Congress if he could keep a diamond box given to him by the King of France (the answer was ok).

This issue was dormant for nearly two centuries until President Jimmy Carter affirmatively asked whether or not the blind trust in which he placed his peanut farm was actually "blind" (it was). And then came Donald Trump. With scores of companies in dozens of countries, it would be easy for foreign entities who want his support on a matter to put money in his pocket. Indeed, why would such a country *not* send delegations to the Trump Hotel in DC—to use an obvious and real example—to make a decision maker who loves money and loyalty happy?

There's now massive evidence of self-dealing by a president who, to quote Oscar Wilde, "can resist anything except temptation." *Insatiable* is a word that comes to mind.

- "Lobbyists representing the Saudi government reserved blocks of rooms at President Trump's Washington, DC, hotel within a month of Trump's election in 2016—paying for an estimated 500 nights at the luxury hotel in just three months, according to organizers of the trips and documents obtained by the *Washington Post*. "In all, the lobbyists spent more than $270,000 to house six groups of visiting veterans at the Trump hotel, which Trump still owns," according to David A. Fahrenthold and Jonathan O'Connell.
- "Former Gov. Paul LePage of Maine and his staff members paid for more than 40 rooms at Washington, DC's Trump International Hotel

during a two-year period, spending at least $22,000 in Maine taxpayer money at a business owned by the president's family." Scott Thistle and Kevin Miller, *Portland Press Herald* (2/17/19)

- "Trump made 290 visits to his own businesses during the first 970 days of his presidency. That's 290 taxpayer-funded promotional visits to businesses he still profits from." Citizens for Responsibility and Ethics in Washington (2/24/19)
- Trump appears to violate the emoluments clause on *himself*. According to the Government Accountability Office, every time Trump heads to Mar-a-Lago—his "Winter White House"—it costs taxpayers around $3.4 million. During the 2018 midterm campaign, Trump spent $37,000 a month for office space in Trump Tower. Wrote Public Citizen's Rob Weissman, "To have a purported billionaire taking money from people who are contributing $10 and $20 increments to bulk up his own bank account is pretty pathetic."
- CREW has also documented 2130 "conflicts of interest" between his public role and his business interests in Trump's first two-and-a-half years in office.[7]

---

7 It now appears likely that a series of lawsuits seeking access to his tax returns and financial records are ripening to the point when state and federal authorities will shortly have access to them—despite Barr's ludicrous argument that only the president's own Justice Department can compel such information under penalty of his criminal prosecution (*Barr v. Trump* is not a case name we expect to see soon). New York officials and prosecutors are especially interested to see if he criminally inflated assets in order to obtain loans. For it's unlikely that his energetic efforts to keep these files secret are based on good government notions of privacy.

- Last, as if the betting window were about to close, there was an outburst of presidential grifting around Labor Day 2019. E.g., as noted, the president was pressuring the G-7 to hold its 2020 meeting at his Trump Doral Miami; wearing a new blue "USA" hat during Hurricane Dorian that went on sale 48 hours later as profitable campaign swag; convincing the Air Force to make out-of-the-way refueling stops at the faltering Prestwick Airport near Trump Turnberry in Scotland; and getting VP Pence and his entourage to stay at his Doonberg resort in Ireland despite being 140 miles away from his scheduled events in Dublin.
- One wit tweeted: "I'm surprised 1600 Pennsylvania Ave hasn't set up on Zillow or AirBnB yet." (@SweetGeekling).

#20. The Lyin' King: The solution was obvious: like Carter, put his holdings in a true blind trust or sell them. Trump had other plans. In a bizarre display just weeks before his inauguration, Trump placed a pile of paper-filled manila folders on his desk (many thought the folders were blank) and claimed they were paperwork he just completed to sign over his businesses in a trust to his sons.

"What I'm going to be doing is my two sons—who are, right here, Don and Eric—are going to be running the company. They are going to be running it in a very professional manner. They're not going to discuss it with me.... These papers are just some of the many documents I've signed, turning over complete

and total control to my sons." (1/11/17)

Oops—he *has* discussed company matters with his sons (no shocker there), and while he may not be managing the firm directly daily, he is profiting from it daily due to how he has maintained his ownership.

There are two major pending cases brought against Trump's alleged violation of the clear language of the Emoluments Clause. One brought by 200 members of Congress and another by the AGs of Maryland and Washington, DC. It only helped these cases when Trump, at the 2019 G-7 meeting in Biarritz, France, said that he intended to hold the G-7 meeting in 2020 at his Trump Doral Miami. Which would mean that foreign delegations wouldn't merely be able to choose to patronize his own facility, but would be *required* to attend and pay.

Nor was his proposal subtle. Sounding far more like a timeshare salesman than a president, he said at his closing presser that "each country can have their own villa or their own bungalow...we have incredible conference rooms, incredible restaurants...it's like such a natural." Fortunately, he assured everyone at his presser that "I'm not going to make any money. I don't want to make money. I don't care about making money." Really?

It turns out that there are limits to the open corruption of steering a fat federal contract to yourself. After acting chief of staff Mick Mulvaney announced on Thursday October 17th that the G-7 would be held at Trump's Doral, on Saturday night October 19th a chagrined Mulvaney announced that Trump had reversed

"There are lines we would never cross and that's mixing business and anything governmental."
Eric Trump (who probably misspoke and meant to say "always cross")

"Self-serving pardons. Self-serving Medals of Honor. Self-serving Ambassadorships. This is a self-serving presidency."

CREW, 5/18/19

himself, since "he was honestly surprised at the level of pushback," i.e., this was an elegant way of admitting that members of both parties gagged on the Gordon-Gekko greed from a president who said he didn't care about money.

10. Last, of course, there is the prospect of Impeachment & Trial as this book went to press. Squeezed between not being allowed to indict and not wanting to exonerate, Mueller clearly implied in his Report's very last line that Congress—with no such restrictions—was probably the best venue to show that "no person in this country is so high that he is above the law." Viz., in the view of the coauthors:

> *If a president who repeatedly obstructs both a criminal investigation into himself as well as an impeachment inquiry and by inaction encourages another Russian intervention to help him win the 2020 election—while daily violating the constitutional prohibition against accepting gifts from foreign officials, extorting the Ukranian president to do him a political "favor," and telling more lies than probably all former presidents combined—aren't impeachable offenses, by which the framers meant "abuse of power," what would be?*

Early in this process, some Members and commentators worried that even if the House impeached, this GOP Senate never would get to the two-thirds needed to convict, which could allow Trump in 2020 to brag that he was "acquitted!" Of course, the 1974 Senate wouldn't "convict" Nixon...until the tape came out where he agreed to hush money to the Watergate burglars. As for a tough Senate vote on Trump's obvious abuses of power, it can be convincingly argued, could it further *endanger* marginal GOP incumbents like Collins and Gardner. *Quién sabe?*

On such a fraught constitutional matter, however, speculation should not supersede one's oath of office. *Fiat justitia ruat caelum* is the principle in Latin, which translates as "Let justice be done though the heavens fall."[8]

Despite years of blatant impeachable offenses, a cautious Democratic leadership refused to consider Impeachment...until the release of a whistleblower's complaint and summary of a conversation between presidents Trump and Zelensky in September of 2019, which famously depicted the former's corruption and triggered a formal House impeachment inquiry. For despite an energetic effort by Trumpistas to ignore the clear meaning of words, conservative Peter Wehner's translation was irresistible: "You want Javelin missiles to help protect you from Russia? Great. Then I have a favor to ask of you: Investigate a political rival of mine. For more details, talk to my personal attorney. Oh, and also the attorney general of the United States."

---

8 Mind you, the Impeachment standard is "high crimes and misdemeanors." Then there are the nonprosecutable sins in the 10 Commandments, such as not bearing false witness, coveting your neighbor's wife, taking the name of the lord in vain ("goddam" being his favorite at rallies), etc. The authors have determined that Trump has likely violated up to eight of the 10 Commandments, which admittedly is not impeachable, but not very consistent with the GOP embrace of "family values," either.

Despite furious and multiple counterattacks from Trump and his defenders in the weeks following, more evidence came out corroborating the Ukranian shakedown; at the same time, other potentially impeachable acts emerged as the House and national media followed lead after lead in what was being called "The Stupid Watergate."

It appears that the die is cast.

For this time, after years of evading accountability for his sins and crimes, Trump flew too close to the sun...and likely wrote the first line of his obituary, whenever that happens. The outstanding impeachment issues as of late 2019 are two:

- First, would the House narrow its focus to only one Article of Impeachment based on the Ukrainian extortion or include other serious ones, as the Nixon and Clinton Impeachments did (for which there is already abundant evidence, largely from the Mueller Report)? These would include: Obstruction of Justice; Abuse of Power; Violation of the Emoluments Clause; Campaign Finance Crimes; and near-Pathological Serial Lying.

   The authors favor this broader approach or else Trumpers will later say, "Well, it was just ONE phone call and doesn't rise to the level of an impeachable offense," and future presidents would think that these other "high crimes and misdemeanors" had been green-lighted by omission.
- Second, would the Senate—with a majority of 53 Republican senators, all self-avowed "constitutional

conservatives"—vote based on their party blood oath or their constitutional oath? Watch for the probability they circle the wagons and try to gaslight their way through the conclusive evidence of guilt...or the growing possibility that one moment 20 or more Republicans (needed to reach the 2/3 supermajority) lock arms and jump together to vote to "remove" because public opinion has shifted in their states to Nixonian levels.

Conclusion.

Based on everything above, Trump's view of The Rule of Law appears pretty straightforward: Is the person implicated a Republican or a Democrat...White or Black...pro-Trump or Never-Trump? Will 45 make money? Who needs a law degree or even a Department of Justice when there are such bright-line tests for corruption?

So if an implicated person is, say, a racist sheriff, adjudicated war criminal, accused sexual predator, Michael Flynn, or Dinesh D'Souza, for a few examples, you get pardons or compliments. But if the person under scrutiny is black or brown, Jeff Bezos, or Hillary Clinton, s/he has a problem.

What if the person is Trump himself? When Trump was asked by ABC's George Stephanopoulos if he'd use information from a foreign source if offered it for 2020, he responded, "I think I'd take it," then offering up a benign hypothetical involving *Norway* as the offering country, still apparently oblivious or indifferent to the fact that a candidate cannot accept anything of value from a foreign country—whether ally or enemy—in our elections. Trump's North Star, according to foreign policy expert Jake Sullivan, instead seems to be "a mafia-style pay-to-play protection racket." Ask the Saudis. Ask the Ukranians.

There now can be only three possible reckonings: the House of Representatives impeaches and dares the Senate to ignore the obstruction, shakedowns, and self-enrichment; a vote on November 3, 2020; and/or POTUS 46 announces a bipartisan *National Reconciliation Commission on Truth and Justice* of retired judges and senators to explain how close we came to an American version of European monarchy or even fascism.

What? European fascism? If a reader thinks it fine to call all Democrats "socialists" or worse, s/he should consider what this sampling of Trumpaganda adds up to: "I alone can fix it"; "lock her up!"; journalists are the "ENEMY OF THE PEOPLE"; "Democrats hate America"; delegitimizing an independent judiciary and liberal judges; demonizing immigrants and people of color; appointing unqualified family members to high positions; embracing and lauding modern authoritarian leaders; suggesting that the US kill the families of suspected terrorists; accusing Speaker Pelosi and Chairman Schiff of "treason"...

...using the White House to denounce and intimidate people exercising their right of speech; engaging in multiple obstructions of justice far beyond Nixon's crimes; suggesting that administration officials violate the law to get his Wall built; glorifying the military, police, and bikers—"tough guys" in his John Wayne imitation; spewing thousands of repeated falsehoods that poison reasoned debate; even toying with a kind of modern "nullification"—a descendant of John Calhoun's pre-Civil War version—by openly considering ignoring a Supreme Court decision (Census case).

All of this is shocking but no longer surprising. A Quinnipiac poll concluded that a significant majority of Americans believe that President Trump engaged in criminality either before (64 percent) or after (45 percent) becoming president. Trump's lifelong contempt for the law is an open secret.

After the rise and fall of Trumpism as a governing ethic, will the United States learn how to never again steer so close to the cliff of authoritarianism? A new POTUS, Congress, and Commission can provide a road map back so that radicals posing as patriots keep their hands off our democracy.

7.
APPOINTEES
ETHICS, SCHMETHICS

When Ike was president, golf thrived. Kennedy nearly killed off the men's hat industry. Obama accelerated the popularity of *Hamilton*. From this perspective of how a president can be a shape-shifter, what vibe is Trump giving off?

As the rest of this book shows, Donald Trump is an avatar of amorality, immorality, and corruption. Nicolle Wallace, a top Bush 43 aide and now an MSNBC show host, marveled in April 2018 how Trump unethically says and does things "that wouldn't even occur to a Bush or Obama."

It's predictable, therefore, that, as president, he would surround himself with similar characters—grifters, kin, zealots, and multimillionaires.

"If there's anything that characterizes basic government operation under President Trump, it is constant grifting."

Ryan Cooper, *The Week* (9/8/17)

As of this writing in mid-2019, there is no office of the inspector general—the internal watchdog for most executive bureaucracies—at *12* federal agencies, including the Department of the Interior, the Department of Education, Homeland Security, the CIA, and the Environmental Protection Agency. Ethics and good governance are of such a low priority that 45 doesn't even bother appointing the internal officials legally tasked with ensuring them.

Let's take a look at what's going on inside some of those agencies.

"Lincoln had a team of rivals. Trump has a team of Morons."

NYT columnist Paul Krugman (1/14/19)

Department of Education: Betsy DeVos
Education Secretary Betsy DeVos is Trump's dream pick for Education Secretary—she's a billionaire heiress who never

attended public school and is sister of Erik Prince, the Darth Vader of the military-industrial complex. That is, she's a dream secretary if the dream were a nightmare.

DeVos seems to have nothing but contempt for the very education system it is her job to run. As a former Republican Party chairperson in Michigan and a chair of the American Federation for Children, she has been a leading champion of "school choice," mostly by advocating for the proliferation of charter schools, which has resulted in the mass defunding of neighborhood schools in her home state. In the words of the *Detroit Free Press*, DeVos's advocacy in Michigan has led to a "deeply dysfunctional educational landscape," where "parents of school-age children have plenty of choices," but quality is "in short supply."

To get a sense of DeVos's contempt for public education, as well as her ineptitude when it comes to education policy, one need look no further than her confirmation hearing:

When asked whether guns have any place in schools: "In Wapiti, Wyoming, I think probably there—I would imagine that there's probably a gun in the school to protect from potential grizzlies." (1/17/17)

When asked about testing to measure for proficiency versus testing to measure for growth in schools: "I think, if I'm understanding your question correctly around proficiency, I would also correlate it to competency and mastery so that you—each student is measured according to the advancement that they're making in each subject area."
Senator Al Franken (D-Minnesota): "Well that's growth. That's not proficiency..."
DeVos: "The proficiency is if they've, like, reached a third-grade

As of the Fall of 2019, with the departure of John Bolton—Trump's third national security advisor—seven cabinet-level appointees were ousted by presidential tweet.

level for reading, etc."

Franken: "No, I'm talking about the debate between proficiency and growth—what your thoughts are on them."

DeVos: "Yes. Well I was just asking to clarify —"

Franken: "This is a subject that has been debated in the education community for years. It surprises me that you don't know this issue..." (1/17/17)

Senator Tim Kaine (D-Virginia): "And if confirmed, will you insist on equal accountability in any K-12 school or educational program that receives federal funding, either public, public charter, or private?"

DeVos: "I support accountability."

Kaine: "Equal accountability for all schools that receive federal funding?"

DeVos: "I support accountability."

Kaine: "Is that a yes or a no?"

DeVos: "That's a—I support accountability."

Kaine: "Do you not want to answer my question?"

DeVos: "I support accountability." (1/17/17)

In addition to her desire to corrupt the public-education system, DeVos is corrupting the very office of the Secretary of Education. When government ethics officials first went through her financial-disclosure paperwork in early 2017, it identified *102* financial entanglements with potential conflicts of interest. And somehow, despite purportedly divesting from all of those interests, she and her husband still made nearly $60 million during her first year in office—roughly 288 times the $208,000 a typical cabinet-level federal employee makes. At the same time, by the end of 2018, her office had somehow spent $12 million on its security detail.

Environmental Protection Agency: Scott Pruitt

Speaking of appointees eager to be fifth columns dismantling their own agencies, let's talk about Trump's EPA. 45's initial pick to head the agency was Scott Pruitt, a former Oklahoma politician who, in his bio as Oklahoma attorney general, described himself as a "leading advocate against the EPA's activist agenda." In this case, the White House vetting worked because they got exactly what they wanted.

Pruitt's contempt for environmental regulation and his pro-fossil fuel trivializes "a wolf in sheep's clothing." Because of his serial ethics abuses in Oklahoma and closeness with lobbyists, his vetting form upon taking the EPA job even had a section titled "allegations of coziness with big energy companies."

His tenure was so racked by ethics violations—some related to his anti-EPA attitudes, some just run-of-the-mill corrupt—it's impossible to list them all. Here's a representative sample:

- Pruitt spent exorbitant amounts of government money on travel. He traveled four times on private and military jets rather than flying commercial, costing taxpayers $60,000; he spent around $14,000 during the summer of 2018 just flying (first class) around his home state of Oklahoma; and he spent $68,000 in taxpayer money on first-class flights and top hotels during seven months in 2017 and 2018, including $20,000 for a four-day trip to Morocco.
- In classic corrupt politician form, Pruitt had his staff perform obviously inappropriate personal tasks for him, like finding a job for his wife and fetching him snacks.
- Pruitt's administration is alleged to have deliberately avoided creating written records of some official meetings and keeping secret calendars so as to avoid

- unsavory revelations from Freedom of Information Act requests.
- Pruitt was extremely tight with lobbyists during his time as head of the EPA. He lived for about six months in an apartment, owned by a health care lobbyist whose husband lobbied the EPA, for which he paid significantly less than the market rate. And lobbyists worked with the EPA to plan Pruitt's aforementioned expensive overseas trips, including the $20,000 trip to Morocco as well as a $30,000 trip to Italy.
- There were nonsensical, seemingly random items, including $43,000 for a soundproof booth in his office.

Ironically, when Pruitt finally resigned in July 2018, it wasn't because he was too close with lobbyists or too loose with taxpayer money. The final straw was Pruitt overstepping his boundaries with Trump: according to the *New York Times*, Trump requested Pruitt's resignation after it leaked that Pruitt had asked the president to fire then-Attorney General Jeff Sessions so that he could abandon his post at the EPA to take over the Justice Department.

Surprise! Less than a year after his ouster, Pruitt was working as a lobbyist for a coal company in Indiana.

Although Pruitt's replacement is better in terms of out-and-out corruption ("more disciplined," as the *New York Times* describes), Andrew Wheeler is a former fossil-fuel lobbyist who wants to take Pruitt's regulatory rollbacks even further (see Chapter 2 for the Trump administration's degradation of the environment).

Department of the Interior: Ryan Zinke

Perhaps the most scandal-ridden agency in the Trump

administration has been the Department of the Interior, headed, for the first two years of 45's presidency, by Ryan Zinke.

According to a count by Citizens for Responsibility and Ethics in Washington (CREW), 16 months into his tenure as Secretary of the Interior, Zinke was tied up in no fewer than 18 federal investigations. The topics of those investigations include:

- An incident during which the Interior Department, rejecting recommendations from federal experts, blocked a Native American casino project after meeting with lobbyists representing a major competitor, MGM Resorts.
- The deletion of any mention of humanity's role in climate change in a National Parks Service report after Zinke testified to Congress that he would not censor scientific reports.
- Zinke's private involvement in a negotiation with the oil company Halliburton to secure a land deal that would include a microbrewery for Zinke.
- $139,000 in taxpayer funds spent on replacing three sets of doors in Interior Department offices.
- Alleged phone calls from Zinke to Senators Lisa Murkowski and Dan Sullivan, both of Alaska, threatening to block energy policies that would have brought jobs to the state after Murkowski voted against Trump's repeal of Obamacare.

In January 2019, Zinke resigned by sending Trump a nearly illegible letter written in red marker. His deputy, David Bernhardt, a former oil-industry lobbyist, was confirmed as his replacement in April. And, like EPA administrator Andrew Wheeler, it doesn't look like Bernhardt is going to be much more ethical than his predecessor. Just four days after his confirmation, he was under ethics investigations for using his former position as acting secretary to advance a policy pushed by a former lobbying client, for continuing to work as a lobbyist after filing legal paperwork declaring that he had ceased lobbying, and for halting the release of a report pointing to the harmful effects of a certain pesticide.

Treasury Department: Steven Mnuchin

Paying for luxurious travel with government money seems to be somewhat of a theme in Trump's Cabinet: perhaps their taking an ethical clue from the owner of Mar-a-Lago, taking the mixing of public service and self-service to be standard operating procedure. One of the earliest scandals among Trump's appointees came in August 2017, when Treasury Secretary Steven Mnuchin's actress wife of two months, Louise Linton, posted a photo on Instagram of her and her public-servant husband stepping off of a government plane in Kentucky. There was no reason for Linton to go on the trip, and there was no reason Mnuchin had to spend money on a government plane—the trip, to lobby for Trump's tax cuts, pretty obviously called for a solo commercial flight. But Linton treated it like a luxurious vacation—she even hash-tagged the clothing brands she was wearing, right alongside #daytrip and #usa.

When confronted about the post (and about the general inappropriateness of the trip) by one Instagram user, Linton wrote: "Did you think this was a personal trip?! Adorable! Have you given more to the economy than me and my husband? Either as an individual earner in taxes or in self sacrifice to your country. I'm pretty sure we paid more taxes toward our day 'trip' than you did. Pretty sure the amount we sacrifice per year is a lot more than you'd be willing to sacrifice if the choice was yours."

Oy! There's a lot of elitism to unpack there. *The New Yorker*'s Jia Tolentino perhaps did the best job of summing up the whole situation: "In a few aggrieved sentences, Linton managed to frame her husband's three-hundred-million-dollar net worth as a burden, her six months in Washington as harrowing public servitude, and an ordinary American as a contemptible member of the economic underclass."

As Senator Ron Wyden (D-Oregon) put it: "You don't need a giant rulebook of government requirements to just say yourself, 'This is common sense. It's wrong.' That's just slap-your-forehead stuff." (9/13/17)

And that's not all for Mnuchin and Linton. In April 2019, the Office of Government Ethics rejected Mnuchin's 2017 financial-disclosure form. Evidently, Mnuchin agreed upon his confirmation to divest from a limited liability corporation in the film industry after it was deemed that his connection to the company raised conflict-of-interest concerns. And he did divest. But his wife didn't—rather, she was listed as the CEO.

Mnuchin and Linton: the Bonnie and Clyde of government corruption, only less competent.

We apologize for the repetition, but the point needs to be made that Trump's appointees are just like him—almost comically corrupt. To conclude:

Department of Commerce: Wilbur Ross

The Office of Government Ethics rejected Commerce Secretary Wilbur Ross's financial-disclosure form when it found that he didn't sell stock in a bank despite indicating otherwise, a move that provided the specter of a conflict of interest. Ross's was one of three disclosure forms outright rejected by the OGE since 2017—a practice that, before the Trump administration, was rare, much less three for one administration.

Then there were those times he was accused of lying under oath to hide the racial motivation behind the "citizenship" question on the Census from. Who said that? Chief Justice John Roberts in his decision against Ross's agency. (See Chapter 6, "The Rule of Law(lessness").

And in an obvious effort to set a record for unethical acts within a three-year span for cabinet secretaries, it was widely reported that the Commerce Secretary ordered NOAA officials under his control to defend Trump's weather misforecasting during Hurricane Dorian, giving new meaning to "political... science."

Department of Homeland Security: John Kelly

Before Trump made him his chief of staff, John Kelly was head of the Department of Homeland Security, which oversees such immigration-enforcement agencies as Immigration and Customs Enforcement and Customs and Border Protection. While he wasn't head of DHS during the Trump administration's horrific family-separation policy—which saw thousands of asylum-seeking children ripped from their guardian relatives and placed in cages—he helped to plan the whole ordeal.

Now, according to CREW, "he is on the board of Caliburn International, which runs the largest facility housing migrant children separated from their families at the border." Talk about blood money.

Federal Aviation Administration: Dan Elwell

A *ProPublica* investigation published in March 2019 found that, before he was the acting head of the Federal Aviation

Administration, Dan Elwell, a former airline lobbyist, coordinated directly with former lobbyist colleagues to craft FAA policy.

Furthermore, when Boeing 737 Max's were crashing—leaving 346 dead—around the world, Trump ordered the FAA to keep them in the air (they were later grounded) after Boeing CEO Dennis Muilenburg gave him a ring. According to the *New York Times*, Muilenburg had schmoozed Trump in the past, visiting him personally at Mar-a-Lago and donating $1 million to his inaugural committee.

A League of His Own?

According to Michael Lewis, writing in the September, 2017, *Vanity Fair* about Energy Secretary Rick Perry, "'Perry has no personal interest in understanding what we do and effecting change,' a DOE staffer told me. 'He's never been briefed on a program—not a single one.'"

Hatch Act: Con-way

In 1939, in an effort to keep the executive branch focused on good governance, Congress passed the Hatch Act, which barred most presidential-administration officials from engaging in certain types of political activity, like election campaigning. In recent past administrations, violations of the Hatch Act haven't been much of an issue for federal employees (the Obama administration had one Hatch Act violation, while Hatch Act issues under W. Bush were only revealed after he left office). Not so with Trump.

In November 2018, the US Office of the Special Counsel asserted that six current and former White House officials—principal deputy press secretary Raj Shah, deputy director of communications Jessica Ditto, executive assistant to the president Madeleine Westerhout, director of media affairs Helen Aguirre Ferré, press secretary for vice president Pence Alyssa Farah, and deputy communications director for the Office of Management and Budget Jacob Wood—violated the act by, among other things, tweeting, "Make America Great Again," and "MAGA," Trump's reelection-campaign slogan.

Earlier that year, the office also announced that Trump's counselor, Kellyanne Conway, also violated the Hatch Act when she voiced support for Roy Moore in the 2018 Senate special election in Alabama, and CREW then filed additional Hatch Act complaints, accusing Conway of retweeting MAGA messages. Finally, CREW urged that Trump fire Conway due to her unprecedented number of violations—50 in one year alone. Her contemptuous response to this recidivism, literally, was "Blah, blah." Oh, Conway is a lawyer.

"AN UPDATE ON THE CORPORATE TAKEOVER OF OUR GOVERNMENT," COURTESY OF THE WATCHDOG GROUP PUBLIC CITIZEN (4/11/19)

- A former oil lobbyist runs the Department of the Interior.
- A former coal lobbyist runs the Environmental Protection Agency.
- A former pharma executive runs the Department of Health and Human Services.
- A former Boeing exec runs the Department of Defense.
- A billionaire Amway heiress runs the Department of Education.
- A private equity kingpin runs the Commerce Department.
- A former Goldman Sachs executive runs the Treasury Department.

"Having worked for years as a lobbyist representing many of the very businesses he now regulates, [David Bernhardt] walked into the No. 2 job at Interior with so many potential conflicts of interest he has to carry a small card listing them all."

Juliet Eilperin, the *Washington Post* (11/19/18)

8.
DUMB & DUMBER
CONTAGIOUS INCOMPETENCE

In a 1992 presidential debate, Bill Clinton pronounced chameleon as "sha-meleon." In 2015, while Indian Prime Minister Narendra Modi was visiting the White House, Barack Obama called him "president." These were verbal slipups made by obviously intelligent people.

Donald Trump is not an intelligent person. While it would be forgivable if he occasionally tweeted out a typo or a misspelling—we've all had our struggles with autocorrect—he consistently makes verbal gaffes and asinine comments unprecedented for an Oval Office occupant, a person whose words are beamed to the world and speak for America.

Some political commentators like to point out Trump's political genius. But a savant can still be an ignoramus. He is quick but not deep. And based on the axiom that "a fish rots from the head down," his incompetence is infecting his administration... one that at times resembles a temp agency as people come, go, and are kicked on the way out.

Words Are Hard

"This is a tough hurricane. One of the wettest we've ever seen from the standpoint of water." (9/18/18)

So true. Indeed, residents and aid workers in the Carolinas confirmed that the water from Hurricane Florence was very wet. As the *Intelligencer*'s Jonathan Chait reported, "Whether

"I am not fit for this office and should never have been here."

President Warren G. Harding

Florence is also wet from other standpoints is a question the president did not address."

What makes this gaffe remarkable is that it didn't come out of impromptu remarks or an unexpected question at a press conference. This was Trump's official video statement on Hurricane Florence—pasted together with scenes from the devastation and posted to Twitter. How did Trump *and* his press team think that this wording made him sound even remotely competent?

> *"We have some of our great business leaders—and leaders period—right behind me. I may ask Marillyn Lockheed, the leading women's business executive in this country, according to many..." (3/22/18)*

> *"Thank you, we appreciate it very much Tim Apple." (3/2/19)*

Trump's verbal flubs can make serious moments hilarious. Twice during White House conferences with CEOs, he's replaced the executives' surnames with the names of their companies. First it was Lockheed Martin CEO Marillyn Hewson, whom he called "Marillyn Lockheed." Then it was Apple CEO Tim Cook, whom he called "Tim Apple."

In an effort to make himself seem smart again—and, of course, seeing an opportunity to attack the "fake news" media (see Chapter 10)—Trump bothered to repeatedly lie about the "Tim Apple" gaffe. According to a report from *Axios*, Trump later claimed that he actually said, "Tim Cook Apple," really fast (as if that's any less embarrassing), and he simply said the "Cook" part softly. Then, a day later, he tweeted, *"I quickly referred to Tim + Apple as Tim/Apple as an easy way to save time &*

Having to cancel a trip to Poland on September 1, 2019, Trump announced that he wanted "to Congratulate Poland" on being invaded by Hitler exactly 70 years before.

Former Secretary of State Rex Tillerson told CBS in 2019: *"What was challenging [was] to for me to work for a man who is pretty undisciplined, doesn't like to read, doesn't read briefing reports, doesn't like to get into the details of a lot of things, but rather just kind of says, 'This is what I believe.'"*

words. The Fake News was disparagingly all over this, & it became yet another bad Trump story!"

When you're in a hole...

Peter Baker, the *New York Times*: "[Putin's] comments to the *Financial Times* right before arriving here was that Western-style liberalism is obsolete. I know you probably—"

"Well, I mean, he may feel that way. He's sees what's going on, I guess, if you look at what's happening in Los Angeles, where it's so sad to look, and what's happening in San Francisco and a couple of other cities, which are run by an extraordinary group of liberal people... When you look at Los Angeles, when you look at San Francisco, when you look at some of the other cities—and not a lot, not a lot—but you don't want it to spread." (6/29/19)

The President of the United States doesn't understand basic political terms. Let that one sink in.

Kristen Welker, NBC News: "I just wanted to follow up on the issue of busing. Do you see it as a viable way of integrating schools?"

"Well, it has been something that they've done for a long period of time. I mean, you know, there aren't that many ways you're going to get people to schools. So this is something that's been done...it is certainly a primary method of getting people to schools."

This one is less shocking, considering his record on race (see

Chapter 4). He is also ignorant of one of the major issues in US civil rights history.

> *"The Continental Army suffered a bitter winner at Valley Forge, found glory across the waters of the Delaware and seized victory from Cornwallis of Yorktown. Our Army manned the air, it ran the ramparts, it took over the airports, it did everything it had to do." (7/4/19)*

After this Fourth of July anachronism, Trump first blamed his gaffe on a broken teleprompter. But do you really need a teleprompter to know that there were no airports around in 1776?

Diplomatic Gaffes

> *Mika Brzezinski, MSNBC: "Given the dire foreign-policy issues percolating around the world right now, who are you consulting with consistently so that you're ready on day one [of your presidency]?"*

> *"I'm speaking with myself, number one, because I have a very good brain and I've said a lot of things... My primary consultant is myself and I have a good instinct for this stuff." (3/16/16)*

This should have been the ultimate red flag—for Democrats, for Republicans, for voters, for foreign leaders. Donald Trump, who had been a real estate operator and reality TV star, fancies himself a foreign policy genius, who can navigate the world based on his "good instinct."

> *Pointing to the "nuclear football": "This is what I have for Kim [Jong-un]." (10/9/17)*

"The kidney has a very special place in the heart." (7/10/19), on announcing an initiative to reduce kidney disease.

With so many examples in both categories, *Late Night* host Stephen Colbert began airing a segment in late 2019 to challenge viewers called "Corrupt or Dumb?"

According to reporting from CNN, Trump's incendiary language came not during a meeting about North Korea's nuclear threat, but during a meeting about Hurricane Maria with the governor of Puerto Rico, Ricardo Rosselló. Not only does Trump often say the wrong thing when it comes to diplomatic affairs, he also says them at the wrong time.

To French President Emmanuel Macron: "Let me wipe that little piece of dandruff off you there.... We have to make him perfect." (4/24/18)

Was this a power move, or did Trump just forget where he was and what he was doing? Whatever the case, it was extremely awkward. Thankfully, Macron, displaying the tact of an actual world leader, laughed it off and moved forward with business.

Trump Tower (of Babble)

Asked about the large number of vacant jobs at the State Department, Trump responded, according to Susan Ohanian in *Trump, Trump, Trump: The March of Folly*, "Let me tell you, the one that matters is me. I'm the only one that matters."

At a campaign stop in South Carolina, he attempted to bash Obama's nuclear deal with Iran:

"Look, having nuclear—my uncle was a great professor and scientist and engineer, Dr. John Trump at MIT; good genes, very good genes, OK, very smart, the Wharton School of Finance, very good, very smart—you know, if you're a conservative Republican, if I were a liberal, if, like, OK, if I ran as a liberal Democrat, they would say I'm one of the smartest people anywhere in the world—it's true!—but when you're a conservative Republican they try—oh, do they do

a number—that's why I always start off: Went to Wharton, was a good student, went there, went there, did this, built a fortune—you know I have to give my life credentials all the time, because we're a little disadvantaged—but you look at the nuclear deal, the thing that really bothers me—it would have been so easy, and it's not as important as these lives are—nuclear is powerful; my uncle explained that to me many, many years ago, the power and that was 35 years ago; he would explain the power of what's going to happen and he was right, who would have thought?—but when you look at what's going on with the four prisoners—now it used to be three, now it's four—but when it was three and even now, I would have said it's all in the messenger; fellas, and it is fellas because, you know, they don't, they haven't figured that the women are smarter right now than the men, so, you know, it's gonna take them about another 150 years—but the Persians are great negotiators, the Iranians are great negotiators, so, and they, they just killed, they just killed us." (7/19/16)

With this 90-second monologue about nuclear power, his family history, Iranian negotiators, gender stereotypes, the political spectrum, political prisoners, and his intellectual credentials, Trump may have set a record for most roundabout sentence in presidential-campaign history. At the least, Professor Irwin Corey territory.

"We believe that only American citizens should vote in American elections, which is why the time has come for voter ID, like everything else. Voter ID. You know, if you go out and you want to buy groceries, you need a picture on a card. You need ID. You go out and you want to buy anything, you need ID and you need your picture." (9/30/18)

It's easy to tell when Trump has no idea what he's talking about: He rambles, eventually letting something truly ridiculous slip out. In this case, he reveals his completely out-of-touch lifestyle when he asserts that you need a photo ID to buy groceries. Not to mention the insanity of pretending to worry about largely nonexistent "voter fraud" while refusing to acknowledge the Russian theft of the 2016 election, if not the 2020 race.

What's the principle behind these different approaches? Trump's GOP worries more about minority voters costing them elections than a foreign dictator stealing one for them. If that's not impeachable, what would be?

"We're working very hard on the Internet. [ISIS] used the Internet better than we did for a period of time. They used the Internet brilliantly but now it's not so brilliant and now the people on the Internet that used to look up to them and say how wonderful and brilliant they are [are] not thinking of them as being so brilliant because they've been decimated." (2/6/19)

Photo by Chip Somodevilla/
Getty Images

This one takes a few reads, but after parsing this "sentence," it seems like Trump is saying, now that ISIS has been stripped of almost all of its land, he is going to tweet the remnants of the group into oblivion. Go get 'em.

2019 WHITE HOUSE MEETING ON ISIS BETWEEN TRUMP & NOBEL PRIZE WINNER

Nadia Murad: "They killed my mom, my six brothers."
Trump: "Where are they now?"
Murad: "They are in the mass graves at Sinjar."
Trump: "I know the area very well. It's tough."
...
Trump: "They gave you [your Nobel Peace Prize] "for what reason?"
Murad: "For what reason? I made it clear to everyone that ISIS raped thousands of Yazidi women."
Trump: "Oh really, is that right?"

DID VINCE FOSTER KILL JEFFREY EPSTEIN?

"The unsubstantiated theory points to allegations that Jeffrey Epstein 'had information on the Clintons' and as a result, 'is now dead.' Conservative comedian Terrence Williams tweeted a video suggesting Bill and Hillary Clinton are responsible for Epstein's death, imploring viewers to retweet if they're 'not surprised' by Epstein's suicide. Trump retweeted the video." –Julia Ingram, *Miami Herald*

Trump tweeted August 18, 2019: "Google manipulated from 2.6 million to 16 million votes for Hillary Clinton in 2016 Election! My vote was even bigger than thought." Helluva story if true but… "Not true at all," replied @ MathewChapman. "CNN's fact-checker says even the professor Trump cited on Google election fraud says the President is lying." The usual above-the-fray Hillary pounced August 19 in a tweet aimed at DJT: "The debunked 'study' you're referring to was based on 21 undecided voters…about half the number of people associated with your campaign who have been indicted."

Stable? Genius? Or president who's seen too many Indiana Jones movies?

A new book reports that Trump would repeatedly insist to his Homeland advisors that he had to deliver on his campaign border pledges. So he repeatedly suggested shooting migrants if they threw rocks or shooting them in the legs plus fortifying a border wall with a trench full of snakes and alligators. Anxious staff warned him that such ideas would be illegal and/or ineffective.

Misspellings

One of Trump's key presidential strategies is to bypass the media (see Chapter 10) and communicate directly with the American people. This usually happens through Twitter. The problem with that, however, is that Trump isn't exactly a strong writer—or speller—and evidently won't bother to have someone proof what he writes or dictates.

Truly there are worse things for a president to be, as the other chapters indicate. And of course one can spell poorly and be intelligent. But given the fact that he is the most powerful person in the world—and such errors seem to reflect a larger inclination toward impulsiveness—his tenuous grasp on written English is just another reason to question whether he's fit for this job.

*"I will be campaigning in Indiana all day. Things are looking great, and the support of Bobby **Night** [Knight] has been so amazing." (5/2/16)*

*"I am **honered** to serve you, the great American people, as your 45th President of the United States!" (1/21/17)*

*"Special Council is told to find crimes, **wether** crimes exist or not. I was opposed the the selection of Mueller to be Special Council, I am still opposed to it. I think President Trump was right when he said there never should have been a Special Council appointed because..." (3/21/18)*

*"Great to have our incredible First Lady back home in the White House. **Melanie** [Melania] is feeling and doing really well." (5/19/18)*

*"Despite the constant negative press **covfefe**..." (5/31/17)*

*"Chinese President XI **XINPING** [Jinping] and I spoke at length about the meeting with KIM JONG UN of North Korea." (3/10/18)*

*"Why isn't the FBI giving Andrew McCabe text **massages** to Judicial Watch or appropriate governmental authorities." (8/11/18)*

*"Democrats can't find a Smocking Gun tying the Trump campaign to Russia after James Comey's testimony. No **Smocking** Gun...No Collusion.' @FoxNews" (12/10/18)*

*"Anytime you hear a Democrat saying that you can have good **Boarder** Security without a Wall, write them off as just another politician following the party line." (12/17/18)*

*"Great being with the National Champion Clemson Tigers last night at the White House. Because of the Shutdown I served them massive amounts of Fast Food (I paid), over 1000 **hamberders** etc." (1/15/19)*

"A Confederacy of Dunces"

Vicky Ward, *Kushner, Inc.*: "[Ivanka Trump's] father's reign in Washington DC is, she believes, the beginning of a great American dynasty. 'She thinks she's going to be president of the United States,' Gary Cohn told people after leaving the White House. 'She thinks this is like the Kennedys, the Bushes, and now the Trumps.'"

Best of luck, Ivanka. Anything's possible, especially if you change your last name.

> "According to Mueller, the president asked Corey Lewandowski to convey a message to Sessions. It was a request that Sessions reassert control over the special counsel's investigation...and restrict the special counsel's investigation to interference in future elections." Benjamin Wittes, *The Atlantic* (4/29/19)

Just interference in *future* elections? What is this, Tom Cruise's "pre-crimes unit" from *The Minority Report*?

> Stephen Moore, Trump's pick for a seat on the Federal Reserve: "I'm kind of new to this game, frankly, so I'm going to be on a steep learning curve myself about how the Fed operates, how the Federal Reserve makes its decisions. It's hard for me to say even what my role will be there, assuming I get confirmed." (3/22/19)

> More Moore: "Capitalism is a lot more important than democracy. I'm not even a big believer in democracy." (2009)

Trump's incompetence is not restricted to himself; rather, in his complete mismanagement of the White House, he makes everyone around him look dumb by putting them in positions they're clearly not equipped to handle.

Trump tapped a Fox News personality, Heather Nauert, to represent the US at the United Nations (see Chapter 10), as well as his former private-jet pilot, John Dunkin, to head the Federal Aviation Administration. Fortunately, both eventually declined to move forward with their nominations. Unfortunately, heart surgeon Ben Carson was confirmed as the Housing Secretary (which is admittedly better than making a homebuilder your heart surgeon).

If you don't like to see someone treated as dumb, especially a duly selected president, just ask some of his former White House senior staff, who referred to their boss with superlatives such as:

"[the understanding of] a fifth- or sixth-grader"—former Defense Secretary Jim Mattis

"unhinged"—former Chief of Staff John Kelly

"dumb as shit"—former Economic Adviser Gary Cohn

"a dope"—former National Security Adviser H.R. McMaster

"[the intelligence of] a kindergartner"—H.R. McMaster

"like an 11-year-old child"—former Chief Strategist Steve Bannon

"a moron"—former Secretary of State Rex Tillerson

Additionally, George Conway, the husband of Trump's counselor Kellyanne Conway, has relentlessly disparaged Trump as unfit for the presidency. In March 2019, Conway tweeted screenshots of the *Diagnostic and Statistical Manual of Mental Disorders* to insinuate that Trump displayed signs of narcissistic-personality disorder and antisocial-personality disorder. Guess who couldn't resist dumbly taking the bait?

"George Conway, often referred to as Mr. Kellyanne Conway by those who know him, is VERY jealous of his wife's success & angry that I, with her help, didn't give him the job he so desperately wanted. I barely know him but just take a look, a stone cold LOSER & husband from hell!" (3/20/19)

Kellyanne sided with Trump...George then preemptively released a letter he had sent Trump withdrawing from consideration for any D of J positions.

Some of Team Trump's comments are so ridiculous, they fall

under a category that lawyers call *res ipsa loquitor*—"the thing speaks for itself." Based on Trump's own comments in 2018, "What you are reading and seeing is not really happening," these out-there comments from the president's surrogates are shocking, though not surprising:

Rudy Giuliani, Trump's personal lawyer: "Truth isn't truth." *(8/29/18)*

Wilbur Ross, Secretary of Commerce: "This is a can of Campbell's Soup. In the can of Campbell's Soup, there's about 2.6 cents, 2.6 pennies, worth of steel. So if that goes up by 25 percent, that's about six-tenths of 1 cent on the price of a can of Campbell's Soup. Well, I just bought this can today at a 7-Eleven down here, and the price was $1.99. So who in the world is going be bothered by six-tenths of a cent?" (3/5/18)

Kellyanne Conway, counselor to the president: "You're saying it's a falsehood, they're giving—Sean Spicer, our press secretary, gave alternative facts to that." (1/22/17)

Jared Kushner, real-estate tycoon and multimillionaire: "He opined at an Observer event that he could not understand why people took so much time off around pregnancies. 'After all, there are so many people helping.'" Vicky Ward, Kushner, Inc.

If this assertion alone doesn't convince you, here's more "evidence," as compiled by *NowThis*. Sorry for its length but don't blame us or *NowThis*, since the fault is in the Star:

"Nobody knows more about taxes than I do, and income than I do."

Not brain surgery: Trump at Montana rally in July 7, 2019, comparing himself to Elton John: *"This is the only musical—this mouth. And hopefully the brain attached to the mouth, right? The brain. More important than the mouth is the brain. The brain is much more important."*

BREAKING NEWS: *"I think I am, actually humble. I think I'm much more humble than you would understand."* (7/17/16)

MORE BREAKING NEWS. *"China has total respect for Donald Trump and for Donald Trump's very very large brain."* (9/26/18)

AGAIN: *"Sorry losers and haters, but my I.Q. is one of the highest - and you all know it! Please don't feel so stupid or insecure, it's not your fault."* (5/8/13)

Photo by Mark Wilson/Getty Images

"Nobody knows more about construction than I do."

"Nobody knows more about campaign finance than I do."

"I know more about drones than anybody."

"Nobody knows much more about technology... than I do."

"Nobody in the history of this country has ever known so much about infrastructure as Donald Trump."

"I know that H-1B [visa], I know the H-2B. Nobody knows it better than me."

"I know more about ISIS than the generals do, believe me."

"Nobody knows more about environmental impact statements than me."

"I understand the power of Facebook maybe better than almost anybody."

"I know more about renewables than any human being on earth."

"Nobody knows more about polls than me."

"I know more about courts than any human being on earth."

"I know more about steelworkers than anybody that's ever run for office."

"I know more about golf than Obama knows."

"Nobody knows more about banks than I do."

"Nobody knows more about trade than me."

"I know more about nuclear weapons than he'll ever know."

"I understand the tax laws better than almost anyone."

"I know more about offense and defense than they will ever understand."

"Nobody even understands it but me. It's called devaluation."

"I understand money better than anybody."

"We've got to be nice and cool, nice and calm. All right, stay on point, Donald. Stay on point. No sidetracks, Donald. Nice and easy."

Trump, giving himself advice into a microphone at a campaign stop in Florida (11/3/16)

"I understand the system better than anybody."

"Nobody knows more about debt than I do."

"Nobody knows the game better than me."

"And who knows more about the word 'apprentice' than Donald Trump?"

"I understand politicians better than anybody."

"Who knows the other side better than me?"

"I was the fair-haired boy. Nobody knows more about it than me."

"I know a lot. I know more than I'm ever gonna tell you."

Photo by Ian MacNicol/Getty Images

Citing and Vetting

- According to a *Daily Pennsylvanian* analysis, Trump publicly touted his "Wharton," "Ivy League," or "University of Pennsylvania" education at least 66 times from June 2015 to January 2018. Can you recall Obama even once bragging about being president of the *Harvard Law Review* or Elizabeth Warren mentioning that she taught for 15 years at the same place?

- According to *Politico*, this White House has been so sloppy with its vetting process for appointed positions that the Trump administration had to formally withdraw 62 nominations as of May 2019. At that point in Obama's presidency, he had withdrawn 30 nominations. When Trump later quickly withdrew Rep. John Ratcliffe after articles showed that he had falsified his résumé, he blithely said to the media, which he otherwise calls "fake," "I like when you vet."

- According to the Brookings Institution, in March 2019, turnover among for the Trump administration's senior staff was 66 percent—as compared to 33 percent under George W. Bush after a comparable period and 24 percent under Obama. Not to mention that he set a record by being on his fourth national security adviser and sixth communications director less than three years into his presidency. Only 61 percent of the 714 administration positions requiring Senate confirmation were filled more than two years into Trump's presidency, noted the *Washington Post*.

After all the acrimonious exits and third-tier appointments (Kushner's 29-year-old aide taking over Israeli-Palestinian peace negotiations), by the beginning of his reelection year

Trump's cabinet was not exactly "the best people," but rather a version of the opening *Star Wars* bar scene with its mix of billionaires, reactionaries, and racists drinking away.

Last, qualifying as somewhere between this "Dumb and Dumber" category and simply delusional, there was the much-discussed "SharpieGate" incident as the Category 5 Hurricane Dorian barreled toward possibly Florida and states north and east of it. But not, thankfully, Alabama, despite the Trump Administration's attempt to reverse-engineer reality and mimic the succinct phrase heard throughout Mussolini's reign in Italy: "Il Duce is always right."

When Trump Sharpied a several-days-old official weather map and then had aides threaten federal officials who stood up to him, he came close to George Orwell's conclusion in *1984:* "The party told you to reject the evidence of your eyes and ears. It was their final, most essential command."

9.
AGE OF RAGE
"KNOCK THE CRAP OUT OF THEM, WOULD YOU?"

"There was one performance this year that sank its hooks in my heart. It made its intended audience laugh and show their teeth. It was when the person asking to sit in the most respected seat in our country imitated a disabled reporter, someone he outranked in privilege, power, and the capacity to fight back... Disrespect invites disrespect. Violence incites violence."

—Meryl Streep, 2017

Nuremberg-like rallies with large frenzied crowds extolling their beloved, strutting leader did not begin with Donald Trump, but for now they reflect a lot about him and his followers.

Go back to three weeks before the 2008 election. John McCain's rallies had a supercharged, ugly atmosphere, where threats were made against Barack Hussein Obama ("terrorist!" "traitor!" "kill him!") as he raced to a victory in November with a cratering economy. Speakers at Republican campaign rallies would use Obama's full name as a nod to any concerns about the Democrat's otherism.

At a town hall in Minnesota, a woman said she feared an Obama presidency: "I can't trust Obama. I have read about him and he's not, he's not uh—he's an Arab. He's not—" At that, McCain took the microphone, "No, ma'am. He's a decent family man [and] citizen that I just happen to have disagreements with on fundamental issues and that's what this campaign's all about. He's not [an Arab]." It was a much-lauded moment, though imperfect (so what if Obama were Arab?), and for his trouble, McCain got booed by his own crowd.

"I am tired of him interrupting our president, and I am coming down there to take him and his family out."

James Dean Blevins, 58, of Chicago, in a voicemail threatening Senator Jeff Flake and his family for delaying Brett Kavanaugh's nomination

"According to a new study reported by The Washington Post, counties that hosted political rallies in 2016 with Donald Trump as the headliner saw a 226 percent increase in hate crimes over comparable counties that did not host such a rally in subsequent months."

Vox

McCain, however, gave America Sarah Palin, a shoot-from-the-hip mama bear from Wasilla, Alaska. Her rallies, where she said Obama was "palling around with terrorists who targeted their own country," identified parts of the United States that were "pro-America" and warned ominously that the first plausible black president "is not a man who sees America as you and I do." Her attacks and lack of policy specifics (to put it mildly) drew rebuke from the media but only endeared her more to the Republican base.

By 2015, candidate Trump held a rally of his own where he, too, had a questioner railing about Muslims. The man said, "We have a problem in this country; it's called Muslims." Trump nodded along. Then the man asked, "When can we get rid of them?" No condemnation came from Trump. Instead, the man's paranoia was treated as a valid constituent inquiry: "We're going to be looking at that and plenty of other things."

Photo by Drew Angerer/Getty Images

That kind of rage was passed from Palin to Trump by the likes of, among many others, Fox News's Glenn Beck. In 2010, Beck mapped out on a blackboard his conspiracy theories of a George Soros cabal that eroded American sovereignty—which drove a violent ex-con with a long rap sheet to fire 60 rounds at police en route to starting a revolution and killing as many people as possible at the Tides Foundation because it was funded by Soros and gave grants to the ACLU. (He was intercepted before he arrived at the Tides location.)

In the view of President Obama watching the rise of Trump in 2015: "I see a straight line from the announcement of Sarah Palin as the vice-presidential nominee to what we see today in Donald Trump, the emergence of the Freedom Caucus, the tea party, and the shift in the center of gravity for the Republican Party."

#12. The Hyperbolic and Apocalyptic: This rage then wasn't invented on June 16, 2015, when Donald J. Trump descended his Trump Tower escalator straight into the gutter of saying that Mexicans were "rapists." But since then, like clockwork, he has expertly massaged that rage on the Right each time he rallies his base in towns and cities across Red America.

When Trump is in comfortable company, he tells outlets like Breitbart, *"I can tell you I have the support of the police, the support of the military, the support of the Bikers for Trump—I have the tough people, but they don't play it tough—until they go to a certain point, and then it would be very bad, very bad,"* showing he either doesn't learn or doesn't care (probably both).

#12. The Hyperbolic and Apocalyptic: Even in the face of death threats against journalists, Trump regularly doles out "enemy of the people!" tweets. Just weeks after a Coast Guard lieutenant plotted mass murder and just hours before a white terrorist killed 50 Muslims at Friday prayers in a New Zealand

In his 1996 book, *Love Thy Neighbor: A Story of War,* Peter Maass examined how a civilized society can slide into chaos, where Bosnians started killing their friends and neighbors. Maass interviewed a Balkan journalist, who explained that the Serbian president held the media in his control. "You must imagine a United States with every little TV station everywhere taking exactly the same editorial line—a line dictated by David Duke," journalist Milos Vasic explained. "You too would have war in five years."

mosque, he casually posited what a red-versus-blue civil war might be like and managed to sound like an old-world authoritarian, again bragging about having the support of the police and the military (which is not even true: just 44 percent of troops take a favorable view of Trump's presidency, while 43 disapprove).

Hours after that mosque attack, he shrugged off "white nationalism" as a problem, despite the 30 percent growth in the number of hate groups in the US to a record 1,020 over the prior four years, roughly tracking Trump's campaign debut and his presidency. When confronted with the possible consequences of his words, he offers limp condemnation *("I think it's a shame. I think it's a very sad thing when a thing like that happens. I've expressed that")* while Sarah Huckabee Sanders expressed outrage that anyone would connect him to any assaults by people citing his inspiration.

In a nation of nearly 330 million individuals, obviously Trump can't be held legally accountable for all of their hateful actions. Like those millions, Trump also has First Amendment rights, and his supporters have the right to gather to hear him speak. But when Bernie Sanders and Elizabeth Warren attack our rigged economy, no one is phoning in death threats to Goldman Sachs. No one is beating up investment bankers. White House reporters, however, see February 2017, when Trump branded the media "the enemy of the American people," as a turning point. The president of the White House Correspondents Association says that from that point on, he instructed his family not to touch packages on his stoop and had his son ask him, "Is Donald Trump going to put you in prison?"

Journalist Eugene Robinson had it right in an MSNBC commentary: no one is saying Trump is legally responsible for white nationalists who kill and cite Trump; but since he knows with certainty that his incendiary words will ignite some of his QAnon or white supremacist voters to take things into their own hands, he morally does bear a clear responsibility for the predictable result of his words. What Trump is doing is less than yelling "fire!" in a crowded theater and more like lighting a fuse likely to go off a few blocks away.

Based on his years in counterintelligence at the FBI, Frank Figliuzzi worried in a *New York Times* op-ed on July 31, 2019, that "Trump's violence may lead to violence" because his "rants emboldened white hate groups and reinforced racist blogs." Three days later, the El Paso gunman, targeting Mexicans in his own admission, killed 22 after posting a "manifesto" that repeatedly referred to Trump's words and views. *USA Today* found more than 500 instances where Trump used words like "invasion," "predator," "killer," "criminal," and "animal" when discussing immigration at his rallies.

Was this an aberration, a coincidence? Not when the pipe-bomber, the Pittsburgh synagogue murderer, the El Paso killer of 22, among others, cite the president's repeated hateful language as shaping their pathology. Not when his campaign says that Trump refuses to avoid such trigger words at future rallies.

During Obama's term in office, the number of black victims of hate crimes fell by 23.5 percent. But in the three years since Trump stormed the national stage, there was an 11.5 percent increase, according to the FBI. In 2017, the Anti-Defamation League counted 1,986 anti-Semitic incidents, the biggest annual leap since the ADL began tracking anti-Semitic hate crimes 40 years ago. Wonder who started a new job that year.

There has been violence-provoking language starting with our Revolution. But we've never seen a presidential candidate—or a president—speaking to 10,000 cult-like followers

"Every once in a while I stop short and think 'Remember when that Republican congressional candidate flat out body slammed a reporter because he asked him a question about a CBO score and then he lied about it and got elected and now he's in Congress?'"

Chris Hayes on his "All In" show on MSNBC

"More lies con job Propaganda bye failing CNN garbage."

Cesar Sayoc, Jr., alleged to have sent over a dozen pipe bombs to famous Trump critics

"Donald Trump was praising the bravery of America's 'border security people'—who, in his telling, are facing down '15,000 people marching up'—when he reminded his audience, 'We don't let them and we can't let them use weapons. We can't. Other countries do. We can't. I would never do that. But how do we stop these people?' 'Shoot them!' one rally-goer shouted in reply. The crowd exploded in laughter. The president grinned and shook his head. 'Only in the Panhandle you can get away with that statement, folks,' Trump said to applause."

New York Magazine

who seemed to be all plugged into one socket—they all laugh when Trump coaxes them to laugh, they boo when Trump coaxes them to boo. He's like the conductor of a symphony of hate.

Trump's words inspire others' worst impulses, including his own administration officials and surrogates. Lynne Patton, a HUD official, mocked Representative Ilhan Omar's complaints about death threats after Trump distorted out of recognition Omar's (extremely anodyne) remarks about 9/11, only leading to more death threats for the congresswoman.

#9. Bothsides-ism: Roger Stone, a Trump friend and long-time advisor, taunted critics over impeachment: "Just try it. You will have a spasm of violence in this country, an insurrection like you've never seen." Then Stone warned darkly, "Both sides are heavily armed, my friend. This is not 1974. People will not stand for impeachment."

A would-be pipe bomber sending explosive devices to all the president's loudest critics and a Coast Guard officer seeking to "kill almost every last person on earth"—especially Trump opponents in politics and media—are something very new. These same people blame hip-hop and video games for violence, but not Trumpers' violent words? What exactly do they think of Trump's comment that the famous whistleblower was a "spy... and you know how we used to treat spies?" As if executing a law-abiding whistleblower were not enough, Trump "went there" when he said shortly after that if he were impeached it would lead to a "civil war."

That violence isn't confined to threats toward journalists, Trump's political opponents, or people who oppose his presidency. Commenting on how migrants are treated at the southern border, Trump lamented that *"Our military can't act like a military would act. Because if they got a little rough, everybody would go crazy."* Trump finds restraint to be weakness and feels that the United States' (at least vocal) commitment to human rights ties its hands. It was this belief that led him, just a few months removed from the Tiananmen Square massacre, to praise the Chinese government's response to students protesting in Tiananmen Square (*"...the Chinese government almost blew it. Then they were vicious, they were horrible, but they put it down with strength. That shows you the power of strength."*)

When Trump speaks, his audience is primed by a collective "content bias," validating what author William Davies says about demagogues, that "it really doesn't matter...what is said, but merely how it makes them feel." Trump has no command of facts—could he give anything but the broadest outline on his own tax law or health care?—but at 88 percent approval among Republicans, he has an unrivaled command of his base's emotions.

"Both science and history suggest that people will nurture and act on their prejudices in the worst ways when these people are put under stress, pressured by peers, or receive approval from authority figures to do so."

Dr. Susan T. Fiske, psychologist at Princeton University

"I certainly don't think that the president at any point has done anything but condemn violence, against journalists or anyone else."

Sarah Huckabee Sanders (2/22/19)

Photo by Joe Raedle/Getty Images

"Were/are you a supporter of Donald Trump? As a symbol of renewed white identity and common purpose? Sure. As a policy maker and leader? Dear god no."

Manifesto of gunman in New Zealand mosque massacre

"Staffers flagged a record-high 5,875 incidents of harassment, discrimination, and bullying during the 2017-2018 academic year [in New York City schools], according to state Education Department statistics."

New York Daily News

That's why, when Trump calls a caravan of poor, desperate Hispanic people thousands of miles from Rio Grande an "invasion," his supporters buy it. Only in the dingiest minds can thousands of poor people thousands of miles away, in dirty flip-flops, appear as an existential threat. But that's how Trump and the far right characterized the migrant caravan from Central America and rode the issue through the midterms... to a historic defeat not seen for Republicans since Watergate. Just eleven days before Election Day, though, a gunman killed 11 people in a Pittsburgh synagogue in the first American pogrom, saying that he was incensed by the arrival of migrants in America and the synagogue's support for refugees. Trump referred to it as an "invasion" even *after* the Tree of Life shooting.

He kept that up at least until votes were finally cast, then dropped the issue after the midterms. It was almost too on the nose. That would have been like in, say, 1993 if a soldier had started committing murder because he was so incensed by Bill Clinton's plan to allow gay men and women to serve openly in the military. Except that did happen. In 1993, a Fort Bragg soldier, shouting about Clinton's support for gays in the military, shot and killed four people in a North Carolina restaurant, wounding six others. Of course, Clinton enacted a policy he thought was in America's interest and didn't incite primal animosities and use scare words for political advantage. Trump is different because the Far (F)right is different. Hate is the right's lifeblood, and Trump is just new oxygen.

"Truculent was the word for them. Nixon diehards often seemed moved to support him out of pure spite, relishing how he stuck in liberal America's craw. They didn't really act as if they liked him any better than we did; they just enjoyed the perversity of rooting for him anyway, because they knew that liberal America scorned them as much as it scorned him. How sad for Nixon that his admirers held the same opinion of him as his enemies. Having internalized the elite's contempt...their only available substitute for the pride they'd been denied was to say that they liked being trash, and give the finger. Nixon was the finger."—*The Village Voice*, 1994

"The most powerful engine for a mass movement is the evocation of hatred."

John Adams

10.
MEDIA
"THE ENEMY OF THE PEOPLE"

"I think one of the best names is—you know, I've really started this whole 'fake news' thing. Now they're turned it around and then, now, they're calling, you know, stories put out by different—by Facebook 'fake.'" (10/25/17)

Perhaps the reason "fake news" is Trump's favorite insult for the media is that he thinks he invented the term—even though, according to Merriam-Webster, it has been around since the end of the 19th century. The first time he tweeted about "fake news" wasn't until December 2016—after he had already won the election and after reports about real fake-news farms targeting American voters from places like Macedonia had been proliferating for months.

Bottom line: most politicians have a go-to whipping boy to stay on offense and blame if things go wrong. For Reagan, it was "government" itself. For Bush43, terrorism. For Trump, a media out to get him!

"Fake News"

"@KatyTurNBC... should be fired for dishonest reporting. Thank you @GatewayPundit for reporting the truth. #Trump2016" (12/5/15)

#4. Insult Machine: In her bestselling campaign book, *Unbelievable*, journalist Katie Tur writes, "Imagine someone calling you a liar. Now amplify the experience by a thousand if a presidential candidate calls you a liar. And tack on another factor of ten if that presidential candidate is named Donald J. Trump. Waves of insults and threats poured into my phone—the device buzzing like a shock collar."

Trump's attacks on the press have been central to his presidential brand since the beginning. Tur, the reporter tasked with covering Trump's campaign from start to end for NBC, was the brunt of several of such attacks. As she describes in her book, the kickback from Trump's followers was predictably fierce.

#8. Fear Itself: Trump's repeated attacks on the media in general, and certain reporters and networks in particular, are not simply petulant outbursts. Rather, they're a strategic effort to discredit and weaken a cornerstone of our democracy—a free press, the fourth estate. In July 2018, CNN's Jim Acosta posted a video to Twitter of a crowd making its way into a Trump rally. Rallygoers boo him, scream obscenities, and make thumbs-down gestures. One man makes sure that Acosta sees the writing on his shirt: "F--- the media." "Just a sample of the sad scene we faced at the Trump rally in Tampa," Acosta wrote. "I'm very worried that the hostility whipped up by Trump and some in conservative media will result in somebody getting hurt."

Three months after Acosta posted his video, a Trump supporter mailed over a dozen (luckily defective) pipe bombs to prominent Trump enemies—including CNN's offices in New York City. According to an analysis by the Committee to Protect Journalists, Trump insulted reporters via Twitter 280 times during his campaign.

#12. The Hyperbolic and Apocalyptic: *"The press has become so dishonest.... We have to talk to find out what's going*

"Whoever controls the media controls the mind."

Jim Morrison

"For authoritarians in the strongman style such as Trump, 'the people,' is generally a fungible category understood, tacitly or overtly, as those groups who support the leader— you're either with him or against him. Since (in his eyes) the press is Trump's enemy, it is therefore the enemy of his followers—'the people'— as well."

Greg Sargent,
An Uncivil War

on, because the press honestly is out of control. The level of dishonesty is out of control."

"But I want to just tell you, the false reporting by the media, by you people, the false, horrible, fake reporting makes it much harder to make a deal with Russia." (2/16/17)

Berating the media wasn't just a campaign ploy, but also a way for Trump to deflect from his Oval Office failings. His first press conference as president in February 2017—and the only one for a year—was rife with insults and attacks on the press, setting the tone for, so far, three years of near daily disparagement.

After that maiden presser, his campaign emailed a "Mainstream Media Accountability Survey" to thousands of his supporters. The survey, however, was about as biased ("fake"?) as the worst of the press reports that Trump spent months railing against. Among the questions:

- "Do you believe that people of faith have been unfairly characterized by the media?"
- "Do you believe that the media purposely tries to divide Republicans against each other in order to help elect Democrats?" (That's about as leading a question as one can get.)
- "Do you believe that the media creates false feuds within our Party in order to make us seem divided?" (Or maybe *this* is as leading as it can get.)

#12. The Hyperbolic and Apocalyptic: *"The FAKE NEWS media (failing @nytimes, @NBCNews, @ABC, @CBS, @CNN) is not my enemy, it is the enemy of the American people!" (2/17/17)*

"I think I'm going to spend the first 10 minutes [of a rally] just attacking the media."

ROUGHLY ONE IN TEN TRUMP TWEETS CONTAINS AN INSULT OR CRITICISM OF A JOURNALIST OR NEWS OUTLET.

This undated quote from Bob Woodward's 2018 bestselling book, *Fear*, illustrates how the president revels in his attacks on the media. It's like he's reliving his short-lived professional-wrestling days, hyping up the crowd by trash-talking the villain in the ring.

But *"any* negative polls" are fake news? Really? Who is supposed to believe that?

"So much Fake News about what is going on in the White House. Very calm and calculated with a big focus on open and fair trade with China, the coming North Korea meeting and, of course, the vicious gas attack in Syria." (4/11/18)

#16. Deny/Deny/Deny: Trump rejected as fake news multiple reports that the White House was particularly "chaotic" in the early weeks of spring 2018. Whoops—spoke too soon, since later that month: he had to withdraw his nominee to head Veterans Affairs after accusations of negligence at his previous job; Scott Pruitt, then-head of the EPA, was grilled by a Senate committee about ethics violations, which led to his resignation two months later; Mick Mulvaney, then head of the CFPB and director of the OMB, let it slip that he violated campaign-finance ethics when he was a congressman; and Trump's nominee to direct the CIA, Gina Haspel, was facing a possible negative confirmation vote over her past involvement as a CIA official in torture.

A Republican strategist close to the White House told the *Washington Post*, "It's starting to feel like the early days again,

Photo by Win McNamee/Getty Images

According to the Trump Twitter Archive, between January 2017 and May 2019, Trump had tweeted 430 times about "fake news." He also tweeted 93 times about CNN, 90 times about the *New York Times*, and 70 times about NBC.

with everyone running around red-faced, trying to keep up with the president." Very "calm and collected"...

"Some of the most dishonest people in media are the so-called fact checkers.... I'm telling you, it's just fake news. And you know what, you wouldn't even have to know. You could say it automatically without even knowing." (2/11/19)

Stephen Colbert, impersonating Trump: "In fact, not knowing really helps things, I say. That's why, when it comes to knowing, I say, 'Just say no.'" (2/12/19)

Appreciate how radical Trump's approach is. Brent Bozell, brother-in-law to Bill Buckley, was an incendiary critic of the "liberal media" in the 1960s. His approach was occasionally picked up by Vice President Spiro Agnew ("nattering nabobs of negativism" being one hard-to-forget example), but Richard Nixon's hatred of the media was largely kept contained in the privacy of his Oval Office, as the Nixon tapes indicate. And when he had *one* saucy public exchange with Dan Rather of CBS—Nixon: "Are you running for something?" Rather: "No, Mr. President, are you?"—it was head-turning. Compare that, in retrospect, with 45 (see Chapter 12, "Bully's Pulpit").

(Also, the entire premise of "liberal media" has an ideological slant, since media platforms are businesses largely run by white Republicans with the power to hire, fire, and protect annoyed advertisers; see Eric Alterman's *What Liberal Media? The Truth About Bias and the News*, from 2003.)

The Trump-Fox White House

Should Never-Trumpers regard Sean Hannity and Donald Trump as "Dr. Evil" and "Mini-Me?" Consider:

Sean Hannity, Fox News: "[Russian collusion] is a conspiracy theory cooked up by Obama and the Democrats..." (1/23/18)

Trump, during a speech at Mar-a-Lago: "It's largely a hoax created by the Democrats..." (4/18/18)

Hannity: "...as an excuse for why Hillary Clinton lost the election. That was never supposed to happen."

"...softening the blow of loss, which is, frankly, a loss they never should have had."

Hannity: "The FBI was never actually able to look at the DNC servers."

"Their server—the DNC server—was never gotten by the FBI. Why did the FBI never take it?"

As *Axios* revealed, nearly 60 percent of Trump's typical work day is reserved for "executive time." Multiple reports from insiders and journalists conclude that a large portion of his "executive time" is spent watching Fox News, as the above sequence of interactive talking points indicates.

According to John Avlon, a CNN commentator and former editor-in-chief of *The Daily Beast*, "Typically, talking points have gone from politicians to partisan media. *This* is a two-way street in something close to real time. It's self-reinforcing of the White House's message, and then it increases the tribalism

Under oath at a House Judiciary Committee hearing in the Fall of 2019, Corey Lewindowsky–previously a campaign manager to Trump's 2016 effort–was asked why he lied to MSNBC's Ari Melber when asked if the president ever asked him to get AG Sessions to interfere with the Mueller probe: The wily witness showed he had learned from his master: "I have no obligation to be honest with the media because they're just as dishonest as anyone else."

"Trump has told confidants that he has ranked the loyalty of many reporters, on a scale of 1 to 10. Bret Baier, Fox News' chief political anchor, is a 6; Hannity a solid 10. Steve Doocy, the co-host of 'Fox and Friends,' is so adoring that Trump gives him a 12."

Jane Mayer, *The New Yorker* (3/11/19)

on Twitter, the social-media mobs, all those kinds of things that dumb-down debate and make us meaner and dumber and pettier.... It is an extraordinary two-way relationship, the likes of which we've never seen."

Tucker Carlson, Fox News: "The president of South Africa, Cyril Ramaphosa, has begun seizing land from his own citizens without compensation because they are the wrong skin color. That is literally the definition of racism."

Trump, later that evening: "I have asked Secretary of State @SecPompeo to closely study the South Africa land and farm seizures and expropriations and the large scale killing of farmers. 'South African Government is now seizing land from white farmers.' @TuckerCarlson @FoxNews" (8/22/18)

Trump not only repeats the arguments and words that he hears on Fox News, he also takes them into consideration when crafting policy—including diplomatic policy.

As of March 2019, Trump had granted Fox News 44 interviews, including seven with his favorite Fox personality, Sean Hannity. He granted all other major networks just 10 interviews, and zero to CNN and MSNBC. While Barack Obama occasionally went on Fox, he did not sit for interviews four times more frequently on MSNBC than all other networks combined.

In the example above, Carlson misdescribed a reparations movement for black farmers in South Africa in an apparent attempt to stir up irrational reverse-racism fears among conservatives. After presumably watching that segment, Trump took it a step further, intertwining Carlson's account with a prominent white-nationalist conspiracy theory about the South African government killing white farmers. If that weren't bad enough, Trump then purportedly asked his secretary of state to look into the matter, to which the South African government responded that "South Africa totally rejects this narrow perception which only seeks to divide our nation and remind us of our colonial past."

One of these days, Fox News may provoke a nuclear war. Do they know that could hurt ratings?

Jill Brooke in the *Hollywood Reporter*: "Sitting in [*New York Post* editor Jerry] Nachman's office while he was editing one of my pieces, I heard his secretary yell, 'It's Donald.' Nachman motioned me to 'shhh' and put Trump on speaker. 'Those fucking bitches,' Trump bellowed. 'I want a front-page story tomorrow.'

"Jerry calmly replied, 'Donald, you just don't demand a front-page story. There has to be a story.' 'For all the newspapers I've sold for you, you should give me one.' 'That's not how it works.' 'What gets a front-page story?' Donald asked. 'It's usually murder, money or sex.' Donald fired back: 'Marla says with me it's the best sex she's ever had.' Nachman's face lit up like a firecracker. 'That's great!' he said. 'But you know I need corroboration.'

"'Marla,' Trump yelled into the background. 'Didn't you say it's the best sex you ever had with me?' From a distance, we heard a faint voice: 'Yes, Donald.' Only years later did we learn that Trump sometimes impersonated voices to reporters. I still can't be sure whether the voice in the room was really hers."

Trump also uses Fox News to staff his administration, and vice versa. It used to be controversial when a *single* reporter transitioned only from government to journalism, like Diane Sawyer with the Nixon administration to CBS. Here are seventeen Fox figures either passing through the Fox–Trump administration revolving door or blurring the lines between free press and state TV:

- Bill Shine, a former Fox News executive and producer, spent eight months as Trump's deputy chief of staff and communications director. During his tenure in the White House, Fox was still paying out a $15 million bonus and severance deal to Shine.
- Anthony Scaramucci, a former Fox Business host, spent ten days as Trump's communications director.
- Ben Carson, a former Fox News contributor, is now Trump's Secretary of Housing and Urban Development.
- John Bolton, a former Fox News commentator, was Trump's third national security adviser.
- K.T. McFarland, a former Fox News commentator, was Trump's deputy national security adviser.
- Heather Nauert, a former Fox News anchor, was a State Department spokesperson and was Trump's initial pick to replace Nikki Haley as ambassador to the United Nations.
- Morgan Ortagus, a former Fox News contributor, is now the State Department spokesperson.
- Kimberly Guilfoyle, a former Fox News host, is now working on Trump's reelection campaign...and is dating Donald Trump, Jr.
- Hope Hicks, Trump's former communications director, is now the top public relations officer at Fox Corporation.

- Raj Shah, deputy Communications Director, now Fox SVP.
- Sebastian Gorka, a former national security adviser for Trump, is now a regular on Fox News.
- Mike Huckabee, father of Trump's former press secretary, Sarah Huckabee Sanders, used to have his own Fox News show and is now a Fox News contributor.
- Sarah Huckabee Sanders, beginning September, 2019.
- Pete Hegseth, a Fox News host, and Lou Dobbs, a Fox Business host, have each reportedly been patched into Oval Office meetings by speakerphone to offer policy advice.
- Sean Hannity, a Fox News host, reportedly speaks to Trump almost every night after his show ends. Hannity has also been a "special guest" at a Trump rally, speaking at the podium on stage.
- Roger Ailes, the late chairman and CEO of Fox News and Fox Television Stations, was on Trump's campaign-debate team and was prepared to go into business with Trump on "Trump TV" if, as expected, he lost the 2016 election.
- Rupert Murdoch, the founder of News Corp and 21st Century Fox, reportedly speaks to both Trump and Jared Kushner on a regular, almost familial basis.

It's understandable why Trump would relate to Murdoch—both men have built their power on appealing to down-market media audiences. And by doing so, they upended two Western countries: without Murdoch, the United Kingdom would have never voted for Brexit; without Trump's repeating Murdochian demagoguery to America's Fringe Fourth, he wouldn't be president.

"In late 2018, Trump was heading toward a budget deal with the newly ascendant Democrats until guests and hosts across the network started shaming him, demanding that he not sign any government spending bills that didn't include $5 billion for a border wall. 'Don't listen to squish advisers,' urged Pete Hegseth, a 'Fox & Friends' host. He didn't. He listened to Fox instead and shut down the federal government."

Jonathan Mahler and Jim Rutenberg, the *New York Times Magazine* (4/3/19)

According to reporting by Cliff Sims, on election night in 2016, when it still looked like Trump was going to lose and was preparing to contest the results, he only wanted to talk to one person: Murdoch. *"Somebody get Rupert on the phone and tell him to get ready to make this a big deal if we need to,"* he said.

In fact, Fox News is such a propaganda machine that it's willing to switch its position of virtually any issue just to make Trump look good (and the Democrats look bad). Take the issue of North Korea, for example:

Sean Hannity: *"Obama would willingly negotiate with the leaders of terrorist nations like Iran and North Korea without preconditions."*

Sean Hannity: *"The world will probably be a little bit safer [after Trump meets with Kim Jong-un]. The media should be giving President Trump credit for that."*

Gretchen Carlson: *"I'm not sure there's any real discussing issues with Kim Jong-un [for Obama]."*

Geraldo Rivera: *"[Trump] is so charming. He can deal with people. He can get along with people.... I think that [meeting with Kim] will work out well."*

***

"CNN is fake news. I don't take questions from CNN. CNN is fake news! I don't take questions from CNN." (7/13/18)

"I think you should let me run the country; you should run CNN. And if you did it well, your ratings would be much better.... CNN

should be ashamed of itself having you working for them. You [reporter Jim Acosta] are a rude, terrible person. You shouldn't be working for CNN.... You're a very rude person. The way you treat Sarah Huckabee is terrible. And the way you treat other people are horrible.... When you report fake news, which CNN does a lot, you are an enemy of the people." (11/7/18)

Trump reserves a special kind of hate for one of Fox News's main cable rivals, CNN. In addition to berating CNN reporters, blocking them access from certain events and calling the network "the enemy of the people," he has tried to interfere in CNN's business.

#8. Fear Itself: *The New Yorker*'s Jane Mayer has reported that "Trump ordered Gary Cohn, then the director of the National Economic Council, to pressure the Justice Department to intervene" in a merger between AT&T and Time Warner, CNN's parent company. "According to a well-informed source, Trump called Cohn into the Oval Office, along with John Kelly, who had just become the chief of staff, and said in exasperation to Kelly, *'I've been telling Cohn to get this lawsuit filed and nothing's happened! I've mentioned it fifty times. And nothing's happened. I want to make sure it's filed. I want that deal blocked!'*"

(The Department of Justice did indeed challenge the merger, but both a federal district court and the DC Court of Appeals ruled that the merger was lawful. Most antitrust experts found the administration's challenge unconvincing, since the companies' actions didn't fall within the Justice Department's existing Antitrust Division's guidelines for horizontal mergers, although progressive groups made arguments on bigness grounds generally.)

"This is banana republic stuff—the kind of thing that routinely happens in countries without the rule of law," conservative hawk Max Boot wrote in the *Washington Post*. Trump's repeated slander of any media that question or criticize him undermines one pillar of a democratic America and, until now—excluding Fox, effectively a Pravda on the Hudson—a referee of truth.

> *"Trump insists he is the sole arbiter of truth. Anybody who questions Trump is by definition biased. By his circular logic, any attempt to question Trump is inherently false, since the act of challenging Trump reveals the source to be dishonest. Reporters can try to chase the lies down one by one, but they always lead back into this same logical cul-de-sac." Jonathan Chait, New York Magazine (11/19/18)*

> *Lesley Stahl, 60 Minutes: "It's just me, my boss, and [Donald Trump]—he has a huge office—and he's attacking the press. There were no cameras, there was nothing going on, and I said, 'That is getting tired, why are you doing it? You're doing it over and over and it's boring. It's time to end that.' And he said, 'You know why I do it? I do it to discredit you all and demean you all so when you write negative stories about me no one will believe you.'" (5/23/18)*

To be fair, he's at least one-fourth right—his hard-core base of perhaps 25 percent of America, uncritically pro-Trump because of their "motivated thinking," do react with Pavlovian glee when Trump snarls, "fake media!" Think of a trainer feeding fish to seals.

11.
SECRECY

"WE'RE THE MOST TRANSPARENT ADMINISTRATION EVER, BY FAR."

DAVID LETTERMAN: Why do we want to see President Obama's college records?
DONALD TRUMP: Transparency. Does that make sense to anybody? [Crowd cheers.] Transparency." —2012

Donald Trump's birther campaign wasn't a good government crusade for transparency, but rather an attempted delegitimization based on unnamed sources of America's first black president and a way to stand out among a crowd of GOP aspirants. The second part worked: during the primaries, only 30 percent of Republican voters in polls said they thought that Barack Obama was born in the United States. And of course, Trump steamrolled his sixteen Republican primary opponents.

In the process, he learned that he could make some charge without any evidence—"you wouldn't believe what my people are finding!"—and pay no real penalty. Accusation plus Secrecy was a formula he would not forget.

Or just pure secrecy, as when he refuses to release his taxes, refuses to comply with congressional subpoenas, and refuses to release a whistleblower's complaint that a Trump-appointed Inspector General considered "urgent and serious."

"President Obama is the least-transparent president in the history of this country. There's never been anything like it. We know very little about our president.... If he releases these records, it will end the question[s], and indeed the anger, of many Americans. They'll know something about their president. Their president will become transparent like other presidents." (10/25/12)

"We're bringing back jobs big league. We're bringing them back at the plant level. We're bringing them back at the mine level. The energy jobs are coming back." (2/14/17)

While he spent his early days in office telling miners he'd bring back all their jobs, at the same time he was shielding their owners from embarrassing disclosures. One of the first bills he signed into law repealed a transparency rule that required mining and oil companies to disclose their payments to foreign governments in order to curb bribery and corruption. This gift to big fossil fuel interests was publicly demanded by...exactly no one.

"The White House announced Friday that it would cut off public access to visitor logs revealing who is entering the White House complex and which officials they are meeting, breaking with the Obama administration's practice and returning a cloak of secrecy over the basic day-to-day workings of the government."—The *New York Times* (4/14/17)

This reversal of Obama's policy move would leave the American people in the dark about which activists, lobbyists, and D-list celebrities have threatened Trump's predecessors and, of course, donors. So many donors.

In elevating his electoral college victory, and implicitly drawing attention to his 3 million-vote deficit in the popular vote, Trump revealed his weakness: as a minority president (albeit with a Republican House and the Senate in his first two years) backed by a rabid minority base, his only refuge has been in secrecy. Such as by shielding his tax returns and his administration's actions from the American public like when this "blue-collar billionaire" rolled back an Obama-era regulation that proposed to force airlines to disclose baggage fees for checked and carry-on baggage fees earlier in the process, when customers purchase tickets, which the Trump administration claimed was too hard on airlines.

THINGS TRUMP DOESN'T DO:

- Cover-ups
- Talk to Robert Mueller
- Release his tax returns
- Allow his former advisors to testify before Congress
- Disclose which foreign governments stay at his hotels
- Reveal anything about how Jared Kushner got his security clearance

—Judd Legum

"We recognize that there's a privacy aspect to allowing citizens to come express their views. And that's why we maintain the same policy that every other administration did coming up here prior to the last one."—Sean Spicer (4/17/17)

When the Trump White House closed the visitors' log, they had an interesting logic. As CNN's Chris Cillizza wrote, "That the Obama administration's decision to publicly release most—if not all—visitors to the White House was somehow a less transparent move than the Trump administration's decision to release none of that information. Which is, in a word, ridiculous."

Trump set this standard for transparency so that even his CEO advisory board wasn't immune to his instinct for secrecy. He framed the board's meetings so that they bypassed federal transparency laws that require meetings to be announced in advance and open to the public. Or enraged his own party by ignoring congressional Republicans' demands for the White House to send a report to Congress on the Saudi-sanctioned murder of dissident American journalist Jamal Khashoggi.

Also, the first president in modern times to say he's received numerous "beautiful" letters from the North Korean dictator while refusing to disclose their contents. Guess we'll just have to trust his description as complete and accurate.

After slamming the door on Americans seeing Trump's taxes and ignoring congressional subpoenas as if she were Louis XIV, Conway stretches the bounds of taste by claiming he was not only the most transparent president, but the most accountable while he receives no justice in the face of looting the treasury, record corruption, and an allegation of rape. Still, you gotta love her use of the adverb "definitely," as if her conclusion were the result of a careful comparative study. Actually, her comment *is* completely accurate with only one change: substitute "least" for "most." She can't entirely be blamed, though. When Trump was a failing candidate who seemed sure to face a record rout, after a *Morning Joe* appearance defending Trump, Conway said, according to the show's hosts, "*Bleech*. I need to take a shower." America needs one, too.

President Trump has gone to extraordinary lengths to conceal details of his conversations with Russian President Vladimir Putin, including on at least one occasion taking possession of the notes of his own interpreter and instructing the linguist not to discuss what had transpired with other administration officials, current and former U.S. officials said.—The Washington Post, (1/13/19)

It's more than rich that the same person who suggested a Manchurian Candidate president in the person of Barack Obama,

#20 The Lyin' King: *"This is the most transparent, accountable president perhaps we've ever seen, definitely in modern times."*

Kellyanne Conway
(10/15/18)

who suggested even in the wake of the Orlando Pulse shooting that Obama and ISIS were almost in cahoots *("There's something going on. It's inconceivable. There's something going on.")*, would then meet with America's greatest geopolitical rival, Russia, the same rival that intervened in the presidential election that sent Trump to the White House, and then meet without American translators and taking possession of their notes, only inviting suspicions that look all the more worrying as Trump was effectively cleared of criminal conspiracy by the Mueller findings.

That secrecy extended further into foreign policy as Rex Tillerson, the new secretary of state, ended daily press briefings and, in a break from previous secretaries, traveled to Asia without news media on his plane. Tillerson's successor, Mike Pompeo, would sometimes close off its press briefings to media that weren't "faith-based" and refuse to release its list of attendees or a transcript of the briefing. Just what the (white) working class wanted.

As part of his Very Transparency brand, this president required the signing of nondisclosure agreements of the White House staff. It's an alien notion on Capitol Hill, but one Trump as a candidate pushed for federal employees because of the (well-founded) fear of tell-alls. His NDAs for campaign staffers were unusual, giving wide berth for Trump to sue, extending from the campaign to "all times thereafter" (i.e., the End of Time) and applying to all on his team, paid or unpaid, staffer or volunteer. Historian Russell Riley said, "These people are not working for Donald Trump, they are working for the citizens of the United States of America."

#6. Upside-Downism: When Trump ran against Hillary based partly on her private email account, he said, "Policy decisions will be public and very, very transparent." That may

> *"What [Trump] is a person who demands transparency, which is what the [President Obama's] platform was all about when he decided to run."*
>
> Michael Cohen, 2011

"The E.P.A. had originally forecast that eliminating the Obama-era rule, the Clean Power Plan, and replacing it with a new measure would have resulted in an additional 1,400 premature deaths per year. The new analytical model would significantly reduce that number and would most likely be used by the Trump administration to defend further rollbacks of air pollution rules if it is formally adopted."

—The *New York Times*

have been the first campaign promise he broke. It was followed by the suspension of a rule established by Obama that protected whistleblowers who worked for Department of Energy contractors. That suspension allowed the administration to censor or fail to provide records for 78 percent of Freedom of Information Act requests in 2017.

#6. Upside-Downism: *"I'm talking about a man who declares himself brilliant but directed me to threaten his high school, his colleges, and the College Board to never release his grades or SAT scores."* —Michael Cohen (2/26/19)

When John F. Kennedy said before a gathering of the Western Hemisphere's Nobel laureates, "I think this is the most extraordinary collection of talent, of human knowledge, that has ever been gathered together at the White House, with the possible exception of when Thomas Jefferson dined alone," he surely had no way of knowing that, ten successors later, one would declare himself a "stable genius" upon reports that his underlings mocked him as a "moron," an "idiot," and a "dope" unfit for the office or its intellectual rigors. He had no way of knowing that that successor so feared the release of his high school or college grades or SAT scores that Trump's aides pressured his old military academy to hand over his academic records threatening legal action; and the New York Military Academy moved his files to a secure location, shielded from public view, just in time for his presidential campaign.

He did this all while demanding President Obama's high school and college grades, implying that he could never make it into Columbia or Harvard Law School because, of course, Trump claims (without evidence, his forte) that Obama was a "terrible student." Then with standard flair, he offered $5 million to the charity of Obama's choice if he would disclose his college records. (Anyone shocked that Trump, at the same time, refuses to disclose his?)

#2. Assertions:

"But people do not understand tax returns. I did a filing of over 100 pages, which is in the offices—pity them—with people went and saw that filing, they saw the magnitude of it and they were very disappointed. They saw the detail.... But if I were finished with the audit—I would have an open mind to it. But I do not want to do it during the audit. And no lawyer, even from the other side, they say often. Not always. But when you are under audit, you do not subject it to that. You get it done, and then he released it...Nobody returns a return when it is under audit." (11/7/18)

"Frankly, the people don't care." (4/10/19)

Frankly, they do care about what his taxes say: 67 percent of voters want Trump to release his tax returns, with just 24 percent (his hardened base) saying they don't care to see what's in them.

As a candidate, Trump explained it was all so simple: that he was under audit, and as soon as the audit was complete he'd be happy to share his tax returns. Trump's own IRS commissioner says there is no rule that prohibits the release of Trump's tax returns while under audit. Even Richard Nixon released his tax returns while they were under audit, thus setting the standard for all his presidents...until Trump, who seems to pity average people, for not understanding how audits work for Very Rich People.

TRUMP AND TAXES

5/20/14: Trump says, "If I decide to run for office, I'll produce my tax returns, absolutely. And I would love to do that."

1/24/16: Now a candidate, Trump says in an interview with NBC's Chuck Todd, "I have very big returns, as you know, and I have everything all approved and very beautiful and we'll be working that over in the next period of time, Chuck. Absolutely."

2/11/16: Trump starts to qualify his tax returns' release: "We'll get them out at some point, probably."

2/25/16: Trump points people to read his FEC financial statements, which reveal little, and assures, "They are great!" Trump claims he's been audited for the past 12 years.

2/26/16: The IRS commissioner disputes Trump's claims of being audited

(continued next page)

several years in a row, saying while he cannot comment on a specific case, it'd be "rare."

2/27/16: Trump tweets, "Tax experts throughout the media agree that no sane person would give their tax returns during an audit. After the audit, no problem!"

1/22/17: Kellyanne Conway slams the door on releasing Trump's tax returns, claiming voters "didn't care."

4/7/19: Acting White House chief of staff Mick Mulvaney says Democrats will "never" see Trump's tax returns.

"Customs and Border Protection authorities on Wednesday allowed a group of journalists on a brief, highly controlled tour of the border station in Clint...the agents did not allow the journalists inside any of the cells and prohibited any conversations with the detained children, citing government policies. The agency also barred reporters from bringing cameras or phones inside, threatening to expel anyone who did."

—The *New York Times*

12.
BULLY'S PULPIT
TEDDY ROOSEVELT: "BULLY!" DONALD TRUMP: A BULLY

Target: Colin Kaepernick, NFL players

#8. Fear Itself: *"Wouldn't you love to see one of our NFL owners when someone disrespects our flag to say, 'Get that son of a bitch off the field...'?" (9/22/17)*

It's not surprising that when Colin Kaepernick began his protest against police brutality—against police brutality, not against the American flag—Trump didn't see the complaints as valid. Has Trump ever criticized police misconduct?

Stretching back to the start of his adult life, Trump has demonstrated his racism in denying housing to black applicants in the 1970s and calling for the execution of falsely accused black teenagers in the 1980s. As president, Trump chose an Alabama audience to insult athlete-protesters, the vast majority of whom are black, on behalf of NFL team owners, nearly all white. He may have assumed this was what his crowd craved. After all, he ridiculed his second wife's Georgia family as "dumb southerners" and "hillbillies."

If a player is not standing for the national anthem, Mr. Trump said, "Maybe you shouldn't be in the country."

Target: Michael Cohen

"If anyone is looking for a good lawyer, I would strongly suggest that you don't retain the services of Michael Cohen!" (8/22/18)

"Officials at Salem State University in Massachusetts discovered hateful graffiti spray-painted on benches and a fence surrounding the baseball field, including 'Trump #1 Whites Only USA.'"

The *New York Times* (12/16/17)

"@FoxNews 'Don't forget, Michael Cohen has already been convicted of perjury and fraud, and as recently as this week, the Wall Street Journal has suggested that he may have stolen tens of thousands of dollars....' Lying to reduce his jail time! Watch father-in-law!" (1/18/19)

Let's give Trump some credit. While Nixon kept a private, couple dozen name "Enemies List," Trump's is completely public—and includes at least 598 people, places, and things he's insulted—and grows daily. #11. Nicknames: It includes aides working/lying for him before being publicly drummed out (see: "dog" Omarosa, "sloppy" Steve Bannon)—especially Michael Cohen. The reason was obvious, his fear that Cohen may reveal damaging facts about Trump's financial life or offer a behind-the-scenes portrait of Trump unplugged. He didn't have to wait long: Cohen would testify to Congress about Trump's racist remarks a month later.

Target: Migrants

#20. The Lyin' King: *"...children in question were very sick before they were given over to Border Patrol. The father of the young girl said it was not their fault, he hadn't given her water in days. Border Patrol needs the Wall and it will all end. They are working so hard & getting so little credit!" (12/29/18)*

Few things reveal who Donald Trump is more than his handling of the lives of other people: his dismissal of Puerto Rico post-Hurricane Maria, caging of children, trying to steal health care from tens of millions of Americans, and even cutting off health care from his brother's grandson. Trump targeted the father of a 7-year-old girl who died in a US detention center for migrants. A member of Congress who has visited them described migrant centers as "petri dishes for people to get sick," including babies who often go without baby formula.

Jakelin Caal Maquin traveled 2,000 miles to the US from Guatemala and fell ill with a streptococcus bacteria infection. She died in an El Paso hospital. Trump blamed her father for not providing her with water for a "long period of time," adding, "he actually admitted blame." He actually didn't and said Customs and Border Protection failed to provide water for eight hours. An autopsy report suggested she could have survived with earlier medical intervention. Trump, with the biggest megaphone available, without evidence placed the blame on the girl's father. Was Trump just being careless, cavalier, or cruel?

Target: "Low-life" John Brennan and intelligence agencies

"You look at Brennan, you look at Clapper, you look at Hayden, you look at Comey, you look at McCabe, you look at Strzok and his lover, Lisa Page. You look at other people in the F.B.I. that have been fired, are no longer there.... Certainly I can't have any confidence in the past. But I can have a lot of confidence in the present and the future, because it's getting to be now where we're putting our people in. But in the past, no, I have no confidence in a guy like Brennan. I think he's a total low-life." (7/18/18)

Trump reeled off a string of names that have been his targets, who he believes have caused him to suffer "presidential harassment" as the leader of the free world. Trump regularly attacks the FBI, the CIA, drawing dangerous analogies to Nazi Germany to inflame his victim status...which may mark the first time he's

"[George H.W. Bush] never lost his sense of humor. Humor is the universal solvent against the abrasive elements of life. That's what humor is. He never hated anyone. He knew what his mother and my mother always knew: hatred corrodes the container it's carried in."

Alan Simpson

#6 Upside-Downism: "Further, the President's [Bill Clinton's] repeated lies to the American people in this matter compound the case against him as they demonstrate his failure to protect the institution of the presidency as the 'inspiring supreme symbol of all that is highest in our American ideals.' Leaders affect the lives of families far beyond their own 'private life'...now more than ever, America needs to be able to look to her First Family as role models of all that we have been and can be again."

Rep. Mike Pence, 1998

sincerely condemned Nazis. (The insincere take-back after Charlottesville doesn't count.)

Target: asylum seekers

#12. The Hyperbolic: *"You have people coming, you know they're all met by the lawyers.... And they come out, and they're met by the lawyers, and they say, 'Say the following phrase: I am very afraid for my life. I am afraid for my life.' Then I look at the guy. He looks like he just got out of the ring. He's a heavy-weight champion of the world. It's a big fat con job." (3/24/19)*

When Trump feels blue, he throws a dart somewhere red in the middle of the country, and, wherever it lands, he hosts a rally, where he plays to the worst instincts of a sometimes-packed arena.

At a standard rally in Grand Rapids in 2019, he went back to his golden oldie, attacking desperate migrants in front of crowds cheering for more. Trump then surprised all by attacking a special interest group that priced insulin out of reach of its patients. Only kidding! He went after brown people again. Brown people fleeing desperate poverty or violence caused by US policy back when Trump was calling into tabloids under assumed names.

#17 BLOCK THAT METAPHOR:

"An Orange County high school football game was marred by allegations of racism Monday. At issue were posters allegedly seen at the Friday night game at Aliso Niguel High School against Santa Ana High, where Santa Ana principal Jeff Bishop claimed he saw posters that said, 'We love White' and 'Build the Wall.'"

–CBS Los Angeles (9/10/18)

"After the 2016 presidential election, teachers across the country reported they were seeing increased name-calling and bullying in their classrooms.... Francis Huang of the University of Missouri and Dewey... found higher rates of bullying and certain types of teasing in areas where voters favored Donald Trump over Hillary Clinton in the 2016 election. Seventh- and eighth-graders in areas that favored Trump reported bullying rates in spring 2017 that were 18 percent higher than students living in areas that went for Clinton."

—NPR (1/9/19)

"A school district in Missouri is apologizing after a group of white students turned their backs and waved a Donald Trump sign at the beginning of a basketball game when the opposing team's players who are predominantly black were introduced."

NBC News (12/15/16)

Target: Ilhan Omar

#2. Assertions and Adjectives: *"Look, she's been very disrespectful to this country. She's been very disrespectful, frankly, to Israel. She is somebody that doesn't really understand, I think life, real life, what it's all about. It's unfortunate. She's got a way about her that's very, very bad I think for our country. I think she's extremely unpatriotic and extremely disrespectful to our country." (4/16/19)*

On his long "enemies list," it's the person of Ilhan Omar who combines all the things that most rile Trump—"the way about her," in his own words. Omar is a woman, a person of color, a Muslim, and someone with an opinion contrary to his.

While Omar then faced a deluge of graphic and highly specific death threats for making harmless comments about 9/11, Trump became a human accelerant by having his team edit a video splicing her words ("some people did something") with

"As [New York City] schools have gone soft on discipline, students are tormenting each other more than ever—both in person and online, according to a Post analysis of teacher-generated state data. Staffers flagged a record-high 5,875 incidents of harassment, discrimination and bullying during the 2017-2018 academic year...up more than 300 percent since 2013-2014, when there were 1,344 incidents, and a 60 percent increase from last year, when there were 3,660."

New York Post

images of the horrific attack. Some video they left out: Donald Trump, the day of the attacks, bragging that his building 40 Wall Street was now the tallest in lower Manhattan. Some things they aren't able to find video of—Trump helping with the recovery at Ground Zero, where he claimed he pitched in.

By focusing on Omar, Trump reveals his world view: that the actions of 19 hijackers are representative of 1.9 billion people ("Islam hates us," candidate Trump said). America must not show its fealty to their values; Muslims must prove their loyalty. Being duly elected with nearly 78 percent of the vote and swearing to uphold the Constitution, evidently, does not suffice for Rep. Omar. In attacking Muslims and using his office to focus his attack on her in particular, he's playing with her life. It was keeping in form, considering that one-third of all his tweets in 2018 insulted or attacked someone. Trump's M.O. is the opposite of mothers who instruct us in good manners: "If you don't have something nice to say about someone, don't say it."

"Trash talk turned to hate speech after a high school girls varsity basketball game Tuesday between Mediapolis and Columbus. The message was written sometime before, during or after the game at Mediapolis High School in the home locker room. The message read 'Go back to the border.' Underneath, more red letters spelled 'Go Trump!' Hispanics account for 64.5 percent of the Columbus School District's student population."
The Hawk Eye (2/3/17)

ONE WEEK OF TAUNTS

July 7, 2019: A leaked cable reveals that Kim Darroch, the British Ambassador to the US, refers to the Trump administration as "diplomatically clumsy," "inept," and "uniquely dysfunctional."

July 9, 2019: Trump calls the ambassador *a very stupid guy* and a *pompous fool.*

July 13, 2019: After a new book revealed that Paul Ryan was dismayed at Trump's ignorance of government, Trump says leaders like Ryan *almost killed the Republican Party* because he was "weak, ineffective and stupid." #2. Assertions and Adjectives.

"Back to the Future screenwriter Bob Gale has revealed that Donald Trump was the inspiration for Marty McFly's archnemesis Biff Tannen. Gale spoke to the Daily Beast *about the similarities between Biff and Trump. 'We thought about it when we made the movie! Are you kidding?' Gale told the outlet when asked if he noticed Biff's resemblance to Trump."*

Variety (10/21/15)

13.
WAR & PEACE
HE'S NO METTERNICH

The Middle East

2011: "I can't believe what our country is doing. Gadhafi, in Libya, is killing thousands of people. Nobody knows how bad it is and we're sitting around. We have soldiers all over the Middle East and we're not bringing them in to stop this horrible carnage.... We should stop this guy which would be very easy and very quick." (2/28/11)

2016: "[Hillary Clinton] made a mistake on [intervening in] Libya. She made a terrible mistake on Libya. And the next thing, I mean, not only did she make the mistake, but then they complicated the mistake by having no management once they bombed you-know-what out of Gadhafi. I mean, she made a terrible mistake on Libya." (9/7/16)

2018: "Let's f---ing kill him! Let's go in. Let's kill the f---ing lot of them." (4/7/17) (Trump to Secretary of Defense Jim Mattis, referring to Syrian President Bashar al-Assad after a chemical-weapons attack in Syria, according to Fear *by Bob Woodward.) #18. The 180°*

At a micro level, Trump tried to play the part of the tough guy on Gadhafi in 2011—when it suited him. Then he portrayed himself as the wise, principled conservative noninterventionist—again, when it suited him during the 2016 campaign. Then he turned into President Strangelove when it came to Assad in 2018. Whatever.

Shortly after the "let's f---ing kill him" episode, Trump launched 59 cruise missiles at a Syrian airbase. Pundits—liberal and conservative alike—praised his decisiveness. "Trump just became president," said CNN's Fareed Zakaria. It's a wonder what the media would have said if they knew about his global war-threatening tantrum just a few hours earlier.

#13. The Hyperbolic: *"Jared is such a good lad. He will secure an Israel deal which no one else has managed to get. You know, he's a natural talent, he is the top, he is a natural talent. You know what I'm talking about—a natural talent."* *(1/15/17)*

Oh, we know what he's talking about. In tapping Jared Kushner as the Trump administration's go-to person to solve the Israel–Palestine dilemma—a hydra-headed 70-year-old crisis—the president affirmed Kushner's "natural talent" for, let's face it, marrying his daughter. What an amazing coincidence that the best person in the country to broker peace is a former real-estate executive from his own family.

#20. The Lyin' King: *"I have just returned from a trip [to Saudi Arabia] where we concluded nearly $350 billion of military and economic development for the United States, creating hundreds of thousands of jobs."* *(6/1/17)*

Trump has an incredibly misleading-statement-to-word-count ratio here. In just 28 words, he stretches three different truths:

He Forgot:

- *Trump, in September 2018: "We have to help them.... Tens of thousands of Kurds died fighting ISIS. They died for us and with us and for themselves...but they're great people...I don't forget.*

- *Trump, in October 2019, after green-lighting Turkey's invasion of Kurdish-held territory: "They didn't help us in the second World War [wrong: on side of Allies] they didn't help us with Normandy.... With all of that being said, we like the Kurds."*

1. A majority of that $350 billion is purely aspirational, involving memoranda of understanding that have still not come to fruition, according to the *Washington Post*, which obtained spreadsheets of the deals from the White House.
2. Many of the deals had been announced months earlier and were in the pipeline before Trump claimed credit.
3. Many of the projects are to be implemented in Saudi Arabia, calling into question how many American jobs would actually come out of the deal. Whatever the case, it was never "hundreds of thousands." According to a White House statement, the deal could "potentially" support "tens of thousands of jobs."

"Oil is becoming less and less of a reason [for the US military to stay in the Middle East] because we're producing more oil now than we've ever produced. So, you know, all of a sudden it gets to a point where you don't have to stay there." (11/27/18)

Every once in a while, instead of a string of falsehoods, Trump's lack of a filter results in taboo truths that his fellow Republicans probably wish he kept to himself. Rather than peace, democracy, liberation, or other useful euphemisms for American interventionism, Trump in this statement unashamedly gets at the heart of the reason for US military presence in the Middle East: Oil. Even a stopped clock...

"The Trump administration is putting the finishing touches on its long-awaited Middle East peace plan, three senior officials said on Sunday, and President Trump is likely to present it soon." The New York Times (3/11/18)

"I would say over the next two to three to four months, something like that. That would be the time that I might at least release the plan. It is a very complex situation, but I think we have some brilliant ideas." (9/26/18)

Tick-tock... The world is waiting for the real-estate tycoon's brilliant blueprint for solving one of the world's most difficult geopolitical issues. Forgive us if we're skeptical—especially after Trump has taken significant steps backward in the peace process by moving the US embassy in Israel to Jerusalem and by recognizing Israel's sovereignty over the contested Golan Heights region.

The Korean Peninsula

#13. The Hyperbolic & Apocalyptic: *"Just landed—a long trip, but everyone can now feel much safer than the day I took office. There is no longer a Nuclear Threat from North Korea." (6/13/18)*

"The sanctions are on [North Korea]. The missiles have stopped. The rockets have stopped. The hostages are home. The great heroes have been coming home." (11/12/18)

The same day Trump issued the second of these statements, the *New York Times* reported that "North Korea is moving ahead with its ballistic missile program at 16 hidden bases." The bases "have been identified in new commercial satellite images, a network long known to American intelligence agencies but left undiscussed as President Trump claims to have neutralized the North's nuclear threat." And in January 2019, the Director of National Intelligence wrote in a report that "we continue to observe activity inconsistent with full denuclearization" in North Korea.

While Trump brags "Mission Accomplished," his performance instead sounds like "Mission Impossible."

> *"There is nobody who understands the horror of nuclear more than me." (6/15/16)*

> *"North Korean Leader Kim Jong Un just stated that the 'Nuclear Button is on his desk at all times.' Will someone from his depleted and food starved regime please inform him that I too have a Nuclear Button, but it is a much bigger & more powerful one than his, and my Button works!" (1/2/18)*

> *"So we like South Korea. We've got 32,000 soldiers over there. Thank you very much, United States. They don't pay. They don't pay us, but that's OK. They're very successful." (10/9/18)*

> *"South Korea is costing us $5 billion a year. And they pay— they were paying about $500 million for $5 billion." (2/12/19)*

How generous of the US! Except there are 28,500 US soldiers in South Korea. And Seoul has always paid for roughly half of them. Moreover, the total share of the cost for US troops in South Korea is roughly $1.25 billion, not $5 billion. And the State Department, US Pacific Command, and the Senate Armed Services Committee have all described the troops' presence as mutually beneficial.

When Trump directly asked Mattis why the US was spending so much money to have so many US troops in South Korea, the defense secretary replied, "We're doing this in order to prevent World War III." That raises cost-benefit analysis to a whole new level.

"Basically, [North Korea] wanted the sanctions lifted in their entirety, and we couldn't do that. They were willing to de-nuke a large portion of the areas that we wanted, but we couldn't give up all of the sanctions for that." (2/28/19)

Being loose with the truth is always bad, but never more so than when it's this White House discussing nuclear weapons in the hands of a militant hostile dictatorship. In a rare move soon after this press conference, North Korean government officials called their own conference to deny Trump's assertion, instead claiming that Kim Jong-un asked for partial sanctions relief in exchange for closing his main nuclear complex. And it didn't take long to figure out who was telling the truth: according to a State Department official who briefed the media, Kim asked for lifting United Nations sanctions on the civilian economy, but nothing having to do with armaments.

The vice foreign minister of North Korea told the press that Trump's comments puzzled Kim, and that he "may have lost his will to continue North Korea–US dealings." It would be a massive price to pay for a small slip of the tongue, but that's what happens when a babbler is responsible for delicate matters of war and peace.

"Important actions today from @USTreasury; the maritime industry must do more to stop North Korea's illicit shipping practices. Everyone should take notice and review their own activities to ensure they are not involved in North Korea's sanctions evasion." National Security Adviser John Bolton (3/21/19)

"It was announced today by the U.S. Treasury that additional large scale Sanctions would be added to those already existing Sanctions on North Korea. I have today ordered the withdrawal of those additional Sanctions!" (3/22/19)

Amazing. It takes a special kind of incompetence for a president to directly contradict his national security adviser on Twitter—especially about something as massive as sanctions on a rogue nuclear state. It makes one wonder: when Trump sits down with Kim, does he actually know what he's negotiating?

After you finish cringing at Trump's ineptitude—and how out of touch he often is with the rest of his administration—try to imagine how challenging it must be to have to go on national television to defend him, knowing he's watching, but so are your professional peers. For examples, here are Pompeo and Bolton:

#16. Deny/Deny/Deny:

Jake Tapper, CNN: "Do you think North Korea remains a nuclear threat?"

Secretary of State Mike Pompeo: "Yes."

Tapper: "But the president said he doesn't."

Pompeo: "That's not what he said. I mean, I know precisely —"

Tapper: "He tweeted, 'There is no longer a nuclear threat from North Korea.'"

Pompeo: "Right. What he said is that the—what he said was that the efforts that had been made at Singapore, this commitment that Chairman Kim made, have substantially taken down the risk to the American people..."

Tapper: "Okay. I mean, that's just a direct quote, but I want to move on..." (2/24/19)

Chris Wallace, Fox News: "This is not the first time that the president has taken the word of an autocrat over outside evidence."

National Security Adviser John Bolton: "It's not taking his word. He said, I'm going to take—when he says, 'I'm going to take him at his word,' it doesn't mean that he accepted as reality—it means that he accepts what Kim Jong-un said."

Wallace: "So when he says, 'I take him at his word,' it doesn't mean that he believes Kim Jong-un?"

Bolton: "Well, that's what he said. I think one way to prove that is to give the United States a complete accounting." (3/4/19)

Terrorism

#18. The 180°: *On ISIS in Iraq: "I would take away the oil."*

Seventy seconds later: "I would bomb the hell out of those oil fields." (11/12/15)

Good thing Trump has mostly left battlefield strategy to his generals. It'd be pretty difficult to take away oil that's on fire.

"In the Middle East...not since Medieval times have people seen what's going on. I'd bring back waterboarding. And I'd bring back a hell of a lot worse than waterboarding." (2/6/16)

Trump was so focused on appealing to his base via geopolitical chest-thumping, he has no qualms about violating international law, or rehashing some of the Bush administration's biggest scandals.

THE DEATH-DEFYING HEROISM OF CADET BONE SPURS:

- *"I was down there and watched our police and our firemen down there on 7/11 [sic!] down at the World Trade Center right after it came down."* He wasn't—there's no record that he was there.
- *"I mean 40 Wall Street actually was the second-tallest building in downtown Manhattan and now [after 9/11] it's the tallest,"* he bragged on radio late morning of the attack.
- At a White House event celebrating the enactment of the 9/11 survivors' fund, Trump told the crowd of actual first responders, *"Many of those affected were firefighters, police officers and other first responders. And I was down there also. But I am not considering myself a first responder. But I was down there."* He claims.
- Barbara Res, the VP in charge of construction at the Trump Company, told Lawrence O'Donnell on MSNBC how three Trump casino executives and two crew members were killed in a helicopter crash in 1989. "It wasn't very long after the crash that he was putting out the word that he was supposed to be on that helicopter and at the last minute he got pulled off the plane. In other words, he'd be dead now. That was a total lie promoted by Trump." Res went on to condemn Trump for "making himself part of the story, undermining the fact that three people [from the company] died, just like he is undermining what happened on 9/11."

#2. Assertions and Adjectives: *"You look at what's happening in Germany, you look at what's happening last night in Sweden. Sweden! Who would believe this? Sweden! They took in large numbers [of refugees]. They're having problems like you never thought possible." (2/17/17)*

Trump is, of course, talking about terrorist attacks in Europe—supposedly in Germany and the previous evening in Sweden. According to a Swedish newspaper, however, these were some of the most eventful things to have happened the night before this speech:

- A depressed man (not a refugee or terrorist) set himself on fire and was taken to the hospital.
- A man died in a hospital after a workplace accident.
- Police chased down a drunk car thief in Stockholm.

"We have won against ISIS. We've beaten them badly.... We won." (12/19/18)

"The president has been, I think, as clear as he can be," John Bolton, Trump's national security adviser, later said, adding that 45 "has never said that the elimination of the territorial caliphate means the end of ISIS in toto."
   "In toto"... Right.

Iran

"We cannot prevent an Iranian bomb under the decaying and rotten structure of the current agreement.... Therefore, I am announcing today that the United States will withdraw from the Iran nuclear deal..." (5/8/18)

EM-BAR-RI-SING.
The Indian Government in 2019 had to deny that it asked President Trump to mediate its dispute with Pakistan, after 45 claimed it did in an Oval meeting with the PM of Pakistan. "It has been India's consistent position," said a statement from PM Modi's office, "that all outstanding issues with Pakistan are discussed only bilaterally."

WAR, WHAT IS IT GOOD FOR?

"Afghans seek clarity on Trump's talk of wiping country out," wire service headline of 7/23/19 after Trump said in Oval Office that he could kill "10 million" and "Afghanistan would be wiped off the face of the earth" in 2 to 3 days, but he won't do that.

Almost nine months after Trump reneged on the nuclear deal, Director of National Intelligence Dan Coats asserted that Iran was *still* not undertaking activities to produce a nuclear weapon, and CIA Director Gina Haspel testified that Iran was *still* in compliance with the deal.

But here's the bottom line: The US withdrew from a treaty that took two years to negotiate, on which fourteen other United Nations Security Council members signed off, which every other country in the world save Israel endorsed, and that successfully forced Iran to decommission its nuclear-enabling technology for at least fifteen years. It's hard to think of a more self-wounding action in the Middle East than encouraging Iran to return to its drive to develop a nuclear weapon.

Other international agreements Trump has abandoned as president:

- The Intermediate Nuclear Forces Treaty with Russia (1987)
- The Paris Agreement on climate change with nearly every country on Earth (2015)
- The Trans-Pacific Partnership on trade with 11 other nations (2016)
- The United States–Korea Free Trade Agreement (2012)
- The North American Free Trade Agreement (1994)
- The United Nations Human Rights Council with 47 other nations (1946)
- The United Nations Educational, Scientific, and Cultural Organization with nearly every country on Earth (1945)

"The intelligence people seem to be extremely passive and naïve when it comes to the dangers of Iran. They are wrong!... Perhaps Intelligence should go back to school!" (1/30/19)

"My intelligence people, if they said in fact that Iran is a wonderful kindergarten, I disagree with them 100 percent. It is a vicious country that kills many people.... So when my intelligence people tell me how wonderful Iran is—if you don't mind, I'm going to just go by my own counsel." (2/3/19)

These were Trump's responses to a 42-page report on national security threats from the Director of National Intelligence. Trump, who loves to tout his BS from the University of Pennsylvania's Wharton School of Business, apparently has a gut instinct more reliable than the world's most capable intelligence agencies.

And that gut instinct is leading Trump to trust his "own counsel," which includes Secretary of State Mike Pompeo. He has spent his tenure at the CIA and the State Department Dick Cheney-ing his way into forging connections between Iran and Al Qaeda in order to establish a pretense for war, and then National Security Adviser John Bolton, who had spent much of his career advocating for regime change in Iran.

#2. Assertions: *"What we've done to Iran since I've become president is rather miraculous. I ended the horrible, weak Iran nuclear deal. And I will tell you, Iran is a much different country today than it was two years ago. It's not the same and it won't be the same. And I do believe they want to talk." (1/17/19)*

Indeed, Iran is a "much different country," but not in the way Trump thinks.

"Sometimes I feel like he's on a reality show of some kind when he's talking about these foreign-policy issues. He doesn't realize that we could be headed toward World War III with the kind of comments that he's making."

Senator Bob Corker
(R-Tennessee) (10/8/17)

According to the International Crisis Group, since Trump backed out of the nuclear deal, Iran has done nothing to change its behavior in the region, which was the main goal of the withdrawal. Instead, with US sanctions reimplemented, regular Iranians are feeling the impact, with prices for such crucial goods as medicine and medical products surging. As for Trump's Panglossian view that a more peaceful Iran "wants to talk," in fact in June 2019, the US got within 10 minutes of starting a war with them in retaliation of an American drone they shot down.

> *"Now Obama, with the Iran deal, gave them $150 billion dollars and gave $1.8 billion in cash, in cash, in cash." (9/29/18)*

> *"[Obama] made a horrible deal, giving $150 billion in cash, actual cash, carried out in barrels and in boxes, from airplanes." (4/26/18)*

This story, which the president has told dozens of times, is an example of #The Lyin' King at his most effective. Trump's version of these events is visual, shocking, compelling, and terrible if true...but it's not. The real version is so complicated, however, that it's hard to counter his rapid-fire lies on a talk show. (See the summary on page 181 from the *Washington Post*'s Fact Checker.)

> Secretary of State Mike Pompeo: *"In an important step to counter the Iranian regime's terrorism, the US has designated the Islamic Revolutionary Guard Corps, incl. Qods [sic] Force, as a Foreign Terrorist Organization. We must help the people of Iran get back their freedom." (4/8/19)*

Iranian Foreign Minister Javad Zarif: *"[Trump officials] who have long agitated for FTO designation of the IRGC fully understand its consequences for US forces in the region. In fact, they seek to drag US into a quagmire on his behalf. @realDonaldTrump should know better than to be conned into another US disaster." (4/7/19)*

Jason Rezaian, the *Washington Post*: *"[This] blanket designation is ill-advised and will do little to change Iran's behavior. Even worse, though, it risks putting us one step closer to a military confrontation...yet another blunt and crude move in a situation that calls for more elegant solutions." (4/8/19)*

In April 2019, the Trump administration took its most concrete step to date in provoking war with Iran by designating Iran's Islamic Revolutionary Guard Corps—a state institution—a terrorist organization.

You know you've made a stupid move when the Iranian foreign minister and your (very mainstream) critics are making the same argument.

Venezuela

"[President Nicolas] Maduro is not a Venezuelan patriot. He is a Cuban puppet.... And today I have a message for every official who is helping to keep Maduro in place: The eyes of the entire world are upon you—today, every day, and every day in the future.... We seek a peaceful transition of power, but all options are open." (2/18/19)

"We stand with the Venezuelan people in their noble quest

"There's nobody bigger or better at the military than I am." (6/6/15)

for freedom, and we condemn the brutality of the Maduro regime, whose socialist policies have turned that nation from being the wealthiest in South America into a state of abject poverty and despair.... America will never be a socialist country." (2/5/19)

It's hard to argue that Nicolas Maduro isn't a bad guy. He has been known to violently quell dissent, he's engaged in dubious electoral practices, and his mismanagement has played a significant role in Venezuela's current economic situation, which has seen five-figure inflation, food and medicine shortages, and a mass exodus of economic refugees. But Trump's concern is disingenuous.

For one, Bolton, his national security adviser, has had his targets set on regime change in Venezuela for years. Privatizing the country's oil wealth is just too tempting—as he admitted to Fox Business in January 2019. But the real reason Trump is interested in bad-mouthing the Venezuelan regime is so he can then turn around and compare it to the Democratic Party—specifically its insurgent left wing—whom he accuses of being big bad socialists.

In keeping "all options" on the table in Venezuela—including the option of military intervention, which most experts have said would be a major disaster—Trump is playing with fire. Has anyone shared with him the inglorious legacy of US military involvement in Latin America? Apparently not, since he recently appointed Elliott Abrams as special envoy for Venezuela. Abrams was involved in much of that legacy, including:

- Helping to cover up the El Mozote massacre in 1981,

during which a US-backed Salvadoran military unit slaughtered over 800 people.
- Designing the Reagan administration's policy of supporting the counterrevolutionary Salvadoran government, which killed tens of thousands of civilians.
- Being one of the main architects of the Iran–Contra Affair, then pleading guilty to withholding information from Congress about it.

Problem: reality bites. After six months of Bolton saber-rattling, Maduro's still in charge, and Trump has moved on to a dozen other crises and scandals he can shout about.

The National-Security State

"I have intel people, but that doesn't mean I have to agree. President Bush had intel people that said that Saddam Hussein in Iraq had nuclear weapons, had all sorts of weapons of mass destruction. Guess what? Those intel people didn't know what the hell they were doing, and they got us tied up in a war that we should have never been in." (2/3/19)

Who "didn't know what the hell they were doing"? If President Bush had relied purely on his intelligence staff rather than on Dick Cheney's versions of intelligence, he may have come to a different, war-avoiding conclusion about Saddam Hussein and weapons of mass destruction.

Trump thinks he's making a clever point, but again, in relying on Pompeo, Bolton, and the other warmongers with whom he's surrounded himself over his intelligence agencies, he's setting himself up to make the exact same Bush-era misjudgments on military matters.

Trump speaking to U. N. General Assembly in 2018: *"In two years we have accomplished more than almost any administration in the history of our country."* [Laughter.] *"Didn't expect that reaction but that's ok."*

"The sad fact is that I never heard Mr. Trump say anything in private that led me to believe he loved our nation or wanted to make it better. In fact, he did the opposite."

Michael Cohen, former Trump fixer, under oath in front of the House Oversight Committee (2/17/19)

"President Trump continued to exaggerate the number of jobs generated by US arms sales, both to Saudi Arabia and globally. By the most generous estimate, total US arms sales-related jobs equal two-tenths of one percent of the US labor force. And many of these jobs are located overseas as a result of offset and manufacturing agreements."

William Hartung and Christina Arabia, "Trends in Major U.S. Arms Sales in 2018: The Trump Record—Rhetoric Versus Reality"

#20. Lyin' King: *"I don't think I have the authority to [push through Jared Kushner's security clearance].... I wouldn't—I wouldn't do that.... I was never involved with the security. I know that he—you know, just from reading—I know that there was issues back and forth about security for numerous people, actually. But I don't want to get involved in that stuff."* (1/31/19)

In an unconvincing performance, Trump explained to Maggie Haberman of the *New York Times* that he had nothing to do with his son-in-law gaining top-secret security clearance. But that turned out to be a five-star lie.

Less than a month after the interview, Haberman and other *Times* reporters revealed that Trump ordered his then-chief of staff, John Kelly, to grant Kushner's clearance, despite major concerns from top intelligence and White House officials. Kelly was so miffed by Trump's overreach that he wrote an internal memo explaining how he was "ordered" to grant the clearance, and the White House counsel at the time also wrote a memo—citing the CIA's concerns about Kushner—recommending that he not be granted the clearance.

Imagine that: Kushner—the real-estate heir put in charge of Middle East negotiations; who is accused of having leaked US intelligence to his best buddy Crown Prince Mohammed bin Salman of Saudi Arabia; who was part of the shady group to have met a Russian lawyer about "dirt" on Hillary Clinton in 2016; who didn't disclose meetings with the Russian ambassador on his security-clearance application—needed daddy-in-law's help to get access to top government secrets.

Bonus: Less than a week after the *New York Times*'s Kushner story, CNN reported that Trump also pressured Kelly to grant his daughter Ivanka security clearance. And a couple months later, a whistleblower in the White House told a House committee that senior administration officials granted clearance to *at least 25 people* whose applications had been denied by career intelligence officials. This is nepotism on a scale that would have impressed the Borgias.

In May 2019, National Security Adviser John Bolton said the US was deploying an aircraft carrier strike group to the Middle East to "send a clear and unmistakable message to the Iranian regime."

Number of "unsafe" interactions between US ships and the Iranian military, according to the US Navy:

- 2018: 0
- 2019: 0

> "Trump's reference to $1.8 billion refers to the timing of a settlement of a long-standing claim regarding undelivered aircraft made by Iran on the same day four American detainees...were released. State Department officials have insisted that the negotiations over the claims and detainees were connected, but came together at the same time, with the cash payment used as 'leverage' to ensure the release of detainees."
> –The *Washington Post*'s Fact Checker

Nor did Obama "pay" Iran billions; with sanctions lifted as part of Iran Nuke deal, those funds—Iran's funds—could be returned.

ANDY BOROWITZ, *THE NEW YORKER'S* BOROWITZ REPORT:

"Using some of his harshest rhetoric in recent memory, President Donald J. Trump came out strongly against intelligence on Wednesday morning...

   "He said that he has chosen, instead, to seek advice from his son-in-law, Jared Kushner, and from his elder children, Ivanka, Eric, and Donald, Jr. 'You won't find a trace of intelligence in anything they say,' he boasted.

   "At a briefing for the White House press corps, the President's press secretary, Sarah Huckabee Sanders, denied that Trump's war on intelligence was a new development. 'Intelligence has never played a role in Donald Trump's life,' she said." (1/30/19)

"I'm really good at war. I love war." (11/12/15)

14.
PUTIN
AND HIS SIBERIAN CANDIDATE

Chapter 13 makes clear that Trump loves to cozy up to some of the world's most despotic ruling men. But there's one autocrat with whom Trump's relationship is especially… special. That is, of course, Russian President Vladimir Putin.

Trump's relationship with Putin is still somewhat of a mystery. Though Special Counsel Robert Mueller's report didn't find a provable criminal conspiracy between Team Trump and Team Putin to coordinate Russia's intervention in the 2016 presidential election, they did disclose some 140 contacts between them despite Trump saying previously there were none. Trump's public comments, his history with Russians, and his bizarre deference to Putin raise all sorts of alarms.

At the least, it should prove to be great TV when, during the first presidential debate in the Fall of 2020, the GOP nominee asserts that Democrats are "socialists," as the Democratic nominee calmly replies, "That sounds odd coming from an apologist for the biggest communist in the world…since you're in bed with Putin and side with him over our country."

"Do you think Putin will be going to The Miss Universe Pageant in November in Moscow—if so, will he become my new best friend?" (6/18/13)

"I think [Putin has] done really a great job of outsmarting our country." (10/3/13)

Photo by Drew Angerer/Getty Images

"America is at a great disadvantage. Putin is ex-KGB, Obama is a community organizer. Unfair." (4/17/14)

"He is a strong leader. What am I going to say, 'He's a weak leader?' He's making mince meat out of our president. He is a strong leader..." (2/17/16)

#2. Assertions & Adjectives: Trump spent years bashing President Obama over Twitter—accusing him of being weak, dumb, and unpatriotic. When it came time to campaign for the 2016 election, he contrasted himself as the opposite—strong, smart, and ready to Make America Great Again.

But before 2016, whom did Trump use to present a contrast to the president? Putin, of course. Never mind that he's a murderous tyrant who oversees an oligarchic state—Trump admires Putin because Putin is Trump's model president.

"I think I'd get along very well with Vladimir Putin. I just think so.... Obama and him—he hates Obama, and Obama hates him." (7/31/15)

That Trump thinks in such oversimplified terms is remarkable. "An enemy of my enemy is my friend," even when my enemy is my American predecessor, and my friend is the head of a nation that is often hostile to the one I am vying to lead. That patriotic?

"I got to know [Putin] very well because we were both on 60 Minutes. We were stablemates, and we did very well that night." (11/10/15)

#20. The Lyin' King: "Stablemates?" Trump and Putin were on other sides of the world when they were interviewed by *60 Minutes* in 2015, and they were interviewed at different times. But anything to seem closer to your best buddy, right?

Gesturing to reporters during a meetup with Putin: "Get rid of them. Fake news is a great term, isn't it? You don't have this problem in Russia but we do." (6/28/19)

Oh, great, let's just make jokes about eliminating journalists with the head of state who has seen 26 journalists killed under his watch.

Putin: "[Trump] is a very flamboyant man—very talented, no doubt about that. He is an absolute leader of the presidential race. That's the way we see it today." (12/17/15)

The day after Putin heaped this praise on Trump, Trump repaid the favor by taking to MSNBC's *Morning Joe* to defend Putin from allegations that he has ordered the assassination of journalists:

#12. The Hyperbolic and Apocalyptic: *"He's running his country and at least he's a leader, unlike what we have in this country... I think our country does plenty of killing also."* *(12/18/15)*

Then came Trump's deference to Putin during the 2018 Helsinki Summit, when he took the Russian leader's word over all of his national security experts in his own government:

Photo by Chris McGrath/Getty Images

#16. Deny/Deny/Deny: *"My people came to me. [Director of National Intelligence] Dan Coats came to me, and some others. They said they think it's Russia [who interfered in the 2016 election]. I have President Putin. He just said it's not Russia. I will say this: I don't see any reason why it would be." (7/16/18)*

In the days following the Helsinki summit, Trump tried to retract his statement in the Trumpiest way possible: he tried to convince the press that what he had meant to say was that he didn't see a reason why it "wouldn't" have been Russia. Also, the dog ate his homework.

To make matters worse, post-summit Trump simply refused to brief his team on what went on in his private meetings with Putin. "We are completely in the dark. Completely," a US ambassador in Europe told *The New Yorker*'s Susan Glasser.

In fact, Putin and Trump have met at least *six* times since

On March 10, 2017, in the Oval Office, Trump indiscreetly bragged to the top two Russian diplomats in the Oval Office about how he had just fired James Comey, looking on camera like a giddy Kevin Costner at the end of *No Way Out*, debriefing himself to his Soviet handlers. "He was crazy, a real nut job. I faced great pressure because of Russia," he told the Russians, "that's taken off."

Problem: he mentioned classified intel to them that the CIA worried would expose Israeli intelligence and, worse, told them that he didn't think their "meddling" in 2016 was "a big deal," which obviously gave Putin the green light to again try to boost him in 2020. The Agency then determined that the American president couldn't be trusted to keep classified information secret and so it decided to extract its top covert agent from the Kremlin for his own safety.

(continued next page)

Trump became president, and nobody knows for sure what was said in any of those meetings. Besides the Helsinki summit:

- They first met at a G20 summit in Germany in July 2017. After the conversation, Trump took his interpreter's notes and told him not to disclose what he had heard in the meeting to anyone.
- They met a second time on that Germany trip. Trump pulled a seat next to Putin, and they spoke without any American witnesses.
- After they spoke at a summit in Vietnam in November 2017, Trump seemed to take Putin at his word that he didn't interfere in the 2016 elections.
- In late 2018, Trump spoke to Putin even after claiming that he wouldn't. It only came out weeks later that the conversation occurred without any other Americans present.
- And in June 2019, they met during the G20 summit in Japan.

According to ex-FBI deputy Andrew McCabe, Putin once told Trump that, per Russian intelligence, North Korea didn't have the ability to hit the US mainland with missiles. When FBI staff countered, saying that US intelligence concluded otherwise, Trump reportedly responded:

"I don't care. I believe Putin."

When it comes to national security, how come Russia gets two presidents and we, apparently, get none?

Timothy Snyder, a professor of history at Yale, authored the 2018 book *Road to Unfreedom: Russia, Europe, America*. In it, he outlined at least 50 reasons why Trump might owe a debt to Russia in general and Vladimir Putin in particular, such as:

3. "In 1987, the Soviet state paid for Mr. Trump to visit Moscow, putting him up in a suite that was certainly bugged."

4. "In 2006, Russians and other citizens of the former Soviet Union financed Trump SoHo, granting Mr. Trump 18 percent of the profits—although he put up no money himself."

18. "In October 2015, while running for president, Mr. Trump signed a letter of intent to have Russians build a tower in Moscow and put his name on it. The Trump Organization planned to give its penthouse to Mr. Putin as a present."

26. "A Russian military intelligence officer bragged in May 2016 that his organization would take revenge on Hillary Clinton on behalf of Mr. Putin."

"Russia, if you're listening, I hope you're able to find the 30,000 emails that are missing, I think you will probably be rewarded mightily by our press." (7/27/16)

"If you tell a joke, if you're sarcastic, if you're having fun with the audience, if you're on live television with millions of people and 25,000 people in an arena—and you say something like, 'Russia, please, if you can, get us Hillary Clinton's emails! Please, Russia, please! Please get us the emails! Please!' [Crowd chanting: 'Lock her up!'] So everybody's having a good time; I'm laughing, we're all having fun, and the fake news, CNN and all the others, say, [mocking stern voice:] 'He asked Russia to get the emails.' Horrible." (3/2/19)

Think about it: Trump ran in 2016 screaming about how Hillary Clinton should be in jail for knowingly releasing classified information in emails (which she didn't do) yet in this case did exactly that to Russians directly, no emails needed. Not treason, as defined by the Constitution, but treacherous.

Whose side is this guy on? All of which led one senior German politician to call Trump "a security risk for the entire Western world."

Trump: "Russia would much rather have Hillary than Donald Trump, I can tell you that right now." (3/27/19)

Trump would love to dismiss the media's alarm at his 2016 speech, during which he asked Russia to hack Clinton's emails, as just more Fake News (see Chapter 10). But it turns out that the press was right to be skeptical. According to the Mueller Report, Russian hackers went after Clinton's emails just hours after Trump "joked" about it: "Within approximately five hours of Trump's statement, GRU officers targeted for the first time Clinton's personal office."

After candidate Trump's remarks, Unit 26165 created and sent malicious links targeting 15 email accounts at the domain [redacted], including an email account belonging to Clinton aide [redacted]. The investigation did not find evidence of earlier attempts to compromise email accounts hosted on this domain."

"We are witnessing nothing less than the breakdown of American foreign policy. This week's extraordinary confusion over even the basic details of the Helsinki summit shows that all too clearly." —Susan Glasser, The New Yorker (7/19/18)

Putin, though, when asked if he preferred Trump and thought Trump would have been a more Russia-friendly president than Hillary Clinton: *"Yes, I did. Yes, I did. Because he talked about bringing the US–Russia relationship back to normal." (7/16/18)*

"Withdraw from the Trans-Pacific Partnership...criticize NATO and cast doubt on America's willingness to defend its allies...start a trade war with our closest allies.... There is not evidence that Mr. Putin is dictating American policy. But it's hard to imagine how he could do much better, even if he were." —Susan Rice, former Obama national security advisor and ambassador to the UN, the New York Times (6/8/18)

15.
SPRINGTIME FOR DICTATORS
"UNDER ARTICLE II, I HAVE THE RIGHT TO DO WHATEVER I WANT."

It was a mere three years ago in March of 2016 that Representative Mike Pompeo (R – KS) predicted at a political rally that presidential candidate Donald Trump would be "an authoritarian president who ignored our Constitution."

Garry Kasparov, the brilliant Russian chessmaster who is an expert on authoritarian rulers, said that he understands Trump's attraction to them. "He likes how they don't bother to explain 'why' they take a particular course of action but rather simply say 'why not?'"

The House of Saud

"I have great confidence in King Salman and the Crown Prince of Saudi Arabia, they know exactly what they are doing. Some of those they are harshly treating have been 'milking' their country for years!" (11/6/17)

In this seemingly innocuous statement, Trump defends Saudi Crown Prince Salman's so-called crackdown on corruption, during which he arrested dozens of Saudi princes and officials, detained them at the Ritz Carlton Hotel in Riyadh, shook them down for billions of dollars, tortured some of them, and killed one.

#16. Deny/Deny/Deny: *"It could very well be that the crown prince had knowledge of this tragic—maybe he did and maybe he didn't!... We may never know all of the facts surrounding the murder of Mr. Jamal Khashoggi. In any case, our relationship is with the Kingdom of Saudi Arabia." (11/20/18)*

Yet another example of Trump trying to create his own reality—except a dismembered columnist shot back. Four days *prior* to this statement, the *New York Times* reported that the CIA "has concluded that the Saudi crown prince, Mohammed bin Salman, ordered the killing of the journalist Jamal Khashoggi."

2015: "I like the Saudis. I make a lot of money with them. They buy all sorts of my stuff. All kinds of toys from Trump. They pay me millions and hundreds of millions." (7/16/15)

2017: "Saudi Arabia, I get along with all of them. They buy apartments from me. They spend $40 million, $50 million." (8/21/17)

#20. The Lyin' King: *2018: "And by the way, never did business with them, never intend to do business with [the Saudis]. I couldn't care less." (11/27/18)*

In order to more effectively defend his personal allies in Saudi Arabia from public backlash after the Khashoggi murder, Trump tried to make it seem as though he were acting as an impartial, rational diplomat by separating himself from any personal ties to the Saudis. But he's no objective diplomat, and his charade couldn't escape his own campaign remarks about profiting from the royal family. Or, as the British say, "hoisted with his own petard."

A Saudi prince, for example, paid $20 million for Trump's yacht, "Princess," in 1991, and in 2001 the Kingdom paid $12 million for the entire 45th floor of Trump World Tower. A lobbying firm hired by Saudi Arabia spent $270,000 at the Trump International Hotel in 2016 and 2017. And Saudi business with Trump hotels has seen a significant uptick since Trump took office.

"[Mohammed bin Salman] bragged to the Emirati crown prince and others that [Jared] Kushner was 'in his pocket'.... Indeed, Kushner has grown so close to the Saudi and Emirati crown princes that he has communicated with them directly using WhatsApp, a reasonably secure messaging app owned by Facebook and popular in the Middle East." *The Intercept* (3/21/18)

The love affair between the oligarchic ruling family of Saudi Arabia and the oligarchic ruling family of the United States is "in plain sight." Not only has Trump's son-in-law and appointed Middle East peace envoy, Jared Kushner, gotten buddy-buddy enough with Arab crown princes that he communicates with them via messaging services, but, according to *The Daily Mail*, Kushner may have provided the Saudi crown prince with classified US intelligence on the officials he targeted as part of his above-mentioned corruption crackdown.

That's some next-level international corruption.

North Korea: Kim Don-un

#12. The Hyperbolic and Apocalyptic: *"North Korea best not make any more threats to the United States. They will be met with fire and fury like the world has never seen."* (8/8/17)

"Why would Kim Jong-un insult me by calling me 'old,' when I would NEVER call him 'short and fat'?" (11/11/17)

"When a conservative says that totalitarian communism is an absolute enemy of human freedom, he is not theorizing—he is reporting the ugly reality."

Ronald Reagan (2/6/77)

"Mr. Trump's chumminess with one of the globe's most notorious despots would have been noteworthy under any circumstances. It was all the more striking coming on the heels of the president slamming Justin Trudeau, the prime minister of Canada— one of America's closest allies—as 'weak,' 'meek' and 'very dishonest.'"

The *New York Times* editorial (6/12/18)

Jejune threats and name-calling seem like odd ways to deal with a dictator seeking nuclear capabilities. Luckily, they didn't last for long: eventually, Trump's "fire and fury" turned into... something very, very different.

> *"[Kim Jong-un and I] had great chemistry. You know how I feel about chemistry. It's very important. I know people where there is no chemistry. No matter what you do, you just don't have it. We had it right from the beginning." (6/12/18)*

> *"He wrote me beautiful letters. And they're great letters. We fell in love." (9/29/18)*

It's like a bad rom-com: Two seemingly incompatible characters—one the head of a corporate capitalist superpower, the other leading an isolated communist dictatorship—eventually come to find that they are kindred spirits, united in their admiration for each other's natural despotism.

Trump's remarks bring to mind George W. Bush's comment, in 2001, that he could look in Vladimir Putin's eyes "and get a sense of his soul." At the time, that was widely considered to be a serious blunder, but nothing compared to Trump and Kim falling "in love."

> *"Look, he's the head of his country—he's the strong-head. Don't let anyone think different. He speaks and his people sit up at attention. I want my people to do the same." (6/15/18)*

You gotta hand it to him, Trump is subversive. Only he would be able to turn nuclear-disarmament talks into an office-culture seminar for White House staff.

"Otto Warmbier was a hardworking student at the University of Virginia. On his way to study abroad in Asia, Otto joined a tour to North Korea. At its conclusion, this wonderful young man was arrested and charged with crimes against the state. After a shameful trial, the dictatorship sentenced Otto to 15 years of hard labor, before returning him to America last June—horribly injured and on the verge of death. He passed away just days after his return." (1/30/18)

#3. Performance Artist: *"What happened is horrible. I really believe something very bad happened to him, and I don't think that top leadership knew about it.... I don't believe that [Kim] would have allowed that to happen.... He felt very badly about it.... He tells me he didn't know about it, and I will take him at his word."* (2/28/19)

"It kind of took my breath away to listen to that. I can't but imagine what it must have been like for Mr. Warmbier's parents and the family to hear him say that." John Kirby, former Navy admiral and State Department press secretary (2/28/19)

"Americans know, the world knows, Kim Jong-un knows, and most importantly, the Warmbier family knows that Otto suffered a cruel death inflicted by a brutal regime serving Kim Jong-un." Representative Warren Davidson (R-Ohio) (2/28/19)

Trump believes in a dictator's definition of truth: Whatever the leader says, apparently goes. What do victims of a regime—or all citizens for that matter—think when they hear the American president say that?

(It later came out that Trump approved a plan to pay North Korea $2 million for the release of Warmbier. So much for his criticism of Obama paying Iran money the US had already promised in order to get a nuclear deal off the ground [see Chapter 14].)

Representative Tom Malinowski (D-New Jersey): *"Is Kim Jong-un responsible for maintaining North Korea's system of labor camps?"*
Secretary of State Mike Pompeo: *"He's the leader of the country."*
Malinowski: *"Is he responsible for ordering the execution of his uncle, and the assassination by chemical agent of his half-brother?"*
Pompeo: *"He's the leader of the country."*
Malinowski: *"Was he responsible for the decision not to allow Otto Warmbier to come home until he was on death's door?"*
Pompeo: *"I'll leave the president's statement to stand. He made that statement. We all know that the North Korean regime was responsible for the tragedy that occurred to Otto Warmbier. I met that family. I know those people. I love them dearly. They suffered mightily, sir."*
Malinowski: *"So what's to like?"* (3/29/19)

The Philippines: Rodrigo Duterte

#2. Assertions and Adjectives: *"I just wanted to congratulate you because I am hearing of the unbelievable job on the drug problem.... Many countries have the problem, we have a problem, but what a great job you are doing, and I just wanted to call and tell you that."* (5/2/17)

President Rodrigo Duterte has waged a murderous war on drug use and drug trafficking in the Philippines, calling for the extrajudicial killing of drug users and dealers and unleashing his police to inflict widespread violence. In 2016 and 2017, this so-called "drug war," which Trump endorsed in this phone call to Duterte, claimed more than 12,000 lives.

"Trump often jokes about killing drug dealers.... He'll say, 'You know, the Chinese and Filipinos don't have a drug problem. They just kill them.'" Senior Trump administration official (2/25/18)

At one point, Trump's outward admiration for Duterte could have plausibly been chalked up to ignorance. He doesn't read his intelligence briefings, and he has a tenuous grasp on global affairs in general, especially as they relate to human rights. But this statement, recounted by a senior administration official, says everything we need to know about the president's emerging authoritarianism.

Egypt: Abdel Fattah el-Sisi

"We agree on so many things.... I just want to let everybody know, in case there was any doubt, that we are very much behind President el-Sisi. He's done a fantastic job in a very difficult situation." (4/3/17)

Trump invests a lot of political capital in personal relationships. And while that may work for scoring real-estate deals, it's unclear how currying favor with a despot who has overseen what rights groups call the harshest political repression in Egypt's history advances US national security interests. What

"Hitler massacred 3 million Jews. Now there is 3 million, what is it, 3 million drug addicts [in the Philippines].... I'd be happy to slaughter them. At least if Germany had Hitler, the Philippines would have me. You know my victims, I would like them to be all criminals, to finish the problem of my country and save the next generation from perdition."

Rodrigo Duterte (9/30/16)

"An American president does not lead the Free World by congratulating dictators on winning sham elections."

John McCain (3/20/18)

"Modern tyranny is terror management. When the terrorist attack comes, remember that authoritarians exploit such events in order to consolidate power. The sudden disaster that requires the end of checks and balances, the dissolution of political parties, the suspension of freedom of expression, the right to a fair trial, and so on, is the oldest trick in the Hitlerian book."

Timothy Snyder, *On Tyranny: Twenty Lessons from the Twentieth Century*

is clear is that Trump has interred the human-rights policies of all US presidents since Jimmy Carter. No one today writes of America, in international affairs, as "the shining city on a hill."

"Remember who I'm talking to. [El-Sisi's] a fucking killer. This guy's a fucking killer! I'm getting it done. He'll make you sweat on the phone."

Trump is to murderous strongmen what teenage boys are to professional wrestlers—they both get off on idolizing those whom they perceive to be powerful, even if they're also villains.

Turkey: Recep Tayyip Erdoğan

"President Donald J. Trump spoke today with President Recep Tayyip Erdoğan of Turkey to congratulate him on his referendum victory." White House readout (4/17/17)

"Trump's comments differed in tone from those of the State Department, which urged Turkey to respect the basic rights of its citizens and noted election irregularities witnessed by monitors." The Washington Post (4/17/17)

Trump and his State Department always seem most at odds when it comes to the basic themes of US values: free and fair elections, antiauthoritarianism—democracy. In April 2017, Erdoğan narrowly won a nationwide referendum that greatly expanded his powers as president of Turkey. In addition to concerns from the international community that this was the first step in transitioning Turkey to an "elected dictatorship," international observers also pointed out that as many as 2.5 million votes could have been tampered with in Erdoğan's favor.

When Trump called Erdoğan after the referendum, there was, of course, no mention of any irregularities. No mention of free and fair elections. Only congratulations.

"OK, [Syria]'s all yours. We are done!" (12/14/18)

Trump told this to President Erdoğan during a phone call, per a senior administration official, knowing that Erdoğan was hoping to attack the Kurdish regions in Syria's north. He was eventually forced to eat his words by John Bolton, his national security advisor, who contradicted his boss's plans to withdraw troops from Syria a few weeks later, until Trump precipitously did just that a year later after one phone call from Erdogan, throwing the Middle East into even more turmoil.

Brazil: Jair Bolsonaro

#2. Assertions and Adjectives: *"I also know that [Brazilian President Jair Bolsonaro and I] are going to have a fantastic working relationship. We have many views that are similar."*

"As I told President Bolsonaro, I also intend to designate Brazil as a 'major non-NATO ally,' or even possibly, if you start thinking about it, maybe a NATO ally—have to talk to a lot of people, but maybe a NATO ally—which will greatly advance security and cooperation between our countries."

"I'm very proud to hear the president use the term 'fake news.'" (3/19/19)

It was pretty much a given that Trump was going to go gaga over Brazil's newly elected president, Jair Bolsonaro. The

"Ivana Trump told her lawyer that from time to time her husband reads a book of Hitler's collected speeches, My New Order, *which he keeps in a cabinet by his bed."*

Marie Brenner in *Vanity Fair,* 1990.

KNEEL BEFORE ZOD!
Explaining his unquestioned authority, Trump bragged that had he ordered a soldier to commit a war crime, "the soldier would do it."

"If imitation is the highest form of flattery, authoritarian despots across the globe must be feeling pretty flattered by President Trump."

Brian Klaas, author of *The Despot's Apprentice: Donald Trump's Attack on Democracy* (1/13/18)

fascist (that's not an overstatement) politician—who openly admires Brazil's former military dictatorship, who makes rape jokes, who would like to ban homosexuality, who rails against "gender ideology," who wants to level the Amazon and extract its resources—is often called "the Trump of the tropics." And Trump loves it.

Harvard political science professors Steven Levitsky and Daniel Ziblatt–coauthors of *How Democracies Die*–have identified four warning signs that indicate authoritarianism on a dangerous level:

1. Rejecting or showing weak commitment to democratic rules.
2. Denying the legitimacy of political opponents.
3. Encouraging or tolerating violence.
4. A readiness to stifle or limit civil liberties of opponents, including media.

According to Levitsky and Ziblatt, Trump embodies all four of those warning signs.

"We should definitely be concerned. Unambiguously, Trump checks off all the boxes for a very authoritarian figure." Steve Levitsky, author of *How Democracies Die* (6/15/18)

"The truth unquestionably is, that the only path to a subversion of the republican system of the Country is, by flattering the prejudices of the people, and exciting their jealousies and apprehensions, to throw affairs into confusion, and bring on civil commotion. Tired at length of anarchy, or want of government, they may take shelter in the arms of monarchy for repose and security.

When a man unprincipled in private life desperate in his fortune, bold in his temper, possessed of considerable talents, having the advantage of military habits—despotic in his ordinary demeanour—known to have scoffed in private at the principles of liberty—when such a man is seen to mount the hobby horse of popularity—to join in the cry of danger to liberty—to take every opportunity of embarrassing the General Government & bringing it under suspicion—to flatter and fall in with all the non sense of the zealots of the day—It may justly be suspected that his object is to throw things into confusion that he may 'ride the storm and direct the whirlwind.'"
Alexander Hamilton (1792)

16.
ALLIES
DIPLOMACY BY FRENEMY

"My views on treating allies with respect are strongly held and informed by over four decades of immersion in these issues…. Because you have a right to a Secretary of Defense whose views are better aligned with yours on these and other subjects, I believe it is right for me to step down in my position." —Former Secretary of Defense Jim Mattis (12/20/18)

This is probably the politest "you're an idiot" resignation letter Trump could have hoped for from his secretary of defense. Over the course of two years, Mattis not only had to put up with Trump's nonsensical statements when it came to matters of war and peace (see Chapter 15), he also had to deal with Trump's inflammatory rhetoric toward some of the US's most important and long-standing allies.

The United Kingdom

"If you remember, I was opening Turnberry the day before Brexit. We had an unbelievably large number of reporters there... And all they wanted to talk about was Brexit, and they asked for my opinion. And I think you will agree that I said I think Brexit will happen, and it did happen." [emphasis added]. (7/13/16)

Trump was at Turnberry Golf Club in Scotland the day *after* Brexit, not the day before. Is it prescience when you guess the score of a Yankee game the day after it's been played? *Yes* in Trumplandia.

Two weeks before Brexit, *The Hollywood Reporter* published a profile of Trump that suggested that, apart from having something to do with immigration, Trump had no idea what Brexit was all about:

"'And Brexit ? Your position ?' I ask.

'Huh?'

'Brexit.'

'Hmm.'

'The Brits leaving the EU,' I prompt, realizing that his lack of familiarity with one of the most pressing issues in Europe is for him no concern or liability at all.

'Oh yeah, I think they *should* leave.'" [emphasis added]

#12. The Hyperbolic and Apocalyptic: *"Our country has regained the respect that we used to have long ago abroad. Yes, they are respecting us again. Yes, America is back." (5/25/18)*

"Trump is reviled around the globe and America is going down with its captain." Charles Blow, the *New York Times (10/16/17)*

"I actually told Theresa May how to [conduct Brexit negotiations], but she didn't agree. She didn't listen to me.... She wrecked it."

"I have a lot of respect for Boris. He obviously likes me, and says very good things about me.... He would make a great prime minister." (7/13/18)

**"AMERICA IS BACK."
(5/25/18)**

Unless he meant to say, "America is on its back," the opposite is true. (See poll references below.)
Pew Poll: Confidence in the US President 2015 / 2017
United Kingdom: 76% / 22%
Germany: 73% / 11%
France: 83% / 14%
Canada: 76% / 22%
Mexico: 49% / 5%
South Korea: 88% / 17%
Israel: 49% / 56%
Russia: 11% / 53%

In an interview with the UK's *The Sun*, Trump belittled British Prime Minister Theresa May about Brexit negotiations, even going so far as to assert that her Tory rival, Boris Johnson, would have made for a great prime minister himself. And if the comments themselves weren't tactless enough, Trump made them right before a face-to-face meeting with May to be held later that day (see below).

Imagine what Trump and the GOP would have done if May, while visiting the US, had urged senators to oppose the nomination of Brett Kavanaugh to the Supreme Court the day before his close confirmation vote. (As for Johnson "obviously" liking Trump, here's what he said about the president just a week before: "Imagine Trump doing Brexit. He'd go in bloody hard.... There'd be all sorts of breakdowns, all sorts of chaos.

The White House, via Wikimedia Commons

Everyone would think he'd gone mad. But actually you might get somewhere.")

#3. Performance Artist: *"May I give our relationship, in terms of a grade, the highest level of special. So we start off with special. I would give our relationship with the UK—and now, especially after this two days with your prime minister—I would say the highest level of special. Am I allowed to go higher than that? [Turns to May.] I'm not sure. But's it's the highest level of special."* (7/13/18)

Props to May for keeping a straight face here given Trump's volte-face from only a few hours before. Has any US president *ever* done anything as remotely insulting and erratic to an ally as this?

- *December, 1994:* Buckingham Palace issued this denial after the *New York Post* reported that Prince Charles and Princess Diana would be taking a membership in Trump's soon-to-be-opened Mar-a-Lago: "The story is absolute nonsense. This story was concocted by Mr. Trump to secure publicity for his club. It is a matter of regret that he feels he can use the names of the members of the royal family to do so."
- *June, 2019,* on *Fox* discussing his talks with Queen Elizabeth: *"There are those who say they have never seen the queen have a better time, a more animated time. We had a period where we were talking solid straight. I didn't even know who the other people were. I never spoke to them; we just had a great time."*

The European Union

"I told you @TIME Magazine would never pick me as person of the year despite being the big favorite. They picked [Angela Merkel] who is ruining Germany." (12/9/15)

"What Merkel did to Germany is a shame. It's a sad, sad shame what's happened to Germany.... I have friends in Germany, they want to leave Germany. These are people that two years ago were telling me that it's the greatest place on Earth, and now they want to leave." (3/26/16)

Trump's alienation of close (and important) European allies started on the campaign trail. It's sloppy, tactless, unpresidential—but completely on-brand for Trump, whose supporters love him for supposedly "telling it like it is."

Trump's zero-sum view of global affairs implies that there's no such thing as international cooperation—just play or be played. Well, except when it comes to dictators. Then things get lovey-dovey (see Chapter 15).

Susan B. Glasser wrote in a December 2018 *New Yorker* piece that German chancellor Angela Merkel called for an emergency meeting during the summer NATO summit. She detailed Trump's anger at NATO, which had been presented a case for Ukraine and George to join the alliance. She described his reaction to Merkel in particular:

"His barrage centered on Merkel, Europe's longest-serving democratic leader. 'You, Angela,' Trump chided Merkel. Most of NATO's members had failed to fulfill the goal of spending two per cent of their G.D.P.'s for defense, but Trump focused on Germany's military spending of just over one per cent of

G.D.P."

Trump is a well-known teetotaler. But it's hard to read this *New Yorker* rendition of the 2018 NATO summit without imagining a rambling drunk stumbling into a high-level meeting and making it all about him.

> *"Germany is totally controlled by Russia.... They will be getting between 60 and 70 percent of their energy from Russia and a new pipeline, and you tell me if that is appropriate because I think it's not.... I think it is a very bad thing for NATO and I don't think it should have happened. (7/11/18)*

Speaking of making it all about him, at the NATO summit, Trump couldn't shut up about Germany's pipeline project with Russia and its level of defense spending, even though, shortly before the summit, Merkel promised an increase in the country's defense budget. Trump is able to suck all of the air out of a room by just winging it—even in a room filled with some of the world's most powerful and knowledgeable people.

#4. Insult Machine: *"I think what's happened to Europe is a shame. I think the immigration—allowing the immigration to take place in Europe is a shame. I think it changed the fabric of Europe. And unless you act very quickly, it's never going to be what it was. And I don't mean that in a positive way. I think allowing millions and millions of people into Europe is very sad. I think you're losing your culture." (7/12/18)*

If Trump's obsession with white-nationalist talking points on US immigration (see Chapter 17) isn't enough to convince people that he himself is a white nationalist, perhaps his remarks

*"We don't really
believe the Trump
Administration is going
to become substantially
more normal; less
dysfunctional; less
unpredictable; less
faction riven; less
diplomatically clumsy
and inept."*

Former UK Ambassador
to the US Kim Darroch

about black and brown refugees denigrating the "culture" of other white-majority countries will settle the controversy.

Mexico

#2. Assertions and Adjectives: *"You have some pretty tough hombres in Mexico that you may need help with, and we are willing to help you with that big-league.... And I know this is a tough group of people, and maybe your military is afraid of them, but our military is not afraid of them, and we will help you with that 100 percent because it is out of control—totally out of control." (1/27/17)*

#3. Performance Artist: *"The fact is, we are both in a little bit of a political bind, because I have to have Mexico pay for the wall—I have to.... You cannot say that [you are not going to pay] to the press. The press is going to go with that and I cannot live with that. You cannot say that to the press because I cannot negotiate under those circumstances.... If you are going to say that Mexico is not going to pay for the wall, then I do not want to meet with you guys anymore because I cannot live with that." (1/27/17)*

Trump isn't Stephen Colbert—he isn't able to switch personalities when he's in the spotlight, as the latter did in Comedy Central's *Colbert Report*. With this shockingly irreverent—and leaked—call to Mexican President Enrique Peña Nieto just a week after his inauguration, the president showed that Trump the diplomat is the same as Trump the rally leader is the same as Trump the reality-television star—all of which are absurd in substance and style.

Australia

#4. Insult Machine: *"Look, I spoke to Putin, Merkel, Abe of Japan, to France today, and this was my most unpleasant call because I will be honest with you, I hate taking these [refugees]. I guarantee you they are bad.... They are not going to be wonderful people who go on to work for the local milk people.... I have had it. I have been making these calls all day, and this is the most unpleasant call of the day. Putin was a pleasant call. This is ridiculous."* (1/28/17)

Again, only a week after the start of his presidency, Trump went off on Prime Minister Malcolm Turnbull of Australia when Turnbull mentioned a deal he struck with President Obama to relocate some 1,200 refugees to the United States.

Japan

#12. The Hyperbolic and Apocalyptic: *"I think I can say this: Prime Minister Abe of Japan gave me the most beautiful copy of a letter that he sent to the people who give out a thing called the Nobel Peace Prize.... I mean, it was the most beautiful five-letter—five-page letter. Nobel Prize. He sent it to them. You know why? Because he had rocket ships and he had missiles flying over Japan. Now, all of a sudden, they feel good. They feel safe. I did that."* (2/5/19)

No, Trump probably didn't do "that." Although he has been successful in getting North Korea's Kim Jong-un to the negotiating table, he hasn't yet been able to get Kim to agree to any serious denuclearization. North Korea remains a "serious and imminent" threat to Japan, according to then-Director of

Speaking at the United Nations General Assembly: *"In less than two years, my administration has accomplished more than almost any administration in the history of our country."* (Audible laughter from the audience of world leaders.) *"Didn't expect that reaction, but okay."* (9/25/18)

National Intelligence Daniel Coats. Furthermore, two weeks after Trump revealed that Abe nominated him for the Nobel Prize, a Japanese newspaper revealed that he only did so after the US government "informally" asked him to. Talk about participation trophies!

Canada

> *"PM Justin Trudeau of Canada acted so meek and mild during our @G7 meetings only to give a news conference after I left saying that, 'US Tariffs were kind of insulting' and he 'will not be pushed around.' Very dishonest & weak."* (6/9/18)

Petulance, thy name is Donald. Trump's relations with foreign leaders could provide enough material for an entire semester of high-school psychology. "Now class, this is a textbook example of what we call 'projection.' After Justin stood up to Donald, Donald felt emasculated, so he called Justin 'weak.'"

The White House (official Flickr account), courtesy of Wikimedia Commons

17.
IMMIGRATION
"AND SOME, I ASSUME, ARE GOOD PEOPLE."

"The danger is clear. The law is clear. The need for my executive order is clear." (3/15/17)

The danger *isn't* close to clear: the odds of being killed by a refugee's terrorist attack stand at about 1 in 3.6 billion. Conspicuously absent from his "Muslim Ban" are countries like Saudi Arabia, the UAE, and Lebanon, home to the vast majority of 9/11 hijackers...and are also places that conveniently have Trump properties.

Clumsy fearmongering aside, little about the initial proposed ban was clear—customs agents reported confusion in implementation, it wasn't initially known whether green card holders were included in the ban, and airports were scenes of chaos. One thing that was clear was the intention: to ban Muslims without making it a Muslim ban. According to his TV lawyer Rudy Giuliani on FOX, "I'll tell you the whole history of it: When he first announced it, he said 'Muslim ban.' He called me up, he said, 'Put a commission together, show me the right way to do it legally.'"

"[Apprehensions at] the border down 78 percent. Under past administrations, the border didn't go down—it went up." (7/28/17)

#5. The Unscientific Method: At best, Trump cherry-picked

"Consider the recent tweet from Trump about prayer rugs found near the US-Mexico border: Its foundation was a report that—no joke—was based on the word of an anonymous rancher passing on what she said she heard from unnamed sources in the US Border Patrol. How do you even fact-check such a claim?"

The Intercept

data and completely ignored the huge drops in unauthorized immigration at the southern border before his administration. From 2000 through 2016, apprehensions dropped by about three-quarters. Bush and Obama combined sent more than 6,000 additional troops to the border at a cost of $1.3 billion. Obama signed a $600 million bill to heighten border security and hire 1,000 new border control agents (on top of 250 new ICE agents). While Trump appears to assume that history began with him, past administrations *did* do this.

"We love the Dreamers. We think the Dreamers are terrific." (9/1/17)

He definitely has a weird way of showing it: throwing 800,000 American-raised kids' lives into uncertainty, siccing his attorney general on them, shutting down the government over their status, using them as bargaining chips when his demands failed. Considering that more than nine in ten Dreamers are employed, nearly half are in school, and most don't remember their life prior to their arrival; in the United States, his decision to toy with their lives was especially cruel: they provided their personal information and illegal status to the government, believing that it wouldn't be turned against them.

It was also unwise, since deporting DACA recipients could reduce the gross domestic product by more than $400 billion over the next decade. Then again, he left it to his then-attorney general, Jeff Sessions, to inform the country about his decision on DACA. A profile in courage.

"I've been to detention facilities where I've walked up to these individuals that are so-called minors, 17 or under. I've

looked at them and I've looked at their eyes, Tucker—and I've said that is a soon-to-be MS-13 gang member. It's unequivocal." —Mark Morgan, acting director of Immigration and Customs Enforcement

Wow. Sounds like someone to take to the betting window at Belmont.

A Chronology of Child Separation:

- March 2017: Then-Secretary of Homeland Security John Kelly admitted to CNN that the Trump administration was weighing separating children from their parents to deter illegal immigration: "I am considering in order to deter more movement along this terribly dangerous network.... I am considering exactly that."
- Spring 2018: The *New York Times* reports that more than 700 children had been separated from their parents, including 100 children under the age of four.
- May 2018: Attorney General Jeff Sessions announced the enforcement of a zero-tolerance policy at the border: "If you cross the border unlawfully...we will prosecute you. If you're smuggling a child, then we're going to prosecute you, and that child will be separated from you, probably, as required by law. If you don't want your child separated, then don't bring them across the border illegally."
- June 3, 2018: Senator Jeff Merkley (D.—OR) travels to the US southern border to view a child detention center,

Photo by Pete Marovich - Pool/Getty Images

where children were separated from their parents, as the Trump administration ramps up its zero-tolerance policy.

- June 17, 2018: First Lady Melania Trump pressured the president to reunite families saying, through a spokesperson, that she "hates to see" the separations—and placed the blame on both sides.
- June 18, 2018: ProPublica releases audio of separated children crying out for their parents, providing a flashpoint in the crisis. A reporter plays the recording at a White House briefing while DHS Secretary Nielsen was speaking, who was later asked if the recording and images of the child detentions are an unintended policy consequence and said, "I think that they reflect the focus of those who post such pictures and narratives."
- June 20, 2018: Trump signs the executive order that was intended to reverse the policy, saying "We are going to keep the families together. I didn't like the sight or the feeling of families being separated. This will solve that problem." But since the order was signed, 81 children were separated from their families through November and hundreds of families remain separated as of March 2019.
- April 2019: The federal government reports in court filings that it may take up to two years to identify thousands of immigrant children separated from their families at the southern border. This follows the government revealing it separated thousands more children than initially believed.

#12. The Hyperbolic and Apocolyptic: *"So here are just a few statistics on the human toll of illegal immigration. According to a 2011 government report, the arrests attached to the criminal alien population included an estimated 25,000 people for homicide, 42,000 for robbery, nearly 70,000 for sex offenses, and nearly 15,000 for kidnapping. In Texas alone, within the last seven years, more than a quarter-million criminal aliens have been arrested and charged with over 600,000 criminal offenses.... Sixty-three thousand Americans since 9/11 have been killed by illegal aliens. This isn't a problem that's going away; it's getting bigger." (6/22/18)*

It's not. Here he throws a lot of statistics at his listeners that paint a picture of marauding gangs of criminal aliens when the facts don't remotely support that. He used discredited data cited by white supremacist Rep. Steve King. He also makes a lot of falsehoods: by definition an "alien" is a noncitizen and includes legal and nonlegal immigrants, and combined arrests and convictions.

The numbers are deeply misleading: using both arrests and convictions, and, in the case of the "600,000" criminal offenses over a misleading time period, data covering their entire criminal careers, not within the last seven years. But numbers have never exactly been Trump's thing (as a candidate he said that undocumented immigrants could number "3 million. It could be 30 million." The last Department of Homeland Security estimate in 2012 put that number around 11.4 million.)

"I don't think we like sanctuary cities up here in Nevada. By the way, a lot of people in California don't want them, either. They're rioting now. They want to get out of their sanctuary cities." (10/20/18)

This was a complete fabrication uttered at a rally in Nevada, one not even peddled by a hyped-up *Fox & Friends* story.

A 16-year-old Guatemalan boy held in Yuma, Arizona, said he and others in his cell complained about the taste of the water and food they were given. The Customs and Border Protection agents took the mats out of their cell in retaliation, forcing them to sleep on hard concrete. A 15-year-old girl from Honduras described a large, bearded officer putting his hands inside her bra, pulling down her underwear, and groping her as part of what was meant to be a routine pat down in front of other immigrants and officers. The girl said "she felt embarrassed as the officer was speaking in English to other officers and laughing" during the entire process, according to a report of her account.

—NBC News

"Rather than talking about putting up a fence, why don't we work out some recognition of our mutual problems, make it possible for them to come here legally with a work permit, and then while they're working and earning here they pay taxes here? And when they want to go back, they can go back, and they can cross. And open the border both ways by understanding their problems."

Ronald Reagan, 1989

"Why are we having all these people from shithole countries come here?" the president said [and] also suggested the United States should admit more people from countries like Norway instead."

Fox News, (1/11/19)

Governor Jerry Brown's spokesman, who was asked about any riots in California, said, "Short answer: no." Here's the long answer: no. Followed up by a reporter, Trump said, "they want to get out." Asked if he considered *that* a riot, he simply ignored the question.

"Sadly, it looks like Mexico's Police and Military are unable to stop the Caravan heading to the Southern Border of the United States. Criminals and unknown Middle Easterners are mixed in." (10/22/18)

"They're not coming in. We're going to do whatever we have to, they're not coming in." (10/23/18)

"We will consider that the maximum we can consider that because they are throwing rocks viciously and violently. You saw that three days ago. Really hurting the military. We're not going to put up with that. If they want to throw rocks at our military, our military fights back. We're going to consider it. I told them to consider it a rifle. When they threw rocks like they did at the Mexican military and police, I say consider it a rifle." (11/1/18)

Facing strong headwinds during the midterm elections, Trump dragged his party further to the far right and doubled down on racist demagoguery, portraying a "caravan" of thousands of poor, shell-shocked refugees from across Central America as menaces to life and liberty in America. Far from the MS-13 recruits of Fox News's fevered imagination, they were mostly 4,000 people who were out of work and out of hope in their home countries and looking to get out of harm's way.

About two weeks before Trump made the caravan *the* central

issue of the midterms, about 160 people left San Pedro Sula, Honduras—the murder capital of the world just a few years ago—and within just three days the caravan had grown to about 1,600 people. Along the way, some gave up because of exhaustion and fear, and some died.

#8. Fear Itself: Facing the threat of losing the House and potentially, though less likely, the Senate, the Trumpified Republican Party ran remorselessly on the caravan "issue." Trump deployed 5,200 troops to the border while the migrants (with a price tag that could top $200 million) were more than 1,000 miles away, which would be something on the order of if a president were faced with an invasion of Salt Lake City and sent troops to Kansas City to respond.

Fortunately, since American voters cared more about health care costs than Honduran migrants, it didn't swing the election. Trump quickly forgot the issue, but a world away, some people didn't. The Nigerian army defended their brutal use of force (killing 40 rock-wielding protesters) by posting a video of Trump's own words justifying shooting back. The Nigerian army posted—where else but Twitter?—and wrote: "Please Watch and Make Your Deductions."

"Remember this: President Obama separated children from families." (11/1/18)

No he didn't. While Obama's immigration policies *were* much criticized by immigration advocacy groups, he did detain families together, rather than ripping families apart. Trump meanwhile separated 2,600 children from their parents, with hundreds still not reunited.

"We're not letting them into our country. And then they never

show up, almost, it's like a level of 3 percent. They never show up for the trial. So by the time their trial comes, they're gone, nobody knows where they are." (11/1/18)

#20. The Lyin' King: He should know a thing or two about trials—he's been sued hundreds of times—and of course seven of his top campaign and political aides were convicted of crimes connected to the Mueller probe. But when it comes to trials for immigrants, he's not even close: they have an attendance rate of 72 percent. His shutdown tantrum in January 2019 actually slowed the rates of trials and has created a years-long backlog of cases.

"Many of those workers have said to me, communicated… stay out [keep the government shut down] until you get the funding for the wall. These federal workers want the wall." (12/25/18)

Shorter Trump: Merry Christmas; out-of-work federal workers want my racist wall, too. Except they don't, or there's no data to prove that—the assertion "many of those workers have said to me" being, on its face, absurd. He's in touch with many federal employees who don't want their pay?

"The wall will also be paid for indirectly by the great new trade deal we have made with Mexico." (1/8/19)

"Mr. Trump campaigned on a promise to build a 1,000-mile-long wall to be paid for by Mexico. In late October 2017, prototypes for this wall were unveiled but no construction on new portions of the wall has commenced, in part because of a lack of funding."—the New York Times (12/12/18)

This lie is at least a concession of defeat in his central campaign promise, but it's still a lie. He's misreading economics and flunking any understanding of trade deficits—since a country doesn't lose money in a trade deficit, so it can't earn it back. Either way, the (minimum) $18 billion price tag won't be paid by reworking NAFTA, or through a treaty not yet even ratified by Congress.

"[T]here is a growing humanitarian and security crisis at our southern border." (1/9/19)

Which he caused, since the separation of children from their parents and detention centers for "tender age" kids (read: babies) began with his administration. Border apprehensions have dropped by 75 percent in the past two decades, but if he's looking for humanitarian crises north of the border, he has plenty to choose from—Flint going without clean water for four years, 45 million uninsured, the gun violence epidemic—that he's done nothing to help.

"You'll have crime in Iowa, you'll have crime in New Hampshire, you'll have crime in New York without a wall." (1/10/19)

He could mean the mass shootings that continue unabated—the ones that he blames victims for being unarmed—but what he won't say is native-born Americans commit crimes at a significantly *higher* rate than immigrants, documented or not. Despite Trump's repeated claims that more undocumented immigrants means more crime, a study in the journal *Criminology* looking at a nearly-quarter century of data found just the opposite: its authors concluded, "Increases in the

"Over two-thirds believe America's openness to people from all over the world is essential to who we are as a nation. Only a quarter say 'if America is too open to people around the world, we risk losing our identity as a people.'"

Mark Mellman, pollster

undocumented immigrant population within states are associated with significant decreases in the prevalence of violence."

*"During the campaign, I would say, 'Mexico is going to pay
for it.' Obviously, I never said this and I never meant they're
going to write out a check. I said, 'They're going to pay for it.'
They are. They are paying for it with the incredible deal we
made, called the United States, Mexico, and Canada USMCA
deal."(1/10/19)*

This was the biggest hit of his campaign, the "Free Bird" of
Trump rallies everywhere—and an obvious lie. The "wall" line
was later revealed to have been inserted by staff into speeches
so that he'd remember to talk about immigration, but it turned
out he needed no hints to pitch racist lies to the American voter. But now it's his albatross, worthy enough to leave 800,000
without paychecks for weeks. But maybe he meant *New* Mexico (and the other 49 states)?

#20. The Lyin' King: *"The Rio Grande area where I was yes-
terday, you just have to look at it to see how dangerous it is.
El Paso, Texas went from one of the most unsafe parts or cities
in the United States to one of the safest cities in the United
States as soon as they put up the wall. They built a wall and
fencing apparatus that blocked people. So they went from
one of the most dangerous cities to one of the safest cities, all
within a very short period of time." (1/11/19)*

As is the case when Trump speaks at length, there are plenty
of lies to unpack. In selling his wall, he sells out El Paso, a city
that was never among the most unsafe in the US. El Paso has
long trailed the national average for violent crime but peaked

in 1993—when crime peaked across the US. From 1993 to 2006, crime fell by more than a third. A border fence was built in 2008, and from 2006 through 2011, El Paso's violent crime rate actually *increased* by 17 percent.

> *"I built a lot of wall. I have a lot of money and I built a lot of wall." (2/15/19)*

Since he's been president, no new miles of the border wall have been added, no matter how many times he says or implies it. Contracts have been made and preparations are ready, but, despite hundreds of times making this promise on the campaign trail, he hasn't kept it—and Mexico is definitely not paying up.

He *is* building a wall between himself and reality as walls close in on him but is not actually building a *wall*. Some long-standing border fencing is being repaired, but no new wall has been built since noon on January 20, 2017. He's happy with steel slats, though!

> *"90% of the drugs don't come through the port of entry. 90% of the drugs and the big stuff goes out to the desert." (2/25/19)*

It's the opposite: according to the US Customs and Border Protection's own statistics, in the first 11 months of 2018, 90 percent of heroin, 88 percent of cocaine, 87 of methamphetamine, and 80 percent of fentanyl was seized at legal crossing points.

> *"If we build a powerful and fully designed see-through steel barrier on our southern border, the crime rate and drug problem in our country would be quickly and greatly reduced. Some say it could be cut in half." (1/19/19)*

"Some say?" Who–Steve Miller? Barron Trump? Here 45 is ignoring the fact that ports of entry are the primary entry source. *Trump himself noted in his State of the Union: "Human traffickers and sex traffickers take advantage of the wide-open areas between our ports of entry to smuggle thousands of young girls and women into the United States and to sell them into prostitution and modern-day slavery." (2/5/19)*

Trump's own Justice Department reports that human trafficking prosecutions have dropped by 18 percent and most of the DOJ's trafficking cases it highlights involve US citizens far from the southern border. Although the *New York Times* reported that there have been "horrific" cases of human trafficking—the duct-taped-at-the-border variety—the Paper of Record noted, "If the president was suggesting that such savagery occurs daily on America's southern border, then he was indeed exaggerating."

#1. Cherry-Picking: Many of the cases have been premised on a single case of a Mexican woman at the US border who was smuggled in by another woman to serve as a pregnancy surrogate but was instead forced to engage in domestic work. The United Nations' International Organization on Migration has found that in analyzing a decade of data on 90,000 trafficking victims, 79 percent of trafficking go through ports of entry, like airports, where a wall won't make a dent.

"Two weeks ago, 26 were killed in a gunfight on the border a mile away from where I went." (2/15/19)

Here's where he almost gets the number right—almost—but then gets his geography all wrong. There were about two dozen bodies found as a result of gang clashes in Mexico about 130 miles from the border. But a mile away from McAllen, Texas, where he visited? No, but it could have been in one of the *Sicario* sequels Trump cribs from.

"Nobody shows up [for immigration hearings]. Three percent of the people come back for a trial. It's insane." (3/2/19)

What's insane is that Trump ended a program in June 2018 that saw a 100 percent attendance rate by asylum seekers, not three percent, but 100 percent. The Inspector General at Homeland Security reports that they had a 99 percent rate of check-ins and appointments with ICE. Maybe he should talk to someone?

QUESTION at Rose Garden Press Conference: "...there's a lot of reporting out there, there's a lot of crime data out there, there's a lot of Department of Homeland Security data out there that shows border crossings at a near record low..."
TRUMP: *That's because of us. But it's still—excuse me...*
QUESTION: That shows undocumented immigrants committing crimes at lower levels...
TRUMP: *It's still massive numbers of crossings.*
QUESTION: Shows undocumented criminals—or undocumented immigrants committing crimes at lower levels than native-born Americans. What—what do you say to...
TRUMP: *You don't—you don't really believe that stat, do you? Do you really believe that stat?"*
The "stat" in dispute came from Trump's own Department of Homeland Security.

"Any time a refugee or immigrant committed a gruesome crime in the United States... Stephen Miller would come down to the comms office demanding a press release."

Cliff Sims, former White House communications aide

"Nobody knows anything. Nobody says anything—just lies. They said they were taking them for questioning, and we were only going to be apart for a moment. But they never came back."

Juana Francisca Bonilla de Canjura, of El Salvador, whose daughters Ingrid, 10, and Fatima, 12, were separated from her at the border

"America represents something universal in the human spirit. I received a letter not long ago from a man who said, 'You can go to Japan to live, but you cannot become Japanese. You can go to France to live and not become a Frenchman. You can go to live in Germany or Turkey, and you won't become a German or a Turk. But anybody from any corner of the world can come to America to live and become an American.'"
—Ronald Reagan, 1988

"May we never forget immigration is a blessing and a strength."—George W. Bush, 2019

"We know that family separation causes irreparable harm to children. This type of highly stressful experience can disrupt the building of children's brain architecture. Prolonged exposure to serious stress—known as toxic stress—can lead to lifelong health consequences."—Colleen Kraft, MD, president of the American Academy of Pediatrics

"Any deaths of children or others at the Border are strictly the fault of the Democrats and their pathetic immigration policies that allow people to make the long trek thinking they can enter our country illegally. They can't. If we had a Wall, they wouldn't even try!" (12/29/18)

"Marco Antonio Muñoz, an immigrant from Honduras, committed suicide in a Texas jail after being separated from his wife and child. Muñoz was found dead on the morning of May 13, less than a week after Sessions implemented the 'zero tolerance' policy that led to these family separations. He had been planning to seek asylum with his wife and three-year-old son, according to the Washington Post, which first reported

the story. 'They had to use physical force to take the child out of his hands,' a Border Patrol agent told the Post.—Mother Jones

DHS Secretary Kirstjen Nielsen: "Sir, they are not cages, they are areas of the border facility that are carved out for the safety and protection of those who remain there while they're being processed."

Rep. Bennie Thompson: "Don't mislead the committee."

Rep. Bonnie Watson Coleman: "Does it differ from the cages you put your dogs in when you let them stay outside?"

Secretary Nielsen: "Yes...it's larger, it has facilities, it provides room to sit, to stand, to lay down —"

Rep. Watson Coleman: "So does my dog's cage."

House Homeland Security hearing, 3/6/19

#2. Assertions and Adjectives: *"I've seen some of those places, and they are run beautifully. They're clean. They're good. They do a great job.... In all cases, if you look, people that came from unbelievable poverty, that had no water— they had no anything where they came from—those are people that are very happy with what's going on, because, relatively speaking, they're in much better shape right now."* *(7/5/19)*

Trump wouldn't know what an organization "run beautifully" would look like if it slapped him in the face with a Trump Steak. (Check out Trump's EPA, his handling of Hurricane Maria.) Some things run against Trump's claim, namely, facts: there had been no deaths of migrant children in custody in the ten years prior to January 20, 2017. During the first half of Trump's first term, there have been seven deaths of immigrant

"I am not going to pay for that fucking wall."

Vincente Fox, former Mexican president (2/25/16)

"I would cite you to the Apostle Paul and his clear and wise command in Romans 13, to obey the laws of the government because God has ordained them for the purpose of order. Orderly and lawful processes are good in themselves and protect the weak and lawful."

Jeff Sessions, citing the Biblical verse Romans 13 to defend Trump immigration policies, a handy verse that has been cited previously to defend slavery, by Nazi sympathizers and defenders of apartheid in South Africa.

"VP saw 384 men sleeping inside fences. On concrete w/ no pillows or mats. They said they hadn't showered in weeks, wanted toothbrushes, food. Stench was overwhelming."

Tweet by Josh Dawsey, *Washington Post,* White House pool reporter 7/22/19

children in U. S. custody. At these marvelously run facilities children have mouth sores from eating such nutrient-deficient foods.

Donald Trump might just be confused and might need to make a call to his own DHS inspector general, whose report in July 2019 first documented the deplorable conditions. If that weren't enough, the *New York Times* ran two front-page stories involving a half-dozen investigative reporters writing some 5,000 words further documenting what the children were enduring.

So: who to believe—the adjectives of a president who is a waterfall of lies or his own DHS and the several corroborating media outlets? Rhetorical question? Not for the fourth of American adults enthralled by whatever 45 says.

"They've had to become nurses, they've had to become janitors all because the Democrats refused to change the loopholes on asylum laws.... The Fake News Media, in particular the Failing @nytimes, is writing phony and exaggerated accounts of the Border Detention Centers. First of all, people should not be entering our Country illegally, only for us to then have to care for them.... I think it's a disgrace and the New York Times is basically a partner with the Democrats." (7/7/19)

Maybe Trump started to have doubts that the detention centers weren't being run so marvelously. Photos from inside the camps were being released. Children were drawing pictures of themselves behind bars. Historians backed up the claims that they shared parallels with concentration camps. Then, credible accusations of sexual abuse started to pile up, so what does he do when faced with such charges—attack the press.

Old faithful. It doesn't have to be true (check out how the *New York Times* treated Hillary Clinton's private email server, and Whitewater, and Uranium One, and...). The truth is never a litmus test for Trump; it just has to work.

Pence kept up a tough-guy routine when he stared the problem Trump created in the face—or rather, in the faces of scores of dirty, underfed, underhoused migrants desperate for showers and toothbrushes. Also, the president of the anti-immigrant Federation for American Immigration Reform explained the conditions away by saying the administration "doesn't want the detention to be Club Med," explaining that one way to deter migrants is to "make the experience unpleasant."—The *New York Times* (7/16/19)

"[U]nder President Obama you had separation [of migrant families]. I was the one that ended it." (6/24/19)

Perhaps it's because of guilt regarding what he knows are the deplorable conditions children are facing at the border—standing-room-only cells, accusations of sexual abuse, sleeping on the floor, woefully inadequate food—but more likely it's amoral gaslighting that guides Trump's decision to deflect blame for family separations at the border to President Obama. A director of the Immigration Clinic at the University of Texas Law School says the notion that Obama began the separation policy is "preposterous." A top Obama administration domestic policy advisor did say a similar policy was considered until it was ruled out as heartless. Not a problem for this White House.

Trump on Obama: "Repubs must not allow Pres Obama to subvert the Constitution of the US for his own benefit &

because he is unable to negotiate w/ Congress." (11/20/14)

In the last week of August, 2019, the Trump-Miller-Bannon axis reached for inspiration from America's dark nativist past to keep America white for as long as possible. How else to interpret their cascading proposals?

In the wake of the El Paso massacre of Latinos, Trump in August 2019 sought to destabilize the lives of people struggling to get by: authorizing ICE raids at a Mississippi food plant; denying flu vaccines to undocumented children even as several died in detention of the flu; considering blocking migrant children from public schools; proposing holding migrants in detention indefinitely; denying new arrivals if they might ever use a "public benefit" (social security in 40 years?); and targeting for deportation gravely ill children receiving emergency care for cancer and cystic fibrosis. Said one mother told to go to Guyana, "I feel like I'm signing my son's death warrant." (Here, awful publicity led to a reversal.) The latest: imposing new limits on citizenship of children born abroad to American service members.

When Ronald Reagan was fraying the social safety net, the liberal Democrat Speaker of the House confronted him with the human costs of his budget cuts, using the example of a young woman who lost her parents—and her Social Security benefits. Reagan summoned an aide, "Let's see if we can take care of this girl." The Speaker, Tip O'Neill, exasperated, "I'm not here to talk about one girl. I'm using her as an example."

Will there even be one such moment of clarity from the heartless, soulless Donald John Trump?

EPILOGUE:
"ON BETRAYAL," BY RALPH NADER
"DEAR TRUMP VOTER, IF YOU'RE LISTENING..."

This book would not have been possible without the Electoral College (EC) and 535 people most Americans have never heard of...period. The Electoral College is our Founders' poison chalice. Its present function, in close races, is to suffocate the majority popular vote and hand the presidency over to the loser. In 2016, that loser was Donald J. Trump. He received nearly 3 million fewer votes than Hillary Clinton nationwide.

I need not burden further the majority of voters who know what Trump and his Trumpsters are doing to America and its people. They were not fooled by Trump, supposedly running against "the elites" even while he has been serving and enriching these ruling classes beyond their dreams of avarice.

It's Trump supporters whom I want to address. They are the ones stereotyped by their critics as being all alike in their hatreds, resentments, closed minds, prejudices, and fears. While Trump supporters may hoot and holler alike at his mass rallies, people like them defy such stereotypes back home where they live, work, and raise their families. When asked, they call themselves Republicans, conservatives, or patriots. Down home they want many of the same things in life as neighbors who call themselves liberal or similar names.

Both want clean and fairly counted elections. They want law enforcement against business crimes that cheat, bully, and harm them and that sell bad things on television to their children, bypassing parental authority. They are angry over big business and the superrich not paying their fair share in taxes, even as they can afford to buy politicians. Who doesn't object to all those maddening fine print contracts that deny shoppers the benefits and services they've already paid for, as with their health insurance or their private pensions?

Both want their cars recalled when there is a manufacturing defect. Both want safe medicines, clean food, air, water, and a safe, respectful workplace. They expect their taxes to be used to repair or upgrade their community's roads, schools, drinking water, and public transit systems. Probably many Walmart workers voted for Trump, but that doesn't mean they think it's fair for them to be paid a wage they can't possibly live on while their top boss makes $12,000 *an hour* plus huge benefits. During his campaign, by the way, Trump, the vastly overpaid failed gambling czar, asserted that American workers were "overpaid." How do his supporters let him get away with that?

The commercial drive to overcome more important civic and human values doesn't distinguish between conservatives and liberals, between Republicans and Democrats. They're all fodder for profit. Did you know that every major religion warned its faithful not to give too much power to the merchant class? More than two thousand years ago, merchants even then were running roughshod over civilized values in their quest for profits or riches.

Today they know how to get you in so many ways and to get away with it. Only a democratic society can make these big corporations our servants, not our masters, by subordinating their commercial greed to the supremacy of the law and to civic values that allow people to enjoy freedom and justice.

I've always been amazed at the success that so many politicians have with voters using a few repeated phrases—is the candidate boldly saying out loud what certain voters have been thinking about unpopular populations and keeping it to themselves? So when the only other presidential candidate with a chance at winning in a two-party duopoly is disliked, someone like a Trump, even as a corporate welfare king, can make the sale. A quick sale if he can sum up real resentments about job losses to imports and immigrants, and the fact that the people are being forgotten by the Democratic Party, whose leading operatives are consorting with Wall Streeters and other bigwigs for lucrative retainers.

Many Trump voters felt that way about their labor union leaders, as well. Trump may be losing the trade war, with tariffs raising consumer prices or losing farmer markets, but, hey, at least he is trying to make sure foreign countries don't take us to the cleaners. For "five-minute voters," who don't give themselves the chance to dig deeper, as they do with the details of their sports teams, the key role of US corporations exiting America for these foreign countries with their cheap labor may be missed.

And recall when Trump told them during the campaign that "the drug companies are getting away with murder" and yet has done nothing as president, well hey, at least he is talking about the rip-offs. (Drug companies are laughing as they collect more subsidies and tax breaks from Uncle Sam.) Their "pay-or-die" business just got 13 percent more expensive on the average this year.

Trump scoffs at the climate crisis. All those intensifying heat waves, hurricanes, rising sea levels, tornados, floods, droughts, and wildfires are no evidence of man-caused climate disruption, which he calls a "hoax." Whom do you trust—your eyes and the climate scientists, whose warnings have been accurate for years? Or the "beautiful, clean coal" booster—Donald Trump?

Presidential behavior, in a modern social media age, can be very contagious. And not just for preteens sassing their parents in ways imitative of Trump's outlandish behavior or talk. For example, when talking politics with people, I mention his chronic, pathological lying in tweets and speeches day after day, saying things that clearly just aren't so. Somebody always says, "Well, all politicians lie," which may well be true. But just as there is a difference between coffee that is hot, boiling, or scalding, a difference in degree can become a deadly difference in kind. Especially when the lies and their false scenarios are stacked and backed by the power and delusions of the President of the United States.

But the price of a Fake President is a continuing betrayal—betrayal of the people who believed and put him in office. When he says the economy is so rosy and it clearly isn't for a majority of people having trouble paying their bills even after going into deep debt, they've been betrayed. Trump then pretends as if there were nothing he can do to provide health care for 80 million people without insurance or underinsured...when in reality he is pushing Congress to repeal health insurance for millions of people. Or when he says industrial jobs are coming back and factories are returning and they have not, his lies hide his broken campaign assurances and evade accountability. And the cycles of betrayal continue.

For which his voters pay a big price when the cheering stops. His incorrigible mendacity about too many regulations by our health and safety agencies standing up to the corporate crime wave helps his corrupt deregulators sabotage their own agencies. Sure, there is sometimes too much paperwork and poorly conceived or too weak regulations. But overall, for example, aren't you glad to learn there is less lead in your children's blood, no more lethal asbestos filling your lungs, and far fewer fatalities, broken bones, or amputations in motor vehicle law crashes? Chalk all that up to federal regulatory law enforcement finally saying No to corporate profits over people's lives.

Sometimes it's useful to know a little history about other people, no better than us, who stood up together for justice and got a better living standard across the board. I'm speaking of the people of Western Europe getting themselves together after their countries were destroyed during World War II. With their multiple party systems (more choices and voices), their larger and stronger labor unions than in the US, and their many consumer cooperatives, they demanded and received as voters full health care; four weeks or more annual paid vacation; decent pensions, wages, and public transit; tuition-free higher education; paid child care; paid individual and family sick leave; and paid maternity leave.

Today in the US, nearly seventy-five years after World War II, which we won, we have none of these necessities for all our people. To these Europeans, the logic was simple. They earned their pay, sent their tax payments to the government, and wanted them *returned* in the form of these necessities that make a more decent life. You don't find many conservatives in those nations wanting to turn the clock back. Margaret Thatcher kept national health insurance.

Then there is our northern neighbor—Canada. In the nineteen sixties, while our country was wasting lives and money blowing apart Vietnam, the peaceful Canadians were laying the groundwork for full Medicare for All. Soon all the Canadian provinces had a health insurance structure called "single payer" (meaning the government as the insurer with private delivery of care). Everybody in, nobody out, with free choice of physician or hospital. No nightmarish networks. Lower drug prices. They cover everyone for half the price per capita than we pay in our gouging complex, profiteering system that still manages to leave 29 million people uninsured and double that number in underinsured fright.

If you've been to Canada, you'll note they act and look a lot like Americans. But at a certain time in their history, without being absorbed in the quicksand of costly foreign wars of choice, Canadians said, "enough is enough," and created a very popular health care insurance system that reduced a lot of anxiety, dread, and fear from their quality of life and work. (See singlepayeraction.org for twenty-five ways full Medicare improves Canadian livelihoods compared to their counterparts in the US.) They demanded it and got it. What's our excuse?

To get votes in 2016, Trump on the stump repeatedly promised that he would abolish the "disastrous" Obamacare and replace it with "great" health insurance. For two years, with a Republican Congress, he did neither. He had no replacement plan for Obamacare. Had he gotten Congress to repeal Obamacare, he would have left 20 million more people without health insurance. He was lucky. Lots of Trump voters in that group.

Let's face it, western Europeans—from Scandinavia to England, France, Germany, Switzerland, the Netherlands, Belgium, Italy, and others—had higher expectations for themselves and their political systems than we do. Sure, their politics are fractious, they fight with one another and endure all kinds of shifting coalitions in their parliament. But eventually they returned to their people lots for their taxes—decent livelihoods, income security through retirement, paid leisure and sick time, and far less anxiety, fear, and dread than our trap-door economy allows.

Many Trump voters read about the great labor leader, Eugene Debs, in their high school and college American history books. One day, near the end of his career in the nineteen twenties, a reporter asked an exhausted Debs what was his greatest regret? He looked at the reporter and said, "My greatest regret? . . . My greatest regret is that the American people under their Constitution can have almost anything they want, but it just seems that they don't want much of anything at all."

I thought of Debs when I observed the muted reaction from the American people to the $4.7 trillion budget Trump sent to Congress in March 2019. There was another staggering increase in the already bloated, wasteful, unaudited military budget. But he did want to dangerously cut Medicaid; food stamps; consumer, environmental health, and safety protections against cancer and other diseases; and Medicare (breaking his campaign promise). But he gave the superrich over a trillion dollars in tax cuts and handed your children the debt. "How Dare He!" did not ring out from all corners of our land.

And whatever happened to Trump's big plans for repairing and upgrading America's infrastructure or public works? His proposed budget has a measly $20 billion each year for 10 years. As a builder of hotels and casinos, he knows this is a pittance but isn't telling you. Fortunately for the people, the House Democrats declared his budget as dead on arrival. The question remains—whose side is he really on? Clearly not the side that *truthfully* loves America and Americans.

He is not on the side of struggling blue collar workers who are abandoned or mistreated by their bosses. Even when confronted with Trump's massive fakery, most of his victimized supporters say a version of "yes, but"—"but" meaning the discovery of any excuse to justify their intuitive embrace. Trumpers may be taken in by steady low unemployment numbers that began falling in 2010, while ignoring stagnant real income and the lack of investment in public works in their communities.

They may be only bemused by his antics with Kim Jong Un,

North Korea's dictator, which don't appear to directly affect their families. They may revel in his intimidating attacks on a free press..."but" like his full backing of Israel's continuing military domination of occupied Palestinian territories, not knowing what that does to our costly wars of choice.

They may see his abhorrent personal behavior with women as distasteful, but then . . . he's only human, like many men they know. As far as his failed business career cheating workers, including undocumented ones, customers, creditors, and the IRS, that to many of his supporters is fake news. Besides, to them he is so rich that he can't be bought. As for his evangelical voters, they know about his infidelities, his many sins and non-Church-going life, and his past support for abortion. They shrug. To them, it's enough that Trump is vocally championing their values and policies from the biggest bully pulpit in the land.

Finally, they may be what Matt Taibbi, in his new book, *Hate Inc.: Why Today's Media Makes Us Despise One Another*, calls "grudge voters." One Wisconsin voter told him, "I usually don't vote, but I'm going Trump because f*** everything."

Pessimism never won a battle or election. So raising the bar of what all voters deserve, it is our hope that *Fake President*, among so many other carefully researched and argued books, will a) better equip those who refuse to reward such a miserable person with miserable policies, b) perhaps activate some of the 120 million nonvoters—nearly as many as all those who do vote, and c) encourage betrayed supporters to vote with their heads rather than their fears.

Keep all this in mind, dear Trump supporters. Spend some hours studying the actual records of the presidential candidates and your Congressional candidates. All their talk is cheap without analyzing their actual record—their votes, their advocacy, and their inactions. The 2020 election can be very expensive for you if you don't really unmask what is behind those phony smiles, rehearsed speeches, and shakes of the hand designed to confuse and amuse. Politics is not entertainment. If you like politicians because they say what you think, also question whether they will do what you need.

A president who excites angry voters with racist rants while rewarding his wealthy friends with policies that further enrich them is not a populist, but a phony—the opposite of someone who "tells it like it is." Did you know that the Trump presidency has brought us the first-ever reduction of life expectancy in the US...the stagnation of wages, and an avalanche of cancerous particulates into the water and air of our country? Including his coal country base!

It's time to persuade a large majority of voters that Trump is fundamentally a Fake President who can't be trusted and is destroying the best in America while bringing out the worst. That's a theory of the case that will sway the jury of voters, if they are registered and informed. For the Fox Corporation isn't America. We—the progressive majority—are.

ENDNOTES

PREFACE: FAKING IT

The sixth presidential poll by the Siena Research Institute since 1982 asked 157 scholars, historians, and political scientists to rate on a scale of 1 (poor) to 5 (excellent) the nation's 44 presidents in 20 categories pertaining to their abilities, attributes, and accomplishments. Christine Stapleton. "Trump in Palm Beach: Presidential Poll, *Palm Beach Post*. February 17, 2019.

ESSAY by RALPH NADER

"I can't really say": Sabrina Tavernise. "These Americans are done with politics." *New York Times*. November 17, 2018.
DeGaulle: See Anthony Blinkin. "How America is Losing the Credibility War." *New York Times*. April 18, 2017.

YOUR OWN BULLSHIT DETECTOR

21 Favorite Trump Tricks to Distract, Deflect, and Deceive
Dowd: Bob Woodward. *Fear* (2018). 353.
12,091 falsehoods: Glenn Kessler. "President Trump has made 12,091 false or misleading claims over 928 days." *Washington Post*. August 12, 2019.
Mark Burnett: Patrick Keefe. "How Mark Burnett Resurrected Donald Trump as an Icon of American Success." *The New Yorker*. December 27, 2018.
An early Cassandra: James Poniewozik. "The Real Donald Trump is a Character on TV." *New York Times*. September 6, 2019.
Here's Billy Bush: Jayme Deerwester. "Billy Bush on Trump's lies about Apprentice ratings." *USA Today*. March 17, 2018.
Conspiracy Theories: For more conspiracy theories, see "Aaron Blake, "23 Bizarre Conspiracy Theories Trump has Elevated." *Washington Post*. April 12, 2019.
Birtherism: Greg Price. "'Trump Knows that Republicans are Stupid,' Jared Kushner Allegedly Said to Former Editor." *Newsweek*, May 30, 2017.
Falsehoods: Glenn Kessler. "A year of unprecedented deception: Trump averaged 15 false claims a day in 2018." *Washington Post*. December 30, 2018.

1. HEALTH INSURANCE

They sued, alleging that: Natalie Schreyer. "The Trump Files: When Donald Took Revenge by Cutting Off Health Coverage for a Sick Infant." *Mother Jones*. August 25, 2016.
"It's very easy": Ronald Reagan. "Radio Address on Socialized Medicine." American Rhetoric. 1961
after the outrage: Lori Robertson. "'Millions' Lost Insurance." FactCheck.org. April 11, 2014.
"If you can't": German Lopez. "In 2000, Trump made a powerful argument against his own health care bill." *Vox*. March 24, 2017.
negative anecdotes: Eugene Kiely. "Cruz's Obamacare Whopper." FactCheck.org. February 10, 2017.
"Obamacare is dead": "Remarks by President Trump and Veterans Affairs Secretary Shulkin at Veterans Affairs Listening Session." The White House. March 17, 2017.
not imploding: Michael Hiltzik. "Trump's own figures show that Obamacare is working well for the vast majority of enrollees." *Los Angeles Times*. July 3, 2018.
foreseeable future: Benjy Sarlin. "Study: Obamacare Is Not Collapsing." NBC News. July 10, 2017.
slashing by 70 percent: Dylan Scott, "The Trump administration's latest steps to undermine the Affordable Care Act, explained." *Vox*. July 12, 2018.
"navigators": Tami Luhby. "Trump slashing Obamacare advertising by 90%." CNN. August 31, 2017.
The Senate bill: Benjy Sarlin and Jane C. Timm. "Fact Checking Trump's Remarks on Health Care." July 24, 2017.

a nihilist few: Ashley Kirzinger, Bianaca DiJulio, Bryan Wu, Mollyann Brodie. "Kaiser Health Tracking Poll—August 2017: The Politics of ACA Repeal and Replace Efforts." Kaiser Family Foundation. August 11, 2017.

"$12 a year": Ester Bloom. "President Trump says young people pay $12 for health insurance—here's how much it actually costs." CNBC. July 20, 2017.

drastic drop: Ashley Kirzinger, Bianca DiJulio, Liz Hamel, Elise Sugarman, and Mollyann Brodie. "Kaiser Health Tracking Poll—May 2017: The AHCA's Proposed Changes to Health Care." Kaiser Family Foundation. May 31, 2017.

"unreasonable": Lori Robertson. "Selling Insurance Across State Lines." Factcheck.org July 21, 2017.

"We have the votes": Chris Cillizza. "Donald Trump keeps lying about health care repeal. Why?" CNN. September 28, 2017.

95 percent cut: Patrick Ross. "The lies Trump tells on health care." Health Care In America. May 7, 2017.

throwing in $8 billion: Aviva Aron-Dine. "$8 billion comes nowhere close to meeting Republican commitments to people with pre-existing conditions". CNBC. May 4, 2017.

"single most important": Ezra Klein. "Republicans used to have a health care plan. Now all they have are lies." *Vox.* October 31, 2018.

50 to 129 million: The Center for Consumer Information & Insurance Oversight. "Risk: Pre-Existing Conditions Could Affect 1 in 2 Americans." Centers for Medicare and Medicaid Services.

53 percent: Ashley Kirzinger, Bryan Wu, and Mollyann Brodie. "KFF Health Tracking Poll—April 2019: Surprise Medical Bills and Public's View of the Supreme Court and Continuing Protections for People With Pre-Existing Conditions." Kaiser Family Foundation. April 24, 2019.

no alternative: Jane C. Timm. "Fact check: Trump claims GOP is protecting people with pre-existing conditions. Evidence says otherwise." NBC News. October 23, 2018.

86.2 percent: "New poll shows Canadians overwhelmingly support public health care." Health Care Now.

"In recent years": "Remarks by President Trump in State of the Union Address." The White House. February 6, 2019.

70 percent decrease: Office of the Associate Director. "Access to clean syringes." Center for Disease Control.

$5 billion: "Trump once again requests deep cuts in U.S. science spending." *Science.* March 11, 2019.

next decade: Bobby Allyn. "Justice Department Promises Crackdown On Supervised Injection Facilities." NPR. August 30, 2018.

Federal health officials: Rachana Pardhan. "Number of uninsured Americans rises for the first time since Obamacare." *Politico.* September 10, 2019.

2. CLIMATE VIOLENCE

only pledged: Glenn Kessler and Michelle Ye Hee Lee. "Fact-checking President Trump's claims on the Paris climate change deal." *Washington Post.* June 1, 2017.

a snowball: Philip Bump. "Jim Inhofe's snowball has disproven climate change once and for all." *Washington Post.* February 26, 2015.

warmest year: "NASA, NOAA Find 2014 Warmest Year in Modern Record." nasa.gov. January 16, 2015.

"publicize dozens": Helena Bottemiller Evich. "Agriculture Department buries studies showing dangers of climate change." *Politico.* June 23, 2019.

"Man, this guy": John Leguizamo. Twitter. April 4, 2019.

more birds: Susan Milius. "Stop blaming cats: As many as 988 million birds die annually in window collisions." *Washington Post.* February 3, 2014.

by windmills: Emma Bryce. "Will Wind Turbines Ever Be Safe For Birds?" *Audubon.* March 16, 2016.

In 2006: Pilar Melendez. "Trump Hates Windmills—and It Has Nothing to Do With His Bogus Cancer Claims." *The Daily Beast.* April 3, 2019.

tin-hat: Philip Jaekl. "Why People Believe Low-Frequency Sound Is Dangerous." *The Atlantic.* June 19, 2017.

Chait wrote: Jonathan Chait. "Trump Says Wind Turbine Noise Causes Cancer. (It Does Not.)." *New York Magazine*. April 3, 2019.

97 percent: Jason Samenow. "97 percent of scientific studies agree on manmade global warming, so what now?" *Washington Post*. May 17, 2013.

12 years: Jonathan Watts. "We have 12 years to limit climate change catastrophe, warns UN." *The Guardian*. October 8, 2018.

make up stories: Rachel Withers. "Trump is using the Paris protests to push his anti-Paris Agreement agenda." *Vox*. December 8, 2018.

"death cult": Greg Grandin. "The Death Cult of Trumpism." *The Nation*. January 11, 2018.

"two degrees": David Wallace-Wells. *The Uninhabitable Earth: Life After Warming* (2019). 12–13.

"droughts, wildfires": Dahr Jamial. *The End of Ice: Bearing Witness and Finding Meaning in the Path of Climate Disruption* (2019).

"sharks and rays": Elizabeth Kolbert. *The Sixth Extinction: An Unnatural History* (2014). 15.

"all aspects": "Global Warming of 1.5°." The Intergovernmental Panel on Climate Change (2018).

current rate: Philip Alston. "UN Official: U. S. cannot ignore that climate change will force 120 million into Poverty." *The Hill*. July 7, 2019.

effort to discredit: Juliet Eilperin and Missy Ryan. "White House prepares to scrutinize intelligence agencies' finding that climate change threatens national security." *Washington Post*. February 20, 2019.

"demonization": William Happer. Interview with CNBC. July 14, 2014.

"people like me": William Happer. Emails obtained by *Jezebel*. January 20, 2017.

"CO2 famine": William Happer. Interview with *E&E News*. January 25, 2018.

rollbacks: Mark Tutton. "Donald Trump: Climate 'will change back again.'" CNN. October 15, 2018.

"fires cost": *Real Time with Bill Maher*. December 28, 2018.

"world war": Bill McKibben. "A World at War." *The New Republic*. August 15, 2016.

3. WOMEN

"I hate it": Richard Wolffe. "Donald Trump's only fixed position on abortion is his disdain for women." *The Guardian*. July 1, 2018.

"very special": Alexandra Petri. "Trump and I think women are very special." *Washington Post*. November 21, 2017.

"ideal": Dan P. McAdams. "A Psychologist Analyzes Donald Trump's Personality." *The Atlantic*. June 2016.

"Jessica Leeds…": Eliza Relman. "The 23 women who have accused President Trump of sexual misconduct." *Business Insider*. February 25, 2019.

platitudinous statements: "Reproductive Rights Under 365 Days of Trump." ReproductiveRights.org.

"face of a pig.'": Gail Collins. "Well, Socialism Couldn't Give Us Trump." *New York Times*. March 20, 2019.

Title X: Ariana Eunjung Cha. "Trump administration bars clinics that provide abortions or abortion referrals from federal funding." *Washington Post*. February 22, 2019.

"scary time": Maggie Haberman and Peter Baker. "Trump Taunts Christine Blasey Ford at Rally." *New York Times*. October 2, 2018.

"Auntie Stormy": Annie Karni. "Eric Trump Weighs In on Kellyanne Conway's Husband. He Doesn't Like Him." *New York Times*. December 7, 2018.

charged with battery: Anna North. "Trump's long history of employing—and defending—men accused of hurting women." *Vox*. February 9, 2018.

labor force: Heather Long. "Trump claimed more women than ever are working. The reality is much more grim." *Washington Post*. February 5, 2019.

"Women have": Jeva Lange. "61 things Donald Trump has said about women." *The Week*. October 16, 2018.

4. RACE

The New York Years: David Leonhardt and Ian Prasad Philbrick. "Donald Trump's Racism: The Definitive List." *New York Times*. January 15, 2018.

maiden mention: Morris Kaplan. "Major Landlord Accused of Antiblack Bias in City." *New York Times*. October 10, 1973.

twice sued: Michael Kruse. "Trump's Long War with Justice." *Politico*. August 23, 2018.

Trump employees: Jonathan Mahler and Steve Eder. "No Vacancies for Blacks: How Donald Trump Got His Start, and Was First Accused of Bias." *New York Times*. August 27, 2016

Another key: Aaron Blake. "The extensive effort to bury Donald Trump's grades." *Washington Post*. March 5, 2018.

"racially insensitive": Maria Puente. "Trump 'Apprentice' slur tapes: A who's who of people associated with alleged recording." *USA Today*. August 16, 2018.

"I know nothing": Glen Kessler. "Donald Trump and David Duke: for the record." *Washington Post*. March 1, 2016.

Gregory Cheadle: Mark Z. Barabak. "Trump called him 'my African American. But he condemns the president's treatment of black America." *Los Angeles Times*. August 31, 2017.

age-old trope: Rebecca Morin. "'Idiot,' 'Dope,' 'Moron': How Trump's aides have insulted the boss." *Politico*. September 4, 2018.

South Africa land: Jennifer Williams. "Trump's tweet echoing white nationalist propaganda about South African farmers, explained." *Vox*. August 23, 2018.

racist ad: Tom Foreman. "CNN fact checks Trump's racially charged ad." November 2, 2018.

too racist: Michael M. Grynbaum, and Niraj Chokshi. "Even Fox News Stops Running Trump Caravan Ad Criticized as Racist." *New York Times*. November 5, 2018.

Voter fraud: Allan Lichtman. "Voter fraud isn't a problem in America. Low turnout is." *Washington Post*. October 22, 2018.

"a very important thing": Grace Sparks. "Russian trolls tried to turn off African-American voters in 2016, when fewer African-Americans voted." CNN. December 16, 2018.

800 crimes: David A. Graham, Adrienne Green, Cullen Murphy, and Parker Richards. "An Oral History of Trump's Bigotry." *The Atlantic*. June 2019.

Louisiana Senate race: Sam Wang. "Why Trump Stays Afloat." *New York Times*. October 29, 2016.

"Jexodus": Matthew Boxer. "'Jexodus' is a GOP fantasy. That doesn't mean Jews will vote Democratic forever." *Washington Post*. March 22, 2018.

5. CRIME & GUNS

56 percent drop: Julia Fair. "Timeline: How President Trump's positions on gun control have evolved." *USA Today*. October 4, 2017.

across all races: Emily Widra. "Stark racial disparities in murder rates persist, even as overall murder rate declines." Prison Policy Initiative. May 3, 2018.

fewer raw numbers: U.S. Census.

Philly Miurder Rate: Chris Palmer. "Trump said Philly's murder rate is 'terribly increasing.' It's not." Philly.com. January 26, 2017.

"This American carnage": Donald J. Trump. Inaugural Address. The White House. January 20, 2017.

worst year for mass shootings: Sean Coughlan. "2018 'worst year for US school shootings.'" BBC. December 12, 2018.

"That pattern itself": Philip Bump. "How Trump talks about attacks by Muslims and attacks on Muslims." *Washington Post*. March 15, 2019.

dropped by 42 percent: D'Angelo Gore. "Trump wrong about murder rate." Factcheck.org. October 28, 2016.

"Although assault weapons": William J. Eaton. "Ford, Carter Reagan Push for Gun Ban." *Los Angeles Times*. May 5, 1994.

For once, Trump: Chris Smith. "The NRA Spent $30 Million to Elect Trump. Was it Russian Money?" *Vanity Fair*. June 21, 2018.

terrorists exploit: The Editorial Board. "The NRA's Complicity in Terrorism." *New York Times*. June 16 2016.

In 2011: Adam Taylor. "The Islamic State likes America's 'dumb' gun laws, defector says. " *Washington Post*. August 4, 2016.

"*don't be too nice*": Mark Berman. "Trump tells police not to worry about injuring suspects during arrests." *Washington Post.* July 28, 2017.

"*We think*": Elspeth Reeve. "The NRA of 2013 Is Trying to Stop the NRA of 1999 from Destroying the Second Amendment." *The Atlantic.* June 31, 2013.

they did: Louis Jacobson. "Donald Trump wrong that Charlottesville counter-protesters didn't have a permit." Politifact. August 17, 2017.

car attack: Chris Cillizza. "The stunning difference between Trump's reaction to the Las Vegas shooting and the NYC attack." CNN. November 1, 2017.

These "difficulties": German Lopez. "Trump said, "I love the police. But his budget slashes funding that helps hire more cops." Vox. February 12, 2018.

"*The Republicans*": Donald Trump. *The America We Deserve.* 2000.

"*You know why*": Brandon Carter and Alexander Bolton. "Trump to GOP senator: 'You're afraid of the NRA.'" *The Hill.* February 28, 2018.

Trump withdrew: Michael D. Shear and Cheryl Gay Steinberg. "Conceding to N.R.A., Trump Abandons Brief Gun Control Promise." *New York Times.* March 12, 2018.

"*My Administration*": Tessa Berenson. "Read President Trump's Remarks on the Texas School Shooting." *Time.* May 17, 2018.

Obama-era rule: Ali Vitali. "Trump Signs Bill Revoking Obama-Era Gun Checks for People With Mental nesses." NBC News. February 27, 2017.

"*We don't plan*": BBC News. "White House refuses to release photo of Trump gun law repeal." February 16, 2018.

6. THE RULE OF LAW(LESSNESS)

"*I'm fucked.*": Michael Wolff, *Seige (2019).*

tells border agents: Joan Walsh. "We Are No Longer a Nation of Laws." *The Nation.* April 9, 2019.

The Trumps and HUD: Morris Kaplan. "Major Landlord Accused of Antiblack Bias in City." *New York Times.* October 16, 1973.

"*a lawyer is*": Steve Eder. "Donald Trump Agrees to Pay $25 Million in Trump University Settlement." *New York Times.* Nov. 28, 2016...."I won't settle this case!" June 24, 2018.

depositions revealed: Shane Goldmacher. "Trump Foundation Will Dissolve, Accused of 'Shocking Pattern of Illegality.'" *New York Times.* December 18, 2018; James West. "*Honestly*": "Former Models for Donald Trump's Agency Say They Violated Immigration Rules and Worked Illegally." *Mother Jones.* April 2018.

In 1991: Charles Bagli. "Trump Paid Over $1 million in Labor Settlement, Documents Reveal." *New York Times.* November 27, 2017; Massimo Calabresi, "What Donald Trump Knew About Undocumented Workers at His Signature Power." *Time.* August 25, 2016.

workers without papers: Joshua Partlow and David Fahrenthold. "Trump's Gold Course Employed Undocumented Workers— and then Fired Them Amid Showdown Over Border Wall." *Washington Post.* January 26, 2019.

"*a checkbook*": Shane Goldmacher. "Trump Foundation Will Dissolve, Accused of 'Shocking Pattern of Illegality.'" *New York Times.* December 18, 2018; "Attorney General Underwood Announces Lawsuit Against Donald J. Trump Foundation And its Board of Directors for Extensive and Persistent Violations of State and Federal Law." Office of Attorney General Barbara Underwood, press release. December 17, 2018.

Maryanne Trump Barry: Ross Buettner and Susanne Craig. "Retiring as a Judge, Trump's Sister Ends Court Inquiry Into Her Role in Tax Dodges." *New York Times.* April 10 2019; Debra Cassens. "Trump's sister, a federal appellate judge, resigns amid ethics inquiry." *ABA Journal,* April 11, 2019.

reversed a decades-long: Josh Gerstein. "Justice Department Blesses White House Post for Kushner." *Politico.* January 21, 2017; Josh Gerstein. "DoJ Releases Overruled Memos Finding it Illegal for Presidents to Appoint Relatives." *Politico.* October 3, 2017.

like a Forrest Gump: Callum Patton. "The Special Treatment of Ivanka Trump and Jared Kushner is a National Security Issue, Says Former Federal Prosecutor." *Newsweek*. March 13, 2019; Frank Bruni. "Entitlement, Thy Name is Ivanka." *New York Times*. July 3, 2019.

specific insistence: Maggie Haberman, Michael S. Schmidt, Adam Goldman, and Annie Karni. "Trump Ordered Officials to Give Jared Kushner Security Clearance." *New York Times*. February 28, 2019.

You don't have to: Dr. Bonham's Case, 1610.

personally urged: Damion Paletta and Josh Dawsey. "Trump Personally Pushed Postmaster General to Double Rates on Amazon, Other Firms." *Washington Post*. May 18, 2019.

except the military: "Donald Trump Says Bowe Bergdahl Should Have Been Executed." *Chicago Tribune*. Oct. 8, 2015; Christopher Woody. "Trump Army Deserter Bowe Bergdahl's Sentence 'is a complete and total disaster.'" *Business Insider*. November 3, 2017.

Chief Justice John Roberts: Adam Liptak. "Chief Justice Defends Judicial Independence after Trump Attacks 'Obama Judge." *New York Times*. November 21, 2018.

Barr piously warned: Paul Krugman. "The Death of Democracy, American Style." *New York Times*. September 10. 2019.

knife fight: Jennifer Rubin. "When is a summary not a summary?" *Washington Post*. March 31, 2019; Benjamin Wittes. "The Catastrophic Performance of Bill Barr." *The Atlantic*. May 6, 2019.

"no statute": Charles Krauthammer. "Bungled Collusion is Still Collusion." *Chicago Tribune*. July 13, 2017.

"so phony": Aaron Blake. "The 2016 Donald Trump, Jr. interview about Russia is now downright cringeworthy." *Washington Post*. July 11, 2017.

"most unusual": *Washington Post*, https://wapo.st/2JNC8wz ck); Deb Riechmann et. al. "Trump called on spy chiefs for help as Mueller probe began," *AP*, April 21, 2019.

"Russian cut-out": David Corn. Twitter. March 31, 2019.

Blasphemy: Julie Zauzmer. "Trump uttered what many supporters consider blasphemy. Here's why most will probably forgive him." *Washington Post*. September 14, 2019.

"win lots": Brian Naylor. "Trump's Promise to 'Open Up' Libel Laws Unlikely to be Kept." NPR. May 16, 2019.

"his eyes are": Michael Wolff. *Fire and Fury, at 16 (2018)*.

protected speech: *Texas v. Johnson (1989)*. "When the Supreme Court ruled to allow American flag burning." National Constitution Center. June 21, 2018.

win rate: Margaret Talbot. "No Rules." *The New Yorker*. May 13, 2019; Fred Barbash and Deena Paul. "The Real Reason the Trump administration is Constantly Losing in Court." *Washington Post*. March 19, 2019.

"As the president": Donald Trump. Speech at Trump Tower. January 11, 2017.

unquestioned authority: Susan Glasser. "The Secretary of Trump". *The New Yorker*. August 27, 2019.

"Lobbyists representing": David A. Fahrenthold and Jonathan O'Connell. "Saudi-funded lobbyist paid for 500 rooms at Trump's hotel after 2016 election." *Washington Post*. December 5, 2018.

290 visits: CREW. Twitter. February 24, 2019.

$3.4 million: Philip Bump. "Trump's travel to Mar-a-Lago alone probably cost taxpayers more than $64 million." *Washington Post*, February 5, 2019.

CREW has also documented: Anna Massoglia and Karl Evers. "A World of Influence: A Guide to Trump's Foreign Business Interests." OpenSecrets.org. June 4, 2019.

betting window: Natasha Bertrand and Bryan Bender. "Air Force crew made an odd stop on a routine trip: Trump's Scottish resort." *Politico*. September 7, 2019; Eric Lipton. "A Military Stop at a Trump Resort Raises Ethical Questions." *New York Times*. September 10, 2019.

pardon them later: Nick Miroff and Josh Dawsey. "'Take the Land': President Trump wants a border wall. He wants it black. And he wants it by Election Day." *Washington Post*. August 27, 2019.

series of lawsuits: David Enrich, Matthew Goldstein, and Jesse Drucker. "Trump Exaggerated His Wealth in Bid for Loan, Michael Cohen Tells Congress." *New York Times*. February 27, 2019; William K. Rashbaum and Danny Hakim. "New York Attorney General Opens Investigation of Trump Projects." *New York Times*. March 11, 2019. Tom Winter; "N.Y. regulators probing Trump Organization's insurance practices." *New York Times*. March 5, 2019; Paul Waldman. "The wall of concealment Trump build around his finances is beginning to crumble." *Washington Post*. May 23, 2019.

7. APPOINTEES

"grifting": Ryan Cooper. "Steven Mnuchin is a window into the most corrupt White House in history." *The Week*. September 18, 2017.

"As of this": Citizens for Responsibility and Ethics in Washington. Twitter. April 9, 2019.

"dream secretary": Tara Copp. "Here's the blueprint for Erik Prince's $5 billion plan to privatize the Afghanistan war." *Military Times*. September 5, 2018.

DeVos's advocacy: Stephen Henderson. "Betsy DeVos and the twilight of public education." *Detroit Free Press*. December 3, 2016.

potential conflicts: Michael Stratford. "DeVos review identifies 102 financial interests with potential conflicts." *Politico*. January 20, 2017.

nearly $60 million: Lorraine Woellert and Theodoric Meyer. "Trump's wealthiest Cabinet members earned millions in 2017." *Politico*. November 30, 2018.

288 times: Casey Suglia. "What Is Betsy DeVos' Salary As Secretary Of Education? She Claimed She Would Only Take $1." *Romper*. February 8, 2017.

by the end of 2018: David Badash. "Betsy DeVos cost taxpayers $12 million so far." *Salon*. October 5, 2018.

nonprofit colleges: Laura Meckler. "Betsy DeVos to the rescue: For-profit colleges see a savior in secretary." *Washington Post*. November 23, 2018.

loan forgiveness: Katie Lobosco. "DeVos wants to cut budget funding for student loan forgiveness, again." CNN. March 13, 2019.

loan relief: Aimee Pichee. "Student loan relief for public servants: 38,460 applied, only 262 accepted." CBS. April 4, 2019.

women's safety: Peggy Drexler. "Betsy DeVos' huge step back for college women's safety." CNN. July 13, 2017.

1200 probes: Annie Waldman. "DeVos Has Scuttled More Than 1,200 Civil Rights Probes Inherited From Obama." *ProPublica*. June 21, 2018

"cozines": Jonathan Swan, Juliet Bartz, Alayna Treene, and Orion Rummler. "Exclusive: Leaked Trump vetting docs." *Axios*. June 23, 2019.

impossible to list: Eli Watkins and Clare Foran. "EPA chief Scott Pruitt's long list of controversies." CNN. July 5, 2018.

military jets: Rene March. "EPA inspector general investigating Pruitt's travel to home state." CNN. August 28, 2017.

his home state: Sara Ganim, Gregory Wallace, and Rene Marsh. "EPA documents show agency's justification for Pruitt travel." CNN. February 17, 2018.

trip to Morocco: Brady Dennis and Juliet Eilperin. "New documents show nearly $68,000 in recent premium flights, hotel stays for EPA's Pruitt." *Washington Post*. March 20, 2018.

his wife: Lisa Friedman. "Former E.P.A. Aide Says Pruitt Asked Her to Help Find Work for His Wife." *New York Times*. July 2, 2018.

fetching him snacks: Asawin Suebsaeng and Lachlan Markay. "Scott Pruitt Made Public Servants Fetch His Protein Bars and Greek Yogurt." *The Daily Beast*. June 7, 2018.

avoided creating written records: Scott Bronstein, Curt Devine, and Drew Griffin. "Whistleblower: EPA's Pruitt kept secret calendar to hide meetings." CNN. July 3, 2018.

market rate: John Santucci, Matthew Mosk, and Stephanie Ebbs. "EXCLUSIVE: More Cabinet trouble for Trump? EPA chief lived in condo tied to lobbyist 'power couple.'" ABC. March 29, 2018.

nonsensical: Gregory Wallace and Rene Marsh. "GAO: $43,000 soundproof booth for EPA head violated law." CNN. April 16, 2018.

after it leaked: Coral Davenport, Lisa Friedman, and Maggie Haberman. "E.P.A. Chief Scott Pruitt Resigns Under a Cloud of Ethics Scandals." *New York Times*. July 5, 2018.

working as a lobbyist: Emily Hopkins and Chris Sikich. "Embattled former EPA head Scott Pruitt is a lobbyist in Indiana. This is who he works for." *Indianapolis Star*. April 23, 2019.

even further: Coral Davenport. "Pruitt's Successor Wants Rollbacks, Too. And He Wants Them to Stick." *New York Times*. July 27, 2018.

investigations include: Caroline Zhang. "A Guide to the 18 Federal Investigations into Ryan Zinke." CREW. August 9, 2018.

In January 2019: Ryan Zinke. Twitter. January 2, 2019.

Just four days: Coral Davenport. "Interior Dept. Opens Ethics Investigation of Its New Chief, David Bernhardt." *New York Times*. April 15, 2019.

advance a policy: Coral Davenport. "Top Leader at Interior Dept. Pushes a Policy Favoring His Former Client." *New York Times*. February 12, 2019.

ceased lobbying: Coral Davenport. "Trump's Pick for Interior Dept. Continued Lobbying After Officially Vowing to Stop, New Files Show." *New York Times*. April 4, 2019.

pesticide: Eric Lipton. "Interior Nominee Intervened to Block Report on Endangered Species." *New York Times*. March 29, 2019.

best job: Jia Tolentino. "Louise Linton Isn't Mad. You're Mad." *New Yorker*. August 22, 2017.

Evidently, Mnuchin: Meredith Lerner. "Mnuchin's Financial Disclosure the Third Ethics Watchdog Refused to Certify." CREW, April 4, 2019.

rejected Commerce Secretary: Reis Thebault. "Facing ethics violation, Wilbur Ross says he didn't mean to file inaccurate financial disclosures." *Washington Post*. February 19, 2019.

Now, according to: Linnaea Honl-Stuenkel. "John Kelly Cashes in on Child Separation Policy." CREW. May 8, 2019.

A ProPublica investigation: Derek Kravitz and Jack Gillum. "'Happy to Do It': Emails Show Current FAA Chief Coordinated With Ex-Lobbyist Colleagues on Policy." *ProPublica*. March 27, 2019.

Furthermore, when: David Gelles, Thomas Kaplan, Kenneth P. Vogel, and Natalie Kitroeff. "U.S. Under Pressure to Cease Flights of Troubled Boeing Jet." *New York Times*. March 12, 2019.

Hatch Act: Josh Gerstein. "Report: Bush staff violated Hatch Act." January 24, 2011.

In November 2018: Michelle Ye Hee Lee and Juliet Eilperin. "Six White House officials reprimanded for violating the Hatch Act." *Washington Post*. November 30, 2018.

Earlier that year: MJ Lee. "Office of Special Counsel: Conway violated Hatch Act." CNN. March 6, 2018.

MAGA messages: Morgan Gstalter. "CREW files Hatch Act complaint against Kellyanne Conway." *The Hill*. October 23, 2018.

"Having worked": Juliet Eilperin. "Zinke's #2 has so many potential conflicts of interest he has to carry a list of them all." *Washington Post*. November 19, 2018.

8. DUMB & DUMBER

In a 1992: B.J. Leonard. "It's Not 'Shameleon;' Kase Klosed on Klinton." *Tulsa World*. October 27, 1992.

In 2015: "President Modi? Barack Obama's slip of tongue." *News 18*. September 29, 2015.

Chait reported: Jonathan Chait. "Trump Calls Hurricane Florence 'One of the Wettest We've Ever Seen From the Standpoint of Water.'" *New York*. September 18, 2018.

report from Axios: Jonathan Swan. "Scoop: Trump lied to RNC donors about 'Tim Apple' video." *Axios*. March 10, 2019.

"I quickly": Donald Trump. Twitter. March 11, 2019.

A new book reports: Michael D. Scheer. "Angry Demand to shut Border..." *New York Times*. October 2, 2019.

"*According to Mueller*": Benjamin Wittes. "Five Things I Learned From the Mueller Report." *The Atlantic*. April 29, 2019.

"*I'm kind of*": Stephen Moore. Interview with *Bloomberg*. March 22, 2019.

"*Capitalism is a lot*": Stephen Moore. Interview in *Capitalism: A Love Story* (2009), directed by Michael Moore.

"*private-jet pilot*": Isaac Stanley-Becker. "Trump wanted his personal pilot to head the FAA. The critical job is still vacant amid Boeing fallout." *Washington Post*. March 14, 2019.

"*fifth- or sixth-grader*": Bob Woodward. *Fear: Trump in the White House* (2018).

"*dumb as shit*": Michael Wolff. *Fire and Fury: Inside the Trump White House* (2018).

"*kindergartner*": Joseph Bernstein. "Sources: McMaster Mocked Trump's Intelligence At A Private Dinner." *BuzzFeed*. November 20, 2017.

"*like an 11-year-old child*": Gabriel Sherman. "'I Have Power': Is Steve Bannon Running for President?" *Vanity Fair*. December 21, 2017.

"*a moron*": Carol E. Lee, Kristen Welker, Stephanie Ruhle, and Dafna Linzer. "Tillerson's Fury at Trump Required an Intervention From Pence." NBC. October 4, 2017.

"*husband from hell!*": George Conway. Twitter. March 18, 2019.

Kellyanne sided: Kellyanne Conway. Interview with *Politico*. March 20, 2019.

"*Truth isn't truth*": Rudy Giuliani. Interview with MSNBC. August 20, 2018.

"*can of Campbell's*": Wilbur Ross. Interview with CNBC. March 5, 2018.

"*alternative facts*": Kellyanne Conway. Interview with MSNBC. January 22, 2017.

"*He opined*": Vicky Ward, *Kushner, Inc.: Greed. Ambition. Corruption. The Extraordinary Story of Jared Kushner and Ivanka Trump* (2019)

"*total respect*": Donald Trump. Press conference in Washington, DC September 26, 2018.

"*my I.Q*": Donald Trump. Twitter. May 8, 2013.

"*Nobody knows more*": "Everything Donald Trump Is An Expert In, According to Himself." *NowThis*. January 8, 2019.

"*Stay on point*": Donald Trump. Speech in Pensacola, Florida. November 3, 2016.

Daily Pennsylvanian analysis: Alex Graves. "How many times has Trump mentioned his Wharton education? We crunched the numbers." *The Daily Pennsylvanian*. January 17, 2018.

withdraw 62: Andrew Restuccia. "Moore is just the latest casualty of Trump's nomination process." *Politico*. May 2, 2019.

According to the Brookings Institution: Manuela Tobias. "A look at White House turnover under Trump, Obama following Scott Pruitt's exit." *PolitiFact*. July 11, 2018.

Only 61 percent: "Tracking how many key positions Trump has filled so far." *Washington Post*. updated March 25, 2019.

qualifying as: Greg Sargent. "Not just Sharpie-gate: 7 other times officials tried to fabricate Trump's 'truth.'" *Washington Post*. September 5, 2019.

9. AGE OF RAGE

one performance: Daniel Victor and Giovanni Russonello. "Meryl Streep's Golden Globes Speech." *New York Times*. January 8, 2017.

"*I am tired*": Oliver Laughland. "Jeff Flake reveals he has received threats from Trump supporters." *The Guardian*. April 3, 2019.

"*226 percent increase*": Amanda Sakuma. "Hate crimes reportedly jumped by 226 percent in counties that hosted Trump campaign rallies." *Vox*. March 24, 2019.

just 44 percent: Leo Shane III. "Support for Trump is fading among active-duty troops, new poll shows." *Military Time*. October 15, 2018.

casually posited: Tom Nicholson. "Trump: It Would Be 'Very Bad' If My Biker Friends Got 'Tough' On Left Wing Opponents." *Esquire*. March 15, 2019.

isn't confined: Matthew Nussbaum. "Trump defends comments on Tiananmen Square, Putin." Politico. March 10, 2016.

1993: "Soldier Kills 4 People and Hurts 6 in a Restaurant in North Carolina." *New York Times*. August 8, 1993.

Nixon was the finger: Tom Carson. "Our Nixon: Whose Life Was it Anyway?" *The Village Voice*. May 1994.

10. MEDIA

"I think one": Callum Borchers. "Trump falsely claims (again) that he coined the term 'fake news.'" *Washington Post*. October 26, 2017,

"Imagine someone": Katy Tur. *Unbelievable: My Front-Row Seat to the Craziest Campaign in American History* (2017), 68.

Rallygoers boo: Jim Acosta. *Twitter*. July 31, 2018.

Three months after: Madeline Holcombe. "Pipe bomb suspect writes to judge that the 16 devices he mailed were only meant for intimidation." CNN. April 3, 2019.

an analysis: Stephanie Sugars. "From fake news to enemy of the people: An anatomy of Trump's tweets." Committee to Protect Journalists. January 30, 2019.

The survey: Jaclyn Reiss. "Trump campaign sends survey on media bias that is, well, pretty biased." *Boston Globe*. February 16, 2017.

authoritarians: Greg Sargent. *An Uncivil War: Taking Back Our Democracy in an Age of Trumpian Disinformation and Thunderdome Politics* (2018), 132.

"I think": Bob Woodward. *Fear: Trump in the White House* (2018), 271.

A Republican strategist: Philip Rucker, Josh Dawsey, and Ashley Parker. "How a week of triumph for Trump was convulsed by chaos and contradiction." *Washington Post*. April 26, 2018.

"In fact": Stephen Colbert. *The Late Show*. February 12, 2019.

Sean Hannity: Jackie Wattles. "Watch President Trump repeat Fox News talking points." CNN. April 22, 2018.

Axios revealed: Alexi McCammond and Jonathan Swan. "Scoop: Insider leaks Trump's 'Executive Time'-filled private schedules." *Axios*. February 3, 2019.

"Typically": John Avlon. CNN. April 22, 2018.

"Trump has told": Jane Mayer. "The Making of the Fox News White House." *The New Yorker*. March 11, 2019.

After presumably: Any Campbell. "South Africa's White Nationalist Rhetoric Is Thriving, Thanks In Part To Trump." *The Huffington Post*. November 21, 2018.

South African government: South African Government. *Twitter*. August 22, 2018.

Jill Brooke. "The Real Story Behind Donald Trump's Infamous "Best Sex I Ever Had" headline." *Hollywood Reporter*. April 12, 2018.

Morgan Ortagus: Josh Lederman. "Trump to pick Fox News contributor for State Dept spokeswoman." *NBC News*. March 28, 2019.

"Somebody get": Cliff Sims. *Team of Vipers: My 500 Extraordinary Days in the Trump White House* (2019), xvii.

"In late 2018": Jonathan Mahler and Jim Rutenberg. "How Rupert Murdoch's Empire of Influence Remade the World." *New York Times Magazine*. April 3, 2019.

"[Trump] is so charming.": NowThis. June 20, 2019.

"This is banana republic": Max Boot. "If Trump really attempted to ruin CNN, he deserves to be impeached." *Washington Post*. March 5, 2019.

"sole arbiter": Jonathan Chait. "Trump Says in Interview He Is the Sole Arbiter of Truth." *New York*. November 19, 2018.

"It's just me": Lesley Stahl. Interview with PBS. May 23, 2018.

11. SECRECY

"cut off public access": Julie Hirschfeld Davis. "White House to Keep Its Visitor Logs Secret." *New York Times*. April 14, 2017.

In elevating: Danny Vinik. "138 things Trump did this year while you weren't looking." *Politico*. December 29, 2017,

When the Trump White House: Chris Cillizza. "Donald Trump isn't big on the whole transparency thing." CNN. April 17, 2017.

Trump set this: Andrew Desiderio. "Jim Risch tries to calm Republicans furious with Trump." *Politico*. February 22, 2019.

bypass federal transparency: Josh Gerstein. "Trump may be skirting transparency law on advisory boards." *Politico*. February 2, 2017.

ignoring congressional Republicans: Philip Eil. "As president, Trump sings a different tune on 'transparency.'" *Columbia Journalism Review*. January 31, 2017.

"What [Trump] is": Michelle Kosinski and Jennifer Hansler. "State Department bars press corps from Pompeo briefing, won't release list of attendees." CNN. March 19, 2019.

As part of: Brian Bennett. "President Trump's Threats to Former Staffers Reveal a Problem at the White House." *Time*. February 1, 2019.

It's an alien: Josh Dawsey and Ashley Parker. "'Everyone signed one': Trump is aggressive in his use of nondisclosure agreements, even in government." *Washington Post*. August 13, 2018.

His NDAs: Orly Lobel. "Trump's Extreme NDAs." *The Atlantic*. March 4, 2019

"threatening legal action": Aaron Blake. "The extensive effort to bury Donald Trump's grades." *Washington Post*. March 5, 2019.

He did this: Beth Fouhy. "Trump: Obama a "Terrible Student" Not Good Enough for Harvard." NBC. April 25, 2011.

"White House response": John Wagner. "Trump won't release his tax returns because people don't care, top adviser says." *Washington Post*. January 22, 2017.

Frankly, they do: Christopher Wilson. "Trump says people don't care about his tax returns. People say otherwise." *Yahoo! News*. April 10, 2019.

As a candidate: Orion Rummler. "IRS commissioner: No rule against releasing Trump's tax returns while under audit." *Axios*. April 10, 2019.

12. BULLY'S PULPIT

Let's give Trump: "The 598 People, Places and Things Donald Trump Has Insulted on Twitter: A Complete List." *New York Times*. May 24, 2019.

Few things reveal: Shannon van Sant. "Autopsy For 7-Year-Old Migrant Who Died In U.S. Custody Shows She Died Of Sepsis." *NPR*. March 30, 2019.

Jakelin Caal Maquin: David Boddiger. "Trump Lies Again About the Father of a Guatemalan Girl Who Died After Crossing the Border." *Splinter News*. March 30, 2019.

"[George H.W. Bush] never lost": Bret Stephens. "A Presidency Without Humor." *New York Times*. December 7, 2018.

"Further, the President's": Lauren Holter. "Mike Pence Quotes About Impeachment Reveal What He Really Thinks Of Presidents Having Affairs." *Bustle*. August 7, 2018.

"You have people": Brian Klaas. "A short history of President Trump's anti-Muslim bigotry." *Washington Post*. March 15, 2019.

Brown people fleeing: Julin Borger. "Fleeing a hell the US helped create: why Central Americans journey north." *The Guardian*. December 19, 2018.

"allegations of racism": "OC Principals Duel Over Alleged Racist Signs At High School Football Game." *CBS LA*. September 10, 2018.

"Now, research shows": Clare Lombardo. "Virginia Study Finds Increased School Bullying In Areas That Voted For Trump." *NPR*. January 9, 2019.

"Look, she's": Elie Mystal. "Donald Trump Isn't Playing Games With Ilhan Omar—He's Inciting Violence." *The Nation*. April 16, 2019.

"the way about her": Jamelle Bouie. "Why Trump won't stop talking about Ilhan Omar." *New York Times*. April 16, 2019.

Trump's M. O.: Colby Itkowitz and John Wagner. "Trump says he has no regrets about sharing Ilhan Omar video." *Washington Post*. April 16, 2019.

"Trash talk turned": Dan Barry and John Eligon. "'Trump, Trump, Trump!' How a President's Name Became a Racial Jeer." *New York Times*. December 16, 2017.

"Back to the Future screenwriter": Marianne Zumbberge. "'Back to the Future' Writer: Donald Trump Inspired Biff." *Variety*. October 21, 2015.

13. WAR AND PEACE

A majority: Glenn Kessler. "The Trump administration's tally of $350 billion-plus in deals with Saudi Arabia." *Washington Post*. June 8, 2017.

Many of the projects: White House statement. May 20, 2017.

"finishing touches": Mark Landler. "The Mideast Peace Plan Is Nearly Finished. Is It Dead on Arrival?" *New York Times*. March 11, 2018.

The same day: David E. Sanger and William J. Broad. "In North Korea, Missile Bases Suggest a Great Deception." *New York Times*. November 12, 2018.

"we continue": Daniel Coats. "The Worldwide Threat Assessment of the US Intelligence Community." Director of National Intelligence. January 29, 2019.

mutually beneficial: Salvador Rizzo. "President Trump's imaginary numbers on military aid to South Korea." *Washington Post*. February 25, 2019.

When Trump directly: Bob Woodward. *Fear: Trump in the White House* (2018), 305.

Being loose: Eric Talmadge. "Officials say Trump overstated Kim's demand on sanctions." *Associated Press*. March 1, 2019.

Sanctions: John Bolton. *Twitter*. March 21, 2019.

The vice foreign minister: CNN. February 24, 2019.

"Important": Fox News. March 4, 2019.

of course: Jonas Ekman. "In English: This happened in Sweden Friday night, Mr. President." *Aftonbladet*. February 18, 2017.

"in toto": John Bolton. Interview with ABC. March 10, 2019.

still in compliance: Gina Haspel. Congressional testimony. January 29, 2019.

abandoned: Zachary B. Wolf. "Here are all the treaties and agreements Trump has abandoned." *CNN*. February 1, 2019.

his tenure: Ned Price. "Why Mike Pompeo Released More bin Laden Files." *The Atlantic*. November 8, 2017.

regime change: Nilo Tabrizy. "M.E.K.: The Groups John Bolton Wants to Rule Iran." *New York Times*. May 7, 2018.

"What we've done": Donald Trump. Speech at the Pentagon. January 17, 2019.

the main goal: "On Thin Ice: The Iran Nuclear Deal at Three." International Crisis Group. January 16, 2019.

surging: Erin Cunningham. "Fresh sanctions on Iran are already choking off medicine imports, economists, say." *Washington Post*. November 17, 2018.

"Sometimes I feel": Bob Corker. Interview with *New York Times*. October 8, 2017.

"In an important": Mike Pompeo. *Twitter*. April 8, 2019.

"[Trump officials] who have": Javad Zarif. *Twitter*. April 7, 2019.

"blunt and crude": Jason Rezaian, "Why listing Iran's Revolutionary Guard as a terrorist organization is a bad idea." *Washington Post*. April 8, 2019.

five-figure inflation: Steve Hanke. "Venezuela's Hyperinflation Hits 80,000% Per Year in 2018." *Forbes*. January 1, 2019.

For one, Bolton: John Bolton. Interview with *Fox Business*. January 24, 2019.

Less than: Maggie Haberman, Michael S. Schmidt, Adam Goldman, and Annie Karni. "Trump Ordered Officials to Give Jared Kushner a Security Clearance." *New York Times*. February 28, 2019.

Imagine that: Ryan Parry and Josh Boswell. "Exclusive: Saudi crown prince bragged that Jared Kushner gave him CIA intelligence about other Saudis saying 'here are your enemies' days before 'corruption crackdown' which led to torture and death." *The Daily Mail*. April 5, 2018.

"President Trump continued": William Hartung and Christina Arabia. "Trends in Major U.S. Arms Sales in 2018: The Trump Record—Rhetoric Versus Reality." Security Assistance. April 2019.

"The sad fact": Michael Cohen. Testimony in front of the House Oversight Committee. February 27, 2019.

In May 2019: Lucas Tomlinson. *Fox News*. Twitter, May 5, 2019.

In keeping: Frank O. Mora. "What a Military Intervention in Venezuela Would Look Like." *Foreign Affairs*. March 19, 2019; "The risks of military intervention in Venezuela." *The Economist*. February 28, 2019.

Apparently not: Jon Schwarz. "Elliott Abrams, Trump's Pick to Bring 'Democracy' to Venezuela, Has Spent His Life Crushing Democracy." *The Intercept*. January 30, 2019.

Bonus: Less: Pamela Brown and Kaitlin Collins. "President pressured staff to grant security clearance to Ivanka Trump." *CNN*. March 6, 2019.

a whistleblower: Nicholas Fandos and Maggie Haberman. "Whistle-Blower Tells Congress of Irregularities in White House Security Clearances." *New York Times*. April 1, 2019.

"Using some": Andy Borowitz. "Trump Comes Out Strongly Against Intelligence." *The New Yorker*. January 30, 2019.

14. PUTIN

"[Trump] is a very flamboyant man": Vladimir Putin. Remarks in Moscow. December 17, 2015.

"My people": Donald Trump. Remarks in Helsinki, Finland July 17, 2018.

"Completely": Susan Glasser. "'No Way to Run a Superpower': The Trump-Putin Summit and the Death of American Foreign Policy." *The New Yorker*. July 19, 2018.

In fact, Putin: Peter Baker. "Trump and Putin Have Met Five Times. What Was Said Is a Mystery." *New York Times*. January 15, 2019.

Trump spoke: James Politi, Demetri Sevastopulo, and Henry Foy. "Trump sat down with Putin at G20 without US note-taker." *Financial Times*. January 29, 2019.

indiscreetly bragged: Michele Goldberg. "Psst! Don't Tell Trump." *New York Times*. September 10, 2019.

In it, he outlined: Timothy Snyder. *Twitter*. April 14, 2019.

when asked: Vladimir Putin. Press conference in Helsinki, Finland. July 16, 2018.

"Withdraw from": Susan Rice. "How Trump Helps Putin." *New York Times*. June 8, 2018.

15. SPRINGTIME FOR DICTATORS

In this seemingly innocuous: Ben Hubbard, David D. Kirkpatrick, Kate Kelly, and Mark Mazzetti. "Saudis Said to Use Coercion and Abuse to Seize Billions." *New York Times*. March 11, 2018.

Yet another: Julia E. Barnes. "C.I.A. Concludes that Saudi Crown Prince Ordered Khashoggi Killed." *New York Times*. November 16, 2018.

A Saudi prince: "Trump and Saudi Arabia: Deep business ties spark new scrutiny." *CBS and the Associated Press*. October 15, 2018.

A lobbying firm: Erica Orden. "Saudi disappearance puts spotlight on Trump's business ties." *CNN*. October 12, 2018.

Saudi businesses: David A. Fahrenthold and Jonathan O'Connell. "'I like them very much': Trump has long-standing business ties with Saudis, who have boosted his hotels since he took office." *Washington Post*. October 11, 2018.

bragged: Alex Emmons, Ryan Grim, and Clayton Swisher. "Saudi Crown Prince Boasted That Jared Was 'In His Pocket.'" *The Intercept*. March 21, 2018.

"When a conservative": Ronald Reagan. Speech at the Conservative Political Action Conference. February 6, 1977.

Trump's remarks: "Flashback: President Bush on Putin's 'Soul.'" *NBC News*. March 27, 2014.

"Mr. Trump's chumminess": Editorial Board. "Why the North Korea Meeting Was the Trumpiest Moment So Far." *New York Times*. June 12, 2018.

"It kind of": John Kirby. Remarks on *CNN*. February 28, 2019.

"Americans know": Warren Davidson. *Twitter*. February 28, 2019.

"Is Kim Jong-un": House Foreign Affairs Committee Hearing. March 29, 2019.

Duterte has waged: "Philippines: Duterte's 'Drug War' Claims 12,000+ Lives." Human Rights Watch. January 18, 2018.

"Trump often": Jonathan Swan. "Exclusive: Trump privately talks up executing all big drug dealers." *Axios*. February 25, 2018.

"Hitler massacred": Rodrigo Duterte. Speech in Davo City, Philippines. September 30, 2016.

"An American president": John McCain. *Twitter*. March 20, 2018.

Trump invests: John Davidson and Amina Ismail. "Egypt Arrests Leave Few Vocal Critics of Sisi." *U.S. News and World Report*. June 8, 2018.

"Trump's comments": Carol Morello. "Trump calls Erdogan to congratulate him on contested referendum, Turkey says." *Washington Post*. April 17, 2017.

In addition: Shadia Nasralla and Andrea Shalal. "Observer says 2.5 million Turkish referendum votes could have been manipulated." *Reuters*. April 18, 2017.

eat his words: Karen DeYoung and Karoun Demirjian. "Contradicting Trump, Bolton says no withdrawal from Syria until ISIS destroyed, Kurds' safety guaranteed." *Washington Post*. January 6, 2019.

"tropics": "Jair Bolsonaro: Brazil's firebrand leader dubbed the Trump of the Tropics." *BBC*. December 31, 2018.

"If imitation": Brian Klaas. "Want to see where Trump is taking America? Look at Turkey under Erdogan." *Washington Post*. January 13, 2018.

four warning signs: Ryan Sit. "Trump Meets Every Criteria for an Authoritarian Leader, Harvard Political Scientists Warn." *Newsweek*. January 11, 2018.

"Unambiguously": Edward-Isaac Dovere. "Donald dreams of dictators." *Politico*. June 15, 2018.

"The truth": Alexander Hamilton. Letter. August 1792.

16. ALLIES

"My views": Jim Mattis. Resignation letter. December 20, 2018.

Trump was at: John Haltiwanger. "Trump twice repeats falsehood that he was in the UK the day before Brexit and predicted it would happen." *Business Insider*. July 13, 2018.

Two weeks: Zack Beauchamp. "What Trump's bizarre Brexit comments actually reveal." *Vox*. June 1, 2016.

no idea: Michael Wolff. "The Donald Trump Conversation: Politics' 'Dark Heart' Is Having the Best Time Anyone's Ever Had." *The Hollywood Reporter*. June 1, 2016.

Confidence: Pew Research Center. October 1, 2018.

"Trump is reviled": Charles M. Blow. "Trump, Chieftan of Spite." *New York Times*. October 16, 2017.

Imagine what: Alex Spence. "Let Trump Handle Brexit: An Explosive Leaked Recording Reveals Boris Johnson's Private Views About Britain's Foreign Policy." *BuzzFeed News*. June 7, 2019.

Trump's alienation: Elizabeth Markovits. "Trump 'tells it like it is.' That's not necessarily a good thing for democracy." *Washington Post*. March 4, 2016.

"His barrage": Susan B. Glasser. "How Trump Made War on Angela Merkel and Europe." *The New Yorker*. December 24, 2018.

Speaking of: Andrea Shalal and Sabine Siebold. "German leader, defense chief vow boost in military spending." *Reuters*. July 4, 2018.

"We don't": Isabel Oakeshott. "Britain's man in the US says Trump is 'inept': Leaked secret cables from ambassador say the President is 'uniquely dysfunctional and his career could end in disgrace.'" *The Daily Mail*. July 6, 2019.

Furthermore: "Abe nominated Trump for the Nobel at behest of Washington." *The Asahi Shimbun*. February 17, 2019.

17. IMMIGRATION

"The danger": AJ Willingham, Paul Martucci, and Natalie Leung. "The chances of a refugee killing you - and other surprising immigration stats." *CNN*. March 6, 2017.

"I'll tell": Amy B. Wang. "Trump asked for a 'Muslim ban,' Giuliani says—and ordered a commission to do it 'legally.'" *Washington Post*. January 29, 2017.

Obama signed: Miriam Valverde. "False: Trump's claim about illegal immigration under past administrations." *Politifact*. August 3, 2017.

unwise: Noman Merchant. "What happened when Bush, Obama sent troops to Mexico border." *Associated Press*. April 8, 2018.

The numbers: Zachary Basu. "Report: Dreamers contribute $42 billion to annual GDP." *Axios*. January 18, 2018.

Followed up: Julia Ainsley. "Thousands more migrant kids separated from parents under Trump than previously reported." *NBC News*. January 17, 2019.

About two weeks: Meg Kelly. "Fact-checking President Trump's numbers on the 'human toll of illegal immigration.'" *Washington Post*. July 6, 2018.

Fortunately: Linda Qiu. "Trump's Evidence-Free Claims About the Migrant Caravan." *New York Times*. October 22, 2018.

He should know: Dionne Searcey and Emmanuel Akinwotu. "Nigerian Army Uses Trump's Words to Justify Fatal Shooting of Rock-Throwing Protesters." *New York Times*. November 2, 2018.

This lie: Adam Behsudi. "Fact check: Mexico will 'indirectly' pay for a border wall through the new trade deal." *Politico*. January 10, 2019.

Criminology: Christopher Ingraham. "Two studies show that undocumented immigrants are less likely to commit crime than native-born citizens." *Washington Post*. June 19, 2018.

A border fence: Jane C. Timm. "Fact check: Trump claims a wall made El Paso safe. Data shows otherwise." *NBC News*. February 11, 2018.

It's the opposite: Michelle Lee. "Trump does not accurately describe migrant children illegally brought into the United States." *Washington Post*. January 8, 2019.

"Nobody shows": Alan Gomez. "Fact-checking Trump officials: Most drugs enter US through legal ports of entry, not vast, open border." *USA Today*. January 16, 2019.

What's insane: Gillian Edevane. "Donald Trump leans on unverifiable statistics about immigration in blustery CPAC 2019 speech." *Newsweek*. March 3, 2009.

two front-page stories: Zolan Kanno-Youngs. "Squalor Pervasive in Detention Centers." *New York Times*. July 3, 2019.

enduring: Simon Romero, Zolan Kanno-Youngs, Manny Fernandez, Daniel Borunda, Aaron Montes, and Caitlin Dickerson. "Hungry Scared and Sick: Inside Clint's Razor Wire." *New York Times*. July 7, 2019.

POSTSCRIPT

*Percy Shelley, "Ozymandias" [1818]

I met a traveller from an antique land
Who said: "Two vast and trunkless legs of stone
Stand in the desert. Near them, on the sand,
Half sunk, a shatter'd visage lies, whose frown,
And wrinkled lip, and sneer of cold command,
Tell that its sculptor well those passions read
Which yet survive, stamp'd on these lifeless things,
The hand that mock'd them and the heart that fed.
And on the pedestal these words appear:
'My name is Ozymandias, king of kings:
Look on my works, ye Mighty, and despair!'
Nothing beside remains. Round the decay
Of that colossal wreck, boundless and bare
The lone and level sands stretch far away."

ABOUT THE AUTHORS

Mark Green is the former NYC Consumer Commissioner and elected Public Advocate (1990–2001) as well as past president of Air America Radio. Green is the author or editor of 24 books, including two *New York Times* bestsellers—# 1 *Who Runs Congress?* (1972) and *The Book on Bush* (2004). He is the founder of the progressive shadow cabinet @ShadowingTrump, consisting of 21 leading scholars and former officials.

Ralph Nader, America's leading public interest lawyer and consumer advocate, was named by *The Atlantic* as one of the hundred most influential figures in American history, and by *Time* and *Life* magazines as one of the most influential Americans of the twentieth century. He was a four-time candidate for the US presidency, and his first book, the bestselling *Unsafe at Any Speed,* was responsible for US auto safety standards shown to have saved 3.5 million lives over fifty years.